CW00684407

CAVALIER IN THE SKY

Biography of Air Vice Marshal Chandan Singh
MVC AVSM, VrC

Air Vice Marshal Chandan Singh
MVC AVSM VrC

CAVALIER IN THE SKY

Biography of Air Vice Marshal Chandan Singh
MVC AVSM VrC

Major Chandrakant Singh VrC

Published by
LG Publishers Distributors
49, Lane No. 14, Pratap Nagar
Mayur Vihar Phase I, Delhi 110 091
Tel : 011 2279 5641 email: lgpdist@gmail.com

In association with
Maharaja Mansingh Pustak Prakash Research Centre
Mehrangarh Museum Trust, Fort
Jodhpur 342 001

Typeset at
Arpit Printographers, Delhi

Printed at
Sapra Brothers, Noida

Dedicated

*To my country, my people and to the people of Bangladesh and
Tibet for whose freedom AVM Chandan Singh devoted his life*

Contents

FOREWORD

It gives me great pleasure to learn that the Biography of Air Vice Marshal Chandan Singh, MVC AVSM VrC, has been written by Major Chandrakant Singh. The author presents to the readers a work on a brave Cavalier in the sky. In this book AVM Chandan Singh is the main heroic character who has lived life on his terms and lived it well in the service of the country. His presence inspired confidence in his men. To understand him better we have to go back to the influences that have made him the man he is. The foundations were set by his father Col. Bahadur Singh, O.B.E. who had the blessing of my great grand uncle Maharaja Sir Pratap Singhji of Idar, Regent of Jodhpur & commanded the Jodhpur Lancers.

The Chopasani School, established by Maharaja Sir Pratap Singhji for Rajput Boys is the alma mater of Col. Bahadur Singhji and also his brave son AVM Chandan Singh.

The liberation war of Bangladesh was successfully brought to an end after less than two weeks of fighting by the surrender of the Pakistan army on 16th December 1971. Bangladesh and India owe a great debt to Lt. General Sagat Singh and AVM Chandan Singh who made this feat possible by making a bold & direct thrust towards Dhaka by crossing the mighty Meghna river successfully. Without their dynamic initiative & leadership who knows for how long the war would have lingered on and what the final outcome would have been and how many more lives lost.

AVM Chandan Singh received the awards and honors of Ati Vishist Seva Medal in 1962, Vir Chakra 1962, Mahaveer Chakra 1972 and was known as the most highly decorated and outstanding transport Pilot in the Indian Air Force.

I am confident that this book will provoke new thinking and will be found useful for those who are interested in joining the Armed Forces.

I must add a word of appreciation for the author Major Chandrakant Singh, who himself took part in the decisive Meghna crossing in '71 Bangladesh War, has chosen as his subject, this brave flying officer whose story will inspire future generations.

GAJSINGH
MAHARAJA OF JODHPUR

Author's Note

"A doer of things made possible,
He has come to be counted amongst the immortals."
—Dandin *Daskumar Charitra*

The Liberation War of Bangladesh was successfully brought to
an end after less than two weeks of fighting by the surrender of
the Pakistan army on December 16, 1971. The world, but most
of all Bangladesh and India, owe a great debt to Lt General
Sagat Singh and Air Vice Marshal Chandan Singh whose
leadership and hands-on approach helped to accomplish
this feat in less than a fortnight, an unbelievably short time.
Without their dynamic, hands-on, from the front, leadership
we do not know how long the war would have lasted, what
the final outcome would have been and how many thousands
of more lives lost. My friend Maj Gen Randheer Singh has
already written an excellent biography of Lt Gen Sagat Singh
and this is my effort for Air Vice Marshal Chandan Singh.
They are India's greatest war time commanders.

The reader may find that I have often digressed from AVM
Chandan Singh's personal narrative and dealt at length on
the social, historical, geographical and cultural environment
in which he lived his life. These digressions have been
deliberate, for to understand him we have to know about the
influences that have made him the man that he is, particularly
the example set by his own father Col Bahadur Singh OBI,
IDSM, CM, KJSM. When we talk of his father, we cannot but
mention his mentor the great soldier, statesman, sportsman
and patriot Maharajah Sir Pratap Singh of Idar and Prime

Minister of Jodhpur who strode through the late nineteenth and early twentieth centuries like a colossus, a friend of Queen Victoria, Edward VII, George V and Edward Prince of Wales the future Edward VIII, Churchill, Curzon and Kitchener. Friend of Dayanand Saraswati, Swami Vivekanand, patron of the great cricketer Ranjit Sinhji known as Ranji after whom the Ranji trophy is named. He was also the father, uncle or patron of the best polo players in the world in their time. The life and times of Chandan Singh and his father covers a period of almost a century and a half.

We Indians, unlike the British, have scant regard or knowledge of our own history leave alone the history of other nations. So it has been necessary for me to give at least a brief account of the geography and history of the regions that extend all the way from India to Europe encompassing all the countries in between, in which important events in the lives of AVM Chandan Singh and his father Col Bahadur Singh were played out. So reader if you find that I am digressing from the life of the chief protagonist of this biography please forgive me but understand that it is an attempt to inform the reader of events of another era and of places, some of which have outwardly changed beyond recognition but are still beset with problems of the past which have resurfaced with a vengeance and are playing out "Apocalypse Now".

It is the sum total of inherited traits and qualities acquired from the environment that one lives one's life in, that makes a man what he becomes. As naturalists say it is both nature and nurture that make us what we are. My own view is that nurture plays a greater part than nature (inherited traits). Those readers who have served in the Defence Forces will understand, we all know that in our behaviour and outlook we are closer to our present and erstwhile colleagues in the Forces than to our kith and kin with whom we share our DNA. This then is the story not only of his career and accomplishments of which there are many but more of the man himself and the times and places in which he has played his innings.

The subject of this Biography, Air Vice Marshal Chandan

Singh, is a man cast in the heroic mould who has lived life on his terms and lived it well in the service of the country. My only encounter with him while in service was for a brief fifteen minutes on December 9, 1971, when the war had reached a point of decision and I found myself sitting in the hold of a MI-4 helicopter with some of my men. Sitting quietly and inconspicuously in one corner was then Group Capt Chandan Singh, the senior Air Officer in the IV Corps Sector.

We were in the first helicopter to take off and fly across the Meghna to land deep behind the enemy. Both my men and I were beset with uncertainty and anxiety, having been continually in action for the past nine days and having about one third of my men killed or wounded, we were a tired and exhausted company. Only four hours earlier we lad been pulled out of a twenty-four hour long running battle with the Pakistan Army at Ashuganj.

The battle was still raging and though we did not know of it at that time the two battalions 18 Rajputs and 10 Bihar that had replaced us had suffered very heavy casualties. Now instead of some rest we were being launched into this heliborne river crossing operation, an operation of this type which had never before been undertaken by any army in the world leave alone the Indian Army and since then it has not been undertaken again.

His presence was a great confidence booster to my men for if a senior Air Force officer was coming with us he would certainly know what was going on and all would be well. Many years after that event, I called on the Air Marshal at his home in Jodhpur and thereafter have met him several times and gleaned from him in bits and pieces the story of his life which spanned an era that encompassed some of the most momentous events in the history of mankind from the beginning of the twentieth century when the British Empire under Queen Victoria was at its height to the present 'ab ki baar Modi Sarkar'.

This period included the First World War, Second World War, India's Independence and the end of the British Empire and the Princely Order, the 1948/49 War in Kashmir, Indo-China Conflict 1962, Indo-Pak Wars of 1965 and 1971 and many other events that have had a profound influence on our country. He has not only been both a participant and witness but has helped to create this history.

At the time of my first meeting with him after the 1971 War in 2010, I was working on a personal account of the 1971 War and interviewing the veterans of the war to get to know their stories. After meeting him, I decided to put on hold my personal narrative for my own achievements pale into insignificance when compared to his and instead decided to write about Air Vice Marshal Chandan Singh. I know of no one else who has lived life more fully and with accomplishments unmatched by any one else.

The Air Marshal like all truly great men is extremely modest and reticent about his accomplishments and would not say a word about himself, so I was forced to do my research elsewhere till something happened and the Air Marshal began dishing out morsels of information. What emerges is a man whose life and achievements are so astonishing that in any other country by now they would have been the subject of many books and TV documentaries.

He is fortunate to have inherited the right DNA from his father Col Bahadur Singh OBI, another legendary soldier who deserves a biography to himself and whose life and times I have covered in considerable detail in this book. He is also lucky to have lived in a social environment at a time which allowed the full exploitation of his natural talents and professional potential.

Now that I am in my mid-seventies, and like all people of my age, quite cynical about personalities and events, yet I am filled with wonder and admiration at his achievements and have joined the long list of admirers that began sixty-five years ago when he was posted as a squadron commander of King Squadron at the National Defence Academy. To his cadets he was an iconic leader, loved and literally worshipped by all. Even today when the teenage cadets of that time who are now all in their late seventies get together, and like all old soldiers talk of times gone by they cannot help but get sentimental and choke with emotion whenever the conversation comes around to their Squadron Commander of old who like a father held their hand when they were most vulnerable and led them from diffidence and uncertainty of boyhood into becoming the men they are today.

Like his former cadets, I too idolise him and now that he is in his early nineties, God has granted him a well deserved peaceful and contented retirement, good health and the presence of a loving and doting family who like those who have had the privilege to serve with him, revere him.

Keeping this in mind and also the fact that a writer always puts something of himself in his writing as I have done, particularly because the subject is close to my heart, I beg the reader's indulgence and hope that they will understand and forgive my digressions into the bylanes and byways of his historical and geographical world.

I have omitted some accounts at the Air Marshal's insistence because they reflected adversely on some people. He is firm that nothing that would show any colleague of his from any of the Defence Services in a poor light should be mentioned and I have adhered to his wishes against my own inclinations. To lend authenticity and also to give a sense of immediacy, I have reproduced verbatim the accounts of important events by others who were either participants or witnesses to these events.

Since he will not speak about himself it has been difficult to find the real man behind the gold-braided peak cap and a chest full of medals. A man who is India's most highly decorated officer with accomplishments unmatched by any one living today. He has lived his life in several planes, firstly there is his karambhumi (field of action) and quest for knowledge to enable him to perform his varna dharma (duty) and then there is the spiritual, philosophical and unworldly side to him.

I have tried to explore these divergent elements of his life and attempted to record things that influence and concern them. Whether I have succeeded or not I do not know and only the reader can judge. It has been a tough call to pin a man down who moves seamlessly between the two opposing worlds of action and the spiritual. But that trait, many will agree is the hallmark of the truly great.

Once again I beg the reader's indulgence if he thinks that I am often digressing from the story of Air Marshal Chandan Singh himself and getting involved in the extraneous. The fact of the matter is—a life is not lived in a vacuum. It is lived amongst other individuals in a particular time and location. So the geography, people and events connected with his life or having an influence on it cannot be left out particularly when events taking place in these same theatres today continue to affect our lives and politics as they have done in the past.

Many purists and aviators are likely to find some mistakes in the details of the biography but I request them to bear with me for I am not an aviator myself and secondly most of the events whose accounts find a place in the book happened between half a century to a full century before the present. This is not a book on history or of the wars that India has fought nor is it a book of the history of the IAF, it is a book of a man who made history. I have shown the draft to several of my air force friends and incorporated their comments in the book. Some mistakes of omission or commission will still remain for which I seek the reader's indulgence.

The canvas of this biography is huge, encompassing the two world wars, India's Freedom Movement, the shadow of the Raj, Mahatma Gandhi and India's quest to safeguard its borders and interests. It would require someone with the talent of a Margaret Mitchell (*Gone with the Wind*) and a Tolstoy (*War and Peace*) to do justice to it and I claim no such talent but have tried to tell the story as best as I can and as I saw it heard and know.

Publisher's Note

History is a mute witness to magical transformations that the valiant son of Marwar AVM Chandan Singh underwent. From his childhood he had a tremendous urge to earn laurels for his motherland. He had a great passion for flying during his tenure at Rajasthan State Forces and later at IAF. His outstanding services during the Bangladesh war helped our nation to accomplish the mission in such a short time. He truly followed in the footsteps of his father, Col Bahadur Singh, a veteran of Jodhpur Risala.

AVM Chandan Singh has dedicated his whole life to the service of the nation. He has earned a great reputation for his relentless services throughout his career.

I have met him several times along with the author to know about the heroic deeds of his life. AVM Chandan Singh was a modest person and he never mentioned his accomplishments or himself. Indeed I am fortunate to be blessed by this great son of Marwar. His achievements are unparalleled and a source of inspiration for every fellow citizen.

I am grateful to Major Chandrakant Singh for accomplishing this Herculean task. Undoubtedly without his dedicated and selfless hard work it was not possible to publish this book. It is my duty to also mention the support of Shri Sajjan Singh, son of AVM Chandan Singh. He always extended his help for this project.

I conclude by expressing my deep sense of gratitude to our Managing Trustee H.H. Maharaja Gaj Singh Sahib. Under his kind directions and generous patronage MMPP has earned national stature. He is the main source of inspiration behind the progress made by our Institution.

Lastly, I am thankful to the Publisher Mr. Rahul Saxena of LG Publishers Distributors for his cooperation and suggestions.

Dr. Mahendra Singh Tanwar
MMPP Research Centre

1

Patrimony

Country makes a home for men
Men make the country

"....Then there are the Rajputs, who are supposed to be responsible for a thousand Thermopylaes, and not one little Thermopylae as in Greece. That is what the Englishman, Col Tod told us. Col Tod has taught us to believe that every pass in Rajasthan is a Thermopylae. Do these people stand in need of learning the art of defence?" Mahatma Gandhi during the second round table conference at a meeting of the Federal Structure Committee in London in 1931 to discuss India's defence issues in the new world order.

"There is nothing a Rajput treasures more than his honour, horse, sword, village, wine and women. The former three make the latter three possible." Col James Todd, historian and author of *Annals and Antiquities of Rajasthan*.

The Land and People

Marwar or Marusthali is the Western Desert wasteland of Rajasthan. It is mainly sparsely wooded low hills of the Aravalis and its outcrops in the east and stony flat plains or sand dunes in the west which extend across the border into Sindh. The eastern part of Sindh the Umarkot area (now in Pakistan) was once a part of Jodhpur State till it was exchanged by the British for some areas around Ajmer in the middle of the nineteenth century. Interspersed between the hills are a few seasonal rivers which run dry soon after the end of the monsoon.

This land is aptly named, for the name Marwar or Marusthali means the land of death. Before the advent of an irrigation network and of factories which collected and processed bones to produce gelatin for our ice creams and other processed foods, the countryside here used to be littered with the skeletons and carcasses of dead cattle, camels and other animals which provided a feast for vultures and other scavengers.

The whole land was reminiscent of the Skeleton Coast in Namibia. Agriculture was minimal and seasonal and the only means of sustenance was from cattle, goats, sheep and camels. It was not a place fit for humans and animals to live. Into this wasteland inhabited mainly by Bhil and Mina tribes, nomadic sheep and cattle herders and sustenance farmers about a thousand years ago, moved a people who had been driven out of their ancient homelands around Kanauj in the fertile Indo-Gangetic plains by Muslim invaders. They preferred the privations and hardships of the desert to subjugation. Here they made a home for themselves which is today the envy of the whole world.

The monochromatic desert landscape has come alive with the colours of their costumes, their art, architecture, music, food, festivals and culture but mostly by their heroic deeds in defence of their freedom, hard work and perseverance of the people in an environment of security and benevolent rule by the newly arrived Rathores and other Rajput clans.

The people have turned a once wasteland into one of the most prosperous and beautiful parts of India. The vibrancy of their culture and traditions attracts millions of visitors from all over the world who come here to marvel at its wonders not only architectural, but also the colours, costumes and customs of the people. It is today a living repository of what was once the best of India. The people themselves have moved comfortably into the modern world and yet preserve and take great pride in their inherited traditions.

All this is in sharp contrast to the civilisational and cultural developments after the Arab conquest in the Arabian

Peninsula and the North African desert which share similar climatic conditions. Here from a period of a state of high civilisation lasting several thousand years which ended with the Arab conquest after which the rapaciousness and uncivilised behaviour of the new lords, the whole region and people reverted to a state of semi-barbarism which continues even today in the twenty-first century. Proving that it is people who are a more important part than geography in the creation of great civilisations.

Over a millennium of patronage and protection by the Rajput rulers to the mercantile classes has allowed the Marwari trading community of Rajasthan known the world over for their enterprise and thrift to prosper, they have brought into the state industries and trade which with the recent discovery of oil in Barmer will bring more industry and prosperity to the state.

The State of Jodhpur: The Rathore Patrimony

Like all ruling dynasties the world over, the Rathores too claim divine descent, they lay claim to the Sun and Ram as ancestors. But historically we have proof only from about the sixth century when Grahvarman was King of the lower Ganga-Yamuna Doab (land between two rivers) with Kashi (Benaras) as its capital and from whom the original name of the clan Gaharwars is derived. The ancient name for the Ganga-Yamuna Doab was Kaushaldesh the Kingdom of the father of Lord Ram's mother Kaushalyaji. Grahavarman was married to Rajshree the sister of the famous Emperor Harshwardhan of Kanauj during whose reign the Chinese traveller Huen Tsuang visited India. Grahvarman was treacherously murdered by the Parmar King of Ujjain who in retribution was hunted down and killed in battle by Harshwardhan about whom much has been written by the famous Huan Tsuang. In her sorrow Rajshree wanted to commit Sati but Harsha's timely arrival prevented her from committing herself to the flames.

This dynasty continued to rule the Ganga-Yamuna Doab till the end of the twelfth century when it was ousted by Mohammad Ghori. The most famous of Grahvarman's descendants were a father and grandson duo Govindchandra and Jaichandra who ruled from Kanauj in the eleventh and twelfth centuries.

Govindchandra is rightfully remembered as a great king. He was a patron of the arts and many works of literature and religious texts were written in his time. He also built some of the most celebrated temples in North India including the Keshav, Kedar and Vishwanath Temples in Kashi which were later destroyed by Muslim iconoclasts.

His grandson Jaichandra however failed to measure up and it is in his time that North India was lost to Mohammad Ghori and the Rathore branch of the Gaharwars were forced to leave their ancient homeland and seek refuge in the deserts of Rajasthan. Another cadet branch of the Gaharwar clan that was at Benaras had moved earlier southwards into the Vindhya Hills in what is now Bundelkhand and established several small kingdoms which survived till independence when they like Jodhpur merged with the Indian Union.

It would however be wrong to put all the blame for the Muslim conquest of India on Jaichandra as historians have done. More than him I consider the much celebrated Prithviraj Chauhan the King of Delhi who by constant warfare with his neighbours had weakened not only them but himself too. A year before his defeat at Tarain by Ghori he had invaded Bundelkhand (ancient Jijahauti), a surprising and some would say a foolish act for his own sister was married to the Crown Prince of Jijahauti.

He had already antagonised Jaichandra, the ruler of Kanauj who was his maternal uncle by eloping with his daughter Sanjukta and now he did the same with his own brother-in-law. He knew he had not done yet with Mohammad Ghori and yet he antagonised two powers who could have been his strongest allies. In a fiercely contested but inconclusive battle with the Chandelas the rulers of Jijahauti, he lost half his army and he himself was severely wounded. He was saved by his

General Raisinha who himself was mortally wounded and lay dying on the battlefield.

To ward off the vultures and dogs from attacking the wounded Prithviraj, Raisinha cut off pieces of his own flesh and threw them to the dogs and vultures which kept them away from Prithviraj till help arrived. To save his king he sacrificed his own life. The memory of Raisinha lives on today in the name of Raisina Hill where the high institutions of our State including Rashtrapati Bhawan, Houses of Parliament and North and South Block are located. This battle on the banks of the Chambal at Orai is the subject of a famous poem 'Ala Udal' by his court poet Chand Bardai. Chand was his court poet and also author of the *Prithvirajraso*.

These two poems by him the 'Ala Udal' and 'Prithvirajraso' are considered to be the best examples of Hindi poetry in the 'heroic vein' or 'veer ras' and were recited by wandering minstrels in village squares during the monsoon months. Alas television has killed the minstrel and bardic traditions like a many other things.

Another collateral branch of the Gaharwars from a mixed caste union of one the Gaharwar princes with a Brahmin girl had moved even earlier into the Vindhyas in the seventh century and came to be known as the Chandela dynasty who are today famous for having built the temples at Khajuraho. The Chandela dynasty lasted till the time of Sher Shah Suri who treacherously killed the last Chandel King Kirit Shah during the siege of the Kalinjar Fort.

But his daughter Rani Durgawati who after her marriage to Dalpat Rai, the King of Gondwana, on the premature death of Dalpat Rai, became the Ruling Queen Mother and continued the struggle against the Muslim invaders. She died a heroic death on the battlefield while fighting against Akbar's general Asif Khan. Durgawati when wounded in the eye by an arrow snatched a dagger from her mahout and plunged it into her breast preferring death and honour to dishonour or captivity. Today she is a celebrated and iconic figure in Central India and deserves to be better known.

After their forced eviction from Kanauj in 1192 the Rathores wandered in the barren deserts of Rajasthan till the twelfth century when Rao Chanda overthrew the Parihar Ruler of Mandore and established himself there as the new Lord of Marwar. One of Rao Chanda's grandsons, Jodha started the building of the fort of Mehrangarh and moved his court there with the new town of Jodhpur coming up below the Fort. Rao Jodha's sons were as accomplished warriors as him and some of them went on to found new kingdoms of their own such as Bikaner.

New sub-clans emerged from the original Grahawar/ Rathores. The more prominent ones are Jodha, Bika, Mertia and Champawat. The last being Chandan Singh's own clan. Soon after Jodha's time the fate and history of Jodhpur got linked to the Mughals, sometimes in their support but more often in opposition. Being able to muster a force of over fifty thousand horsemen they came to be a power to be reckoned with.

One of the Maharajahs of Jodhpur even decapitated the head of Emperor Shah Jahan's brother-in-law at a durbar in the Dewan-e-Khas in the Red Fort for slighting him in an open durbar. When in the early nineteenth century the British arrived they recognised the military potential of the Rathores and other Rajput Princes and co-opted them as allies. When the British arrived the Rajput Princes were happy to make peace with them for after a turbulent century of unrest and disorder during the decline of the Mughal Empire the British were able to establish order and peace in the land. Moreover the British left them alone to live and govern themselves as they had done before for centuries. Today in independent India the finest and the bravest soldiers still come from here.

In India another group that provides a disproportionate number of soldiers to India's Defence Forces are the Sikhs, many of whom particularly the Phulkian States of Patiala, Nabha, Jind, Faridkot and Kapurthala claim kinship with Rajput clans of Rajasthan. The valour and fighting ability of the Rajputs has been acknowledged time and again by no less a person than Mahatma Gandhi in the speeches he made to students of the Law College in Madras in 1920, in Navsari in 1921 and in Palitana in 1925.

His speech in London in 1931 when the issue of India's defence was discussed, has been quoted at the beginning of this chapter. In all these speeches Mahatma Gandhi has quoted from Tod's account of there being a thousand Thermopylaes in India to Greece's one.

Bagawas: Chandan's Patrimony

The village of Bagawas in the Sojat Pargana is about fifty miles south east of Jodhpur, and towards the south of Bagawas is Mewar, the Kingdom of the Maharana of Mewar now more popularly known as Udaipur. Marwar Junction about forty kms to the west is the nearest railway station to Bagawas. The population of the village today is a few thousand and agriculture is the main occupation, but earlier it was animal husbandry.

Thanks to the extension of electrical transmission lines the farmers are able to pump water from deep bore wells to irrigate their fields. The underground water table is replenished every monsoon from the runoff from the Aravali Hills and the soil being sandy the water percolates deep into the soil where it remains trapped above an impervious under layer of granite and other metamorphic rocks like marble.

In the fields that have no access to irrigation, millets and other monsoon crops are grown and lately Henna cultivation has started in a big way. The henna grown here is considered to be of the highest quality and is not only exported to the rest of the country but is also exported to other countries, particularly Japan where when mixed with indigo it is used as a natural hair dye which gives the hair a dark reddish brown shade favoured by East Asian men and women alike. Henna in its pure form is also the first choice as a colouring agent by Arabs and many elderly South Asians for dyeing their beards and hair a mousy orange-brown. Red hair on the Irish may look fine but on dark skinned Indians and Arabs who do it to disguise their grey hair it looks quite ridiculous. It is believed that the custom of dyeing beards has come down from Muhammad.

Tourism has also picked up, and many old forts, palaces and havelis have been converted into heritage homes and hotels. Thanks to tourism many owners of these heritage properties are now financially more comfortable than they ever were even during the heydays of feudalism. Tourism has provided employment to hundreds of thousands of people directly and also given a boost to the arts and crafts industry in which several millions find employment. One of the chief beneficiaries of tourism is the Air Marshal's own son-in-law, Veerbhadra Singh, the Rawat of Deogarh whose magnificent fort-palace and art collection is the rival of the best in Rajasthan.

Col Bahadur Singh OBI, IDSM, CM, KJSM

Chandan Singh's father Bahadur Singh was born in 1894 in Sadalwas which was the parental village of his mother. It was and still is the custom for expecting mothers to proceed for confinement and delivery of the first born to their parental home for delivery. Sadalwas is a village close to Bera, the chief town of the jagir known by the same name as the town.

The Thakur of Bera was married to Sir Pratap's daughter and was a major feudal lord of Jodhpur. At this time Marwar was passing through trying times, Bahadur Singh's father Thakur Bharat Singh was an independent and fairly affluent landowner in the village of Bagawas which he had to abandon due to the long drought. He had possessed a large herd of cattle all of which perished in the five-year long drought that afflicted Marwar in the late nineteenth century. Reduced to penury he was forced to accept employment as a game keeper in the Maharaja's private shooting reserve at Rs. 6 a month.

The hard work, poor food and below subsistence level wages took a heavy toll on his parents' health and Bahadur Singh was orphaned when he was only about four years old. His father was the first to pass away followed by his mother, just two days later. Bahadur Singh was then taken by his relatives to his mother's parental home to be looked after by her family. His maternal family, were also going through difficult times as the long drought that had afflicted Marwar for several years had affected them too and an extra mouth to feed was a burden. Bahadur Singh even at this tender age was a sensitive boy and sensed that he was a burden on his uncle and aunt. People's memories are short, but those people now in their sixties and seventies would remember that as late as the 1960s people died of starvation in India. The American gift of wheat under Plan 480 was like manna from heaven and at the same time the high yielding hybrid wheat and rice varieties became available which has now made India into a grain surplus state.

Bahadur Singh unable to bear the feeling of hurt of being a burden on his maternal family decided one day to leave his maternal home and walked to Marwar Junction the nearest railway station and boarded a train without a ticket, hungry and in handed down rags like any village urchin. It is unlikely that he knew what he was doing or where he was going and the possible consequences of his action. But as the saying goes 'luck favours the bold'. The last stop was Rai Ka Bagh Station at Jodhpur close to the Rai Ka Bagh Palace, the residence of Sir Pratap who was the Regent of the State during the minority of his nephew the Maharajah.

Here he got down and started walking aimlessly, hungry and in torn and soiled clothes. Fortunately for him he was spotted by some members of the guard at Sir Pratap's residence who took him to the barracks of the Jodha Squadron of Jodhpur Lancers, the barracks were at the foot of Chhitar Hill close to the residence of the legendary Maharajah Sir Pratap Singh. The top of Chhitar Hill is now the location of the magnificent Umed Bhawan Palace which was built a few decades in the 1930s and 40s as a famine relief work when Marwar was passing through another period of drought.

The barracks designed by Col Swinton Jacob are beautiful buildings which bear the stamp of Swinton Jacob's harmonising of Oriental/Rajput exteriors and Western interiors and engineering. These barracks are now used as the Jodhpur University boys' hostel but like nearly all government buildings, are in a sorry state of neglect. At the Barracks he was asked by the Lancers as to who he was and what he was doing there. Displaying the spirit that was to be the hallmark of his life, he replied, "I am Bahadur Singh, son of Thakur Bharat Singh Champawat, a Rajput of Bagawas village."

As luck would have it the off duty Lancer who questioned him also happened to be a Champawat and took him under his wing. On being asked whether he had eaten before his arrival, he replied in the negative. So the cavalryman took him inside to join them for a meal of curried pork and millet (bajra) bread, the like of which he had not had since the death of his parents but was the standard fare of the cavalrymen. Pork was in plentiful supply because wild boar roamed freely on Chhitar Hill which from the 1940s onwards is crowned by the magnificent Umed Bhawan Palace which along with Mehrangarh Fort dominates the skyline of Jodhpur and the surrounding countryside.

The wild boar were not hunted by shooting with rifles. Only ladies were allowed the use of the gun in a boar hunt. The men had to spear them, but some ladies as old paintings show also indulged in equestrian sports including polo and pig sticking. The wild boar once flushed from their hideouts were chased and speared by riders on horseback to provide meat for the sowars (cavalrymen) of Jodhpur Lancers.

Hunting the wild boar on horseback is known as pig sticking. It is an adventurous and dangerous sport and also provided meat for the table. In addition, it was the best possible training for cavalry men. It also had the thrill of the chase and danger of combat as a cornered and wounded boar was a dangerous adversary. Pig sticking as sport and training for war seems to have been prevalent in India for centuries as the frieze from a tenth century temple at Khajuraho shows. Little did they realise that this starving urchin whom they had taken under their wing would one day grow up and command their regiment.

Word about Bahadur Singh's arrival at the Lancer's lines reached Sir Pratap and he arranged to have him accommodated with the Lancers in their barracks. Sir Pratap was a reformist and had started a school in the Lancers' Lines for the children of the sowars. In the early days it was run from a single room. Bahadur Singh was admitted to this school which was the precursor to the Chaopasni School which was under construction at the time. He studied here for about four years till the time the new buildings for the school were ready and the students were shifted to the new school building which is where the school is still located.

The Chaopasni School was started to give the Rajput boys of Jodhpur State a proper education and no tuition and hostel fees were charged so that the parents would be encouraged to send their wards to school. The conservative Rajputs did not give much importance to proper education, thinking that horsemanship and arms training is all that Rajputs needed. Sir Pratap had to cajole and even threaten parents to send their children to school.

The Mayo College at Ajmer had been started some years earlier but was reserved for the wards of the royalty and nobility. The medium of instruction was English, whereas at Chaopasni at that time it was Hindi. The graduates from here were expected to serve in junior and middle level positions in Jodhpur State and they would have little or no contact with the British or the outside world and hence Hindi was considered to be quite adequate.

Life in the Lancers' Lines was not easy for a young boy. He had to run errands for the sowars and help them with odd jobs including care of their horses which he came to love. But the food was excellent and he was comfortably housed. The sowars and their wives were kind and considerate and they all grew fond of this spirited boy and treated him as one of their own. Bahadur fed on a high protein and rich diet both at the school and with the families of the sowars after years of deprivation, developed into a strapping lad taller than all the other boys of his age. The Jodhpur Lancers was to be his home for the next forty years.

Chaopasni School shifted to its present permanent location when the magnificent building was completed, Bahadur Singh along with the other boys moved there. It was at the new location of Chaopasni School when he was about ten or eleven years old that a Swami from the Arya Samaj visited Jodhpur and came to see the school and speak to the boys. Jodhpur had an old connection with the founder of the Arya Samaj, Swami Dayanand Saraswati, who had spent many years here as a guest of Maharajah Jaswant Singh, the elder brother of Sir Pratap.

In fact the Maharajah was so impressed with Swami Dayanand Saraswati's zeal to reform Hindu society and rid it of undesirable practices that he wanted to set an example by introducing reform in his personal and court life. He made a beginning by getting rid of the dancing girls and concubines who were a regular feature of princely courts. One of the concubines Jaan Bai, fearing the loss of her position bribed a cook to poison Swami Dayanand Saraswati who had to be sent to Ajmer for treatment but could not recover and succumbed to the effects of the poison soon afterwards at Bhinai near Ajmer.

The cook was caught and confessed but before Swamiji died he pardoned the cook who out of respect for the wishes of Swami Dayanand Saraswati was not hanged and only imprisoned. The Arya Samaj, a reformist movement that he founded is flourishing and active and has a large following in North India and runs many educational institutions and religious centres.

Among other things the visiting Swami told the boys about the evils of eating meat and the needless and untold pain and hurt inflicted on animals just to provide food for human beings who could just as well subsist on a vegetarian diet. This visiting Swami must have been a very powerful and convincing speaker for about a dozen boys decided to become vegetarian and give up eating meat and subsist on plain dal and millet bread as vegetables were not readily available in most of Marwar except during the rainy season.

After a week or so this was brought to the notice of Sir Pratap who was furious for he considered that a balanced diet of meat and cereals was a prerequisite in the building of the physique required to the making of a good soldier, which was the natural and varna (caste) dharma and calling of every Rajput. He had already persuaded Swami Dayanand to exempt the martial classes from the taboo on eating meat.

He came to the school with a cane in hand and had the errant vegetarians lined up and expressed his severe displeasure and told them that hereafter all boys would revert to being non-vegetarians and if any boy refused he would be flogged. All other boys agreed but Bahadur Singh refused and was flogged with fourteen strokes of his cane by Sir Pratap. On leaving the school, Sir Pratap announced that he would return in a few days and if by then he had not started eating meat he would flog him with twice as many strokes.

Two weeks later, Sir Pratap returned and finding that Bahadur still refused to eat meat flogged him twenty-eight times but Bahadur would not relent. Without saying anything further, Sir Pratap left, perhaps he had spotted some quality in the boy which held promise for future greatness. Sir Pratap was known to be quite liberal in wielding his cane even on sons of the nobility and officers of the State Forces who did not perform as well as he expected of them. He was also known to wield the cane on the members of the Jodhpur Polo Team which included his sons and nephews if they lost an important polo match. He himself was an excellent player and it is under his tutelage that the Jodhpur team became the number one team in India and held that position for over four decades.

Winston Churchill played polo on a few occasions at Jodhpur when he was a subaltern with the 4th Hussars. In his autobiographical book *My Early Years* he says that no team played polo harder than the Jodhpurs, who would charge at full gallop not only at the ball but also at the opposing players and emerging from a cloud of dust leave the opposing players no choice but to give way to avoid injury or worse. Churchill has words of praise for not only Sir Pratap but also two other players, Hurjee and Dhokul Singh.

The former was the father of Major Dalpat Singh MC who fell leading the charge of the Jodhpur Lancers at Haifa. Sir Pratap was a dominant figure in Princely India during the late nineteenth and early twentieth century. He counted amongst his friends the Kings and Queens of England including Victoria, even the Viceroy deferred to him.

Many of the present generation may not know of him. For their benefit I have included as an appendix a short biographical account. Of Sir Pratap and Polo in Jodhpur, I quote Churchill's own words in his biography *My Early Life,*

> "We now have to turn to more serious affairs,......we had arranged for a fortnight at Jodhpur and here we were the guests of the famous Sir Pratap, the Regent of Jodhpur as the Maharajah was still a minor.....
>
> Every evening he and his young kinsmen, two of whom, Hurjee (Hari Singh, a favourite of Sir Pratap) and Dokul Singh were as fine players as India has ever produced, with other Jodhpur nobles, played us in carefully conducted instruction games. Old Pratap, who loved polo next only to war more than anything else in war, used to stop the game repeatedly and point out faults or possible improvements in our play.....
>
> The Jodhpur ground rises in great clouds of red dust when a game is in progress. These clouds carried leeward on the strong breeze introduced a disturbing and somewhat dangerous complication. Turbaned figures emerged at full gallop from the dust cloud, or the ball whistled out of it unexpectedly. It was difficult to follow the whole game and one often had to play to avoid the dust cloud. The Rajputs were quite used to it...

Bahadur Singh was a quick learner and excelled in his class but when he was just fourteen and had passed Class 9 he decided to quit school and join the Jodhpur Lancers. He was under age to be a sowar so was inducted as a syce (groom), something he was not too happy about. But that was how it was to be for the next couple of years. As syce he had to look after the horses and their equipment. Having grown up on the lines of Jodhpur Lancers he knew all the men and the horses which he loved, for this was the only family he knew. Bahadur Singh was dreaming big and never forgot that just a generation before his family were landed gentry and not petty landholders which a series of draughts had reduced them to. As a feudal lord he was entitled to be an officer and not a lowly syce or sowar and moreover he was educated which was more than what some of the officers and junior commissioned officers were.

On one of Sir Pratap's rounds of the Jodhpur Lancers, Bahadur Singh walked up to him and told him that he wanted to be an officer. Sir Pratap surprised at his boldness was taken aback and mumbled something to the affect that soon Bahadur Singh would become one if he worked hard enough. Bahadur Singh was now six feet two inches tall, the tallest and most educated man in the regiment, plus he was an excellent horseman and marksman making him the most distinguished member of the Lancers' community.

Bahadur Singh and the First World War

Many people ignorant of the conditions that prevailed in India during the Raj have disparagingly condemned Indian soldiers who served in the British Indian Army as mercenaries. Among this critical group were and still are a large number of the political class who in their professions and businesses profited immensely from the patronage extended to them by the Raj.

These are today the denizens of Lutyens' Delhi, for having profited immensely by sucking up to the British masters. They became beneficiaries of grants of prime land in New Delhi which allowed them to masquerade as neo-royals. In one generation from petty traders and contractors they have become India's new royalty. Among them were the Thapars, whose father Devan Thapar and Kushwant Singh's father Sujan Singh about whom I have written in greater detail elsewhere in this book. To them and to those whom even today subscribe to this view that Indian soldiers were mercenaries I reproduce below an extract from a letter written in 1914 by Mahatma Gandhi to Lord Chelmsford the then Viceroy of India—

> ...We must give as we have decided to give ungrudging and unequivocal support to the Empire..... I was in-charge of the Indian Ambulance Corps consisting of eleven hundred men during the Boer war....was present at the battles of Colenso, Spionkop and Vaalkranz and Mentioned in Dispatches by Gen Buller.

Earlier during the Zulu War, Gandhi encouraged the British to recruit Indians and argued that Indians should support the war effort to legitimise their claims to citizenship.

During the First World War, Gandhi actively recruited combatants. In a June 1918 pamphlet titled 'Appeal for Enlistment, Gandhi wrote, "To bring about such a state of things we should have the ability to defend ourselves that is, the ability to bear arms and use them when we gain independence. If we have to learn the use of arms with the greatest dispatch it is our duty to enlist ourselves in the Army". Gandhi behind his garb of sainthood was a staunch nationalist and a hard headed pragmatist.

For his support, Gandhi was awarded the Kaiser-e-Hind Medal! It must be remembered that it was during the Boer War that it was the British who first introduced the concept of concentration camps. Hundreds of thousands of Boers—men, women and children were interred and several thousand perished of hunger and disease. Hitler only took a leaf from the British book. The Germans were in the know of what the English had done for it was after all the Germans who were supporting the Boers and supplying them with arms and ammunition to fight the British. The British Commanders-in-Chief in South Africa were Lord Roberts and Kitchener both of whom had India connections and about whom Kipling has written paeans of praise.

On the outbreak of the First World War the Regiment was preparing to sail to France. When one day Bahadur Singh with utmost self-confidence bordering on gumption purchased all the accruements of a Daffadar (sergeant in the Indian Cavalry) and wearing them walked to the office of the Commanding Officer and said, "Daffadar Bahadur Singh reporting for duty." The Commanding Officer taken aback said, "who the devil has promoted you?" To which Bahadur replied, "Sir Pratap", beginning and end of the conversation! Not even the Commanding Officer who was Sir Pratap's nephew could muster courage to check back with Sir Pratap, for such was the awe in which he was held not only by Indian but even by the British. (The readers of today may find it hard to digest that such things could happen, but they must remember that it was the Golden Age of Princely India when the word and wishes of the Maharajah ruled supreme).

And so as a Daffadar, Bahadur Singh moved with the Lancers by train to Bombay and then boarded a steamship on August 29, 1914, for the long journey to Egypt. All the officers and crew of the ship were British and Bahadur Singh always quick on the uptake and with a talent and ear for foreign languages learnt to speak passable English in the two weeks they were at sea before reaching Port Said. Here the Captain of the ship decided to host a banquet for Sir Pratap who having arrived earlier was in Egypt already and was coming on board at Suez to see his men on their way to Cairo.

Sir Pratap's understanding and speaking ability in English was rudimentary so he asked for an interpreter from the officers so that he could converse with the Captain who would be seated next to him at the table, but not one amongst the officers could converse in English. So Sir Pratap asked if there was any one else and was told that there was a Daffadar who could speak English and so Bahadur Singh was detailed to stand behind Sir Pratap and translate for him but Bahadur Singh refused saying that unless he was promoted to the rank of Risaldar he would not do so. The Commanding Officer having no time to find another interpreter had no choice but to promote him to the rank of Risaldar, a rank unique to the Indian army which was higher than that of a non-commissioned officer but lower than that of an officer.

They were known as Viceroy's Commissioned Officers before independence and are now called Junior Commissioned Officers or JCOs in short.) Sir Pratap on seeing Bahadur Singh and that too in Risaldar's rank was surprised and asked him "Bahaduria who has made you a risaldar and where have you learnt English?" To which the reply was, "Hukum it was you who promised me the rank and I presumed that is was what you desired and so the badges of rank, and as for English two weeks on the ship with the crew were enough." Being happy with Bahadur Singh's work as an interpreter at the banquet, Sir Pratap confirmed him in his new rank.

At Port Said the lancers disembarked and rode to Cairo and were given the task to quell any potential rebellion amongst the Egyptians. Their secondary task was to be reserve to meet any threat posed by the Turks to the Suez Canal. Egypt for many centuries had been a part of the Turkish Ottoman Empire and amongst the residents there was some residual sympathy for their co-religionists and former masters.

Most of the Allied troops with the exception of Indians were war time conscripts whose discipline and respect for officers left much to be desired. Even frequent use of the whip which was allowed at this time had little deterrent effect. The Allied High Command was therefore keen to have a well disciplined and reliable force to maintain order in the city and also as a counter to unruly Allied troops, particularly Australian and New Zealanders who after visits to local bars and brothels were involved in many incidents of rioting, looting and even murder. These incidents were triggered generally by brawls originating in the bars and brothels.

In some cases whole units of the Allied Forces were involved. The situation became so bad that eventually many of these units had to be moved out of Cairo and other towns to the Suez Canal Zone. Since there was a danger that the protests from the locals in Cairo could turn into an open rebellion, for as mentioned earlier there was latent sympathy for the Turks amongst the general population, who in many cases were descended from the Turks, the result of centuries of Turkish rule in Egypt.

Besides the law and order problems the other danger was of the spread of venereal diseases amongst the troops, particularly in the contingents from Australia, Canada and New Zealand where in percentage terms it was three times higher than in British Units. But the British themselves had a number ten times higher than that amongst Indian troops of the British Indian Army. However in the troops of the Indian State Forces the figure was negligible. In the rest of the Army at any one time about 11,000 troops which is approximately the number of troops in an army division were out of action on account of sexually transmitted diseases.

In the Middle Eastern Theatre, more soldiers were being treated for STD than battlefield injuries. In the hope that the twin problems of molestation of local women and sexually transmitted disease could be solved if troops could be provided legitimate access to women, organized brothels were set up in the war zones under the supervision of army doctors but statistics of STD amongst troops indicate that this experiment was a failure. The disease lies dormant in the carrier for months before it can be detected. However it is transmitted to those who have come into contact with the carrier during this period.

This was a problem that had to be faced by the army again later during the Second World War and it continues to be so even today in all armies with the added danger of HIV. In the Second World War in the three weeks after landing in Normandy on June 5, 1944 there were over three thousand cases of rape and murder of French women by American troops. This is a problem which all military commanders and historians like to ignore but that does not make it go away. Because when you put hundreds of thousands of young men with very high levels of testosterone in a war zone amongst a civilian population, only very high levels of discipline and moral character can control the problem.

The spread of AIDS in Asia and many other parts of the world can be directly attributed to American Servicemen who starting with the Vietnam War had infected whole populations in South East Asia. These servicemen themselves had become infected with the virus which had become endemic in their home country amongst the gay population of California.

The Indian Army can proudly claim to have mastered the beast within, and by and large it is not a major problem, yet it has to be vigilant for a few cases of HIV have been reported amongst the personnel returning home after UN assignments. Rape by Indian soldiers is rare and it is with full confidence and great pride that I state that we did not have one case of rape reported by our troops in Bangladesh after its liberation in 1971. Nearly all cases of rape and molestation by soldiers reported from Kashmir on investigation have been found to be false, the allegations against the army have been motivated and traced to people sympathetic to Pakistan and on their payroll as has been discovered by the media recently.

Some readers may consider that being a former soldier myself my opinion of the Indian soldier is biased in their favour. However to dispel any doubts about the Indian soldier, I quote two of the most celebrated British Commanders in Chief—Arthur Wellesley, the first Duke of Wellington and Lord Kitchener. For sceptics it will be worthwhile to read the statistics available in the United Nations Records of such cases from troops of all countries who serve in similar conditions and compare them with cases amongst the Indian troops serving with the UN.

Wellington has been known to have famously called the British Tommy 'the scum of the earth'. On the other hand, he has said that even the Battle of Waterloo was more easily won than some of the battles he fought against Indian troops in India. Kitchener in a memorandum written in 1904 states 'soldiers of the Indian Army are of comparatively high social standing; many of them of good birth. Some poor may be, but will take no service except that of a soldier. They possess many sterling and admirable qualities and have proved themselves as excellent fighting men and fit to stand shoulder to shoulder with the best. It follows that they are proud and being sensitive, their sensibilities are easily offended.'

For the Allies, things were not going too well in Europe. The Germans had broken through the Allied defences and there was a real danger of Paris falling to the Germans leading to the total collapse of the Allies. To stem the rout they were desperately in need of reinforcements and the nearest available troops were the Indians in Egypt, so only after a short stay in Egypt and even before they had been operationally deployed in combat the Lancers were ordered to leave their horses behind and were sent by steamship to Europe.

They sailed from Port Said to Marseilles and arrived on October 12, 1914 and from there by train to Orleans where they were issued cold weather clothing and bayonets. For the last fifty miles to the front lines they had to use farm carts or anything else that they could lay their hands on as no motorised transport was available and there was an element of confusion and administrative breakdown.

The British had lost most of their mechanical transport in the hasty retreat after their initial setbacks.

The Allied Forces were also facing a crisis because of low morale of the troops and shortage of manpower to man their defences after their early losses to the German army. So bad was the situation of manpower, that labour battalions from China had to be drafted for digging trenches and other defence works.

There was a danger of the Allied front line collapsing altogether but the timely arrival of an Indian Corps stabilised the Allied Front. But these troops by temperament, training and equipment were more suited for service in the dry and warm climate of the Middle East whereas in France they found themselves in a totally different environment.

Flanders was cold and wet and life in the trenches unpleasant bordering on hell. The cold and wet conditions of trench warfare was something that these men from the desert were unaccustomed to. Fighting static infantry battles was anathema to the cavalry men and there was little opportunity for traditional cavalry charges that Sir Pratap and his Lancers were looking forward to. But whatever the hardships the Indians had to endure them and it is they who helped to halt the advance of the German army.

This fact was conveniently ignored by the British Government and it is only now that they are beginning to acknowledge the importance of the Indian contribution to the war effort. The Germans and Turks however paid handsome tributes to the fighting qualities of the Indians and acknowledged that had it not been for the arrival of Indian army reinforcements they would have broken through to Paris and the war would have ended with a German victory. Marshals Foch, Joffre, General French and General Haig the senior most allied commanders however acknowledged this in their private correspondence and treated Sir Pratap and the senior Indian officers with the highest respect.

Military historians now unburdened of the colonial legacy of their predecessors acknowledge the contribution of the Indian effort in staving off a disaster for the Allies. Some German military historians have confirmed in their writing that had it not been for the arrival of two corps from India they would have encircled Paris and the Allied Armies as was their plan. This plan conceived a decade earlier is known as the Schlieffen Plan named after Gen Eric von Schlieffen, the Chief of the German General Staff prior to the war.

Indian troops in France and Belgium were billeted with local families and this was a new experience for both. For the Indian troops whose only experience of Europeans was of the British in India where the British ruled and lorded over and treated Indians as an inferior race. Here in France the French women found themselves alone, for their own men had been conscripted and were out fighting at the front. They not only welcomed our men into their homes, but treated them as equals, cooked for them, did their washing and looked after them in all sorts of ways something that our men could never imagine the English memsahibs back home doing.

Fighting alongside the British and French troops the Indians for the first time felt that they were equal if not better than them. This knocked the stuffing out of the British propagated canard that the Europeans were a superior race. In any case the Lancers who had seen service in China alongside the British, French, Germans, Americans, Russians and Japanese during the Boxer War already knew that they were second to none.

The French home owners preferred Indians to other nationalities including their own to be billeted with them because the Indians were more disciplined, of cleaner habits and more polite than other troops. Many of our men developed relations with local ladies but it speaks highly of our people that no case of molestation or rape was reported, which cannot be said of troops from other nationalities.

The Indian Muslim troops deprived of female company and lack of privacy preventing them from exercising other popular options, appealed to the King Emperor George V saying that the great Caliph Umar had set a precedent by sanctioning leave to troops once a month to enable them to visit their wives. 'Jorj Pancham', the name by which King George V was referred to by Indian soldiers, was known to be a kind and benevolent ruler, would allow them to avail of this traditional privilege. If it was not possible to grant a long leave of absence even a week or two of local leave would suffice.

It was not necessary to return to India to avail of the benefit granted by Umar, the holy Quran and the Hadith allowed them the privilege of a temporary marriage which facility could be availed of in any rear area of France or England. In 1971 during the genocide in Bangladesh when a news reporter confronted Yayha Khan about the incidence of rapes of Bengali women by Pakistani soldiers, he replied "What do you expect my soldiers in East Pakistan to do to meet their natural needs? Return to the West wing every weekend."

Recently some of the letters sent home by Indian soldiers have been published and they make amusing reading. One soldier writes to a relative that he has saved two hundred and fifty rupees, a princely sum in those days, equal then to about a year's salary and he was proceeding to Paris on three days leave for rest and recreation when he intended to blow up his savings in the brothels. But would the recipient of the letter not let his father know about his intentions.

Another letter which could only have come from a Sikh sepoy has been quoted by Victor Mallet at a function at the UK High Commission to mark the centennial of the war. Balwant Singh writes, "The ladies are very nice and bestow their favours upon us freely. But contrary to the custom in our family, they do not put their legs over the shoulders when they are with a man." Indian troops who had only seen the untouchable memsahibs at home were surprised to be welcomed into the arms of working class French and English girls. These girls treated them as exotic and exciting treats rather than as social underlings.

Immediately on arrival near the front lines, Sir Pratap kept pressing the Allied Command for an old fashioned cavalry charge by the Jodhpur Lancers, but with the advent of trench warfare and massed artillery and machine gun fire, the nature of warfare had changed forever and horses had outlived their usefulness. So the Lancers were put to manning the trenches or kept in the reserve where their reputation for steadfastness would ensure that should the Germans succeed in punching a hole in the Allied Defences, the Jodhpurs would counter attack and fill the breach.

By 1917 with the arrival of tanks on the western front there was no chance that horses would ever be used again except as carriage animals. But the Lancers took part in many actions at Epehy, Villiers Ridge and Cambrai when tanks were used for the first time. Here they fought alongside the Canadian Cavalry Brigade. But all these actions were in a dismounted role. At Cambrai on December 1, 1917, Capt Pobert Trail who was attached to the Jodhpur Lancers from the Guides Cavalry was mortally wounded and awarded the Victoria Cross.

It is interesting to note that another member of the Jodhpur Lancers, Risaldar Govind Singh, who had been temporarily transferred to the 2 Lancers to make up their losses was also awarded the Victoria Cross in the same battle. The Jodhpur Lancers can rightfully claim to be one of the few units of the Commonwealth Armies to have won two Victoria Crosses in this or any war. The age of the war horse was over in Europe but it would be of interest to note that even though the German army in the Second World War was the most highly mechanised army in the world, they still used hundreds of thousands of horses not only as cart horses but also for towing artillery pieces. At the siege of Stalingrad and on other occasions these horses were slaughtered to feed the troops when food ran out. Even during the First War at the siege of Kut Al Amara in Mesopotamia when the Allied troops were besieged, horses and mules were slaughtered for food but Indian troops refused to eat them and many died of starvation while Europeans managed to survive on horse flesh.

At Kut Al Amara in the early years of the war an entire Allied Division surrendered to the Turks once their food and ammunition ran out. For the first time in the history of warfare attempts were made to drop supplies to the beleaguered garrison. In spite of the heroic efforts of the Australian pilots the attempt was unsuccessful with the supplies falling either into the Tigris or on the Turkish positions.

In 1917 the Americans entered the war and millions of reinforcements under the command of General George Pershing had started arriving in France and at about the same time tanks, a British invention made their appearance in large numbers, which provided the key to breaking the stalemate imposed by trench warfare. The Allied Command felt that Indian troops could now be spared from the Western Front and would be better employed in the Middle East where things were not going too well for the Allies who had suffered major reverses, the most famous ones being at Gallipoli and Kut at the hands of the Turks under the command of the legendary Gen Mustafa Kemal. He is now more popularly known as Kemal Ataturk (father of the Turks).

At Gallipoli the Allied troops suffered an ignominious defeat and had to withdraw leaving behind thousands of dead. At Kut Al Amara in 1916 the entire 12 Infantry Division led by British Officers had surrendered to the Turks after a five month siege. Only a few of the twelve thousand Indian troops survived the siege and subsequent imprisonment.

In captivity the British Commanding General Townsend and other British officers disgraced themselves. While they lived in comfort approaching luxury in a resort on Halki Island in the Sea of Marmara and were feted by their captors, the other ranks particularly Indians were starved and tortured. Many died in the long march to the prison camps and the lucky ones were buried in unmarked graves and the unlucky ones no longer able to keep pace with their colleagues fell by the way sides to be eaten by dogs and beetles while still alive too weak from thirst and hunger to drive them away.

According to eye witness accounts, many of the younger prisoners were subjected to un-natural sexual acts to which the Turkish elites like the Mamelukes were addicted to, even Lawrence of Arabia had to suffer the same fate when he was taken prisoner. In his much acclaimed autobiography *Seven Pillars of Wisdom*, he has recounted in detail his experience at the hands of his Turkish captor.

The Ottoman army and governing elites, the heirs to the Mamelukes and Janissaries who in earlier times were the elite troops and governing class of the Ottoman Empire and were by law forbidden to marry and raise families were notoriously famous for being homosexual with a partiality to pre-teen and teenage boys.

To meet its requirement of soldiers and administrators whose loyalty would only be to the Sultan and nobody else, the Ottoman Empire had a system called Devserine which means blood tax. This tax was paid by the Christians and other subjects of the Empire, whereby they were required to surrender their young sons to the state in lieu of money, it is from their ranks after forcible conversion to Islam that the Mamelukes and the Janissary were recruited.

Even today most of the Jihadists belong to groups who as youth have been denied legitimate outlets for their natural human needs with the opposite gender and have been traumatised in childhood by unnatural acts performed on them by their peers. So it is not surprising that they have such an extreme sense of hatred for all humanity and as and when the occasion arises they have no hesitation to indulge in random killing of men, women and children of all faiths, including their own.

A psychological study of the mindset of the Jihadists needs to be carried out and it has to be determined whether it is an inherited trait or is it brought about by the social environment in which they grow up or is it a combination of both?

After more than a century of European conquests this was only the second time in recent history that an Asiatic army had defeated an European Army. The first was a few years earlier when the Japanese defeated the Russians on land and sea. But it took another half a century for the final nail in the coffin of the myth of European superiority to be hammered in. It took millions of deaths during the Second World War, Korea, Vietnam and now Afghanistan and the Middle East for the average Western citizen to realise the wisdom of the saying by the greatest and wisest of the American war time commanders General of the Army Douglas MacArthur that any US president who put American GIs to fight a land battle in Asia should have his head examined.

The decision to relieve Indian troops from Europe and transfer them to the Middle East upset Sir Pratap who was still dreaming and rearing for an old fashioned cavalry charge in Europe with him in the lead. But the Allied Command convinced him that in the Middle East the Jodhpur Lancers would have plenty of opportunity to have his wish fulfilled.

Before leaving France, Sir Pratap decided to give a banquet for the Allied High Command which included the French commanders Marshals Joffre, Petain and British Generals Haig and French. As stated earlier, Sir Pratap's knowledge of English was rudimentary but his understanding of French was absolutely zero. So Sir Pratap's son then studying in England was called to act as interprator. This did not work out as Hanut Singh did not speak either Hindi or Marwari. So Sir Pratap asked for an interpreter from amongst the Jodhpur Lancers. The only one found was Risaldar Bahadur Singh who, as he had done earlier with English, had now mastered French.

However Bahadur Singh refused to be an interpreter, when asked why? He said that all the interpreters in other armies were of the rank of captain and would sit at the table with the dignitaries and not stand behind them like a waiter during the banquet. Unless these two conditions were fulfilled he would not interpret. Sir Pratap tried to reason with him but Bahadur Singh held his ground and Sir Pratap had to promote him and have him seated by his side as there was no one else who was proficient in spoken Marwari, the only language Sir Pratap knew well, whereas his guests could only speak English or French. There was no one including the British colonial officers who could stand up to Sir Pratap and he was known to always get his way, even bypassing the legendary Viceroy of India, Lord Curzon. But Bahadur Singh knew his man and could push the envelope as no one else could.

Life in France had not been a very pleasant experience for the Lancers and they were glad to leave it behind. During the time they had been here they saw the ruthlessness of modern warfare, where killing of both friend and foe was a mechanical process devoid of any honour and chivalry. This was not their concept of how battles should be fought. They saw the effect of poison gas attacks first at Ypres by the Germans and later in other battlefields by both sides. Men blinded and suffering with horrible boils on the skin and slowly choking to death. All this while living in trenches which had become cesspools with floating excreta and parts of human bodies blasted into smithereens by the constant bombardment of artillery, the likes of which had never been seen before.

At places the density of guns was more than one per yard of front. The constant thunder of exploding shells and rattle of machine guns was catatonic and as one soldier describing it said, "the sound appeared to be like a solid, if you put your finger to it you could feel it". Many soldiers could not put up with it and chose suicide or desertion to this life of living hell. Over eighty thousand shell-shocked British troops deserted or showed cowardice in the face of the enemy and were tried by court martial.

About three and a half thousand were convicted to death by firing squads and three hundred actually shot. In the French Army the numbers of executions was over six hundred. Many of the soldiers executed by firing squads were fifteen and sixteen year olds! If this was the state of Western civilisation is it a wonder then that the Jodhpurs and other Indian troops wanted nothing of it? In fact they came away with contempt for Europeans.

On return to Egypt the Jodhpur Lancers were reunited with their beloved chargers that had been left behind when they sailed for France. In France they had to make do with overage horses slightly better than ponies. They now joined Allenby's force in Mesopotamia and along with the Mysore and Hyderabad Lancers formed a part of the 15 Imperial Service Cavalry Brigade, 5 Cavalry Division and the Desert Mounted Corps under the command of a very capable Australian commander, Lt Gen Chauvel.

Here the Jodhpur Lancers were in their element and displayed their full fighting capabilities. In the ensuing battles they proved that they were the finest cavalry in the world and no one was their equal. One of their finest moments was first at the Battle of Abu Talal on July 14, 1918. Abu Talal is in the Jordan valley and was an obstacle in the way of the Allied advance to Jerusalem and was cleared by the Jodhpurs. Major Dalpat Singh the Sqd. Cdr. was awarded the Military Cross for his daring charge and capture of a machine gun post that was holding up their advance.

But the crowning moment was at Haifa on September 23, 1918 and then at Acre, Aleppo and Nahr e Bhist in Lebanon on the Mediterranean Coast. All these places had been the sites of major battles of Alexander the Great over two thousand years earlier but even before Alexander, the Egyptians, Hittite, Hurrians/Mitanni, Assyrians, Persians, and the Israelis had contested for the ownership of this land, which today the Christians, Arabs, Jews and Muslims alike call the Holy Land.

The first battle of which we have a contemporary account is the Battle of Qadesh in 1230 BC between the Egyptian Pharaoh Ramses the Great and the Hittites. For Alexander the Great in his entire campaign the most difficult victory next to his battles in India with Porus and the subsequent engagements with the Mallis in the Central and Lower Indus basin, was a siege of Tyre that lasted more than six months.

Tyre is only a few miles north of the Bay of Haifa. These places had also seen major battles during the Crusades and well before the Crusades battles between the Byzantium and the Arabs at Yarmouk. Later Napoleon came here but had to beat a retreat. This was not only an ancient land and cradle of early civilisations but also a land soaked with the blood of countless millions over several millennia.

This bloodshed continues even today between Arab and Arab, Shia and Sunni, Arab and Kurd, Persian and Arab, Arab and Turk, Turk and Kurd, Yazidi and Muslim, Jew and Muslim and Christian and Muslim and within the tribes and villages of the same ethnic groups. Its capture from the Turks was to have a profound effect on world history. Even today it is the source of most disputes amongst the followers of these religions and ethnic groups, each one of whom claim exclusive ownership of the land.

A few miles north of Beirut at the Nahr al Kalb Bhist also known as the Dog River or Lycus in Roman times because there used to be a statue of a wolf with its mouth open positioned on the northern end of the Roman Bridge. The bridge still stands as a testimony of Roman engineering skill, when the wind was blowing a howling sound like that of a dog would be made by the wind, hence the name. The statue of the wolf disappeared some time after the war, probably looted by some Allied troops.

On the hillside near the bridge are carved memorial

inscriptions by Ramses the Great 1230 BC, Nebuchanazzer of Babylon, 600 BC, Alexander 320 BC, Roman Emperor Caracalla 215 AD, Crusaders 1200 AD, Sultan Barquq 1390 AD Napoleon III in the 19th century and others all bearing testimony to their having passed by here as did the great Greek historian, geographer and travel writer Herodotus in 440 BC. Herodotus has recorded in his writings of having seen the inscriptions of Ramses and Nebuchanazzer.

Today it has been declared a World Heritage Inscription Monument site by UNESCO. More of this later when after another war, Chandan Singh visited this site in 1946 and found that the feat of arms Indian soldiers of his father's generation has also been rightfully acknowledged at this historic site by another inscription. Before he left the Middle East for home another inscription was carved here extolling the feats of arms of Indians in the Second World War. In all there are seventeen inscriptions at the Dog River.

At Haifa the Jodhpur Lancers won a victory which has no parallel in the annals of warfare. The capture of Haifa had become imperative for two reasons first to open a port on the coast to supply the advancing Allied army and secondly an intelligence officer Major Wellesley Tudor Pole who was the Director of Enemy Territory Administration at Cairo reported to his contacts in London which included Lady Blomfield, Lady Paget, Lord Balfour, Lord Curzon and many others that Abdul Baha, the spiritual head of the Bahais and a very influential person with a large following in the Ottoman and Persian empires, was being held as a prisoner by the Turkish governor at Haifa.

The Bahais being pacifists did not support the Turkish war effort. Rescuing Abdul Baha from prison turn his anpporters into sympethours of the Allied. The Turkish governor of Syria, Jamal Pasha suspecting that Abdul Baha was sympathetic to the Allies had him imprisoned and tried for sedition. He was condemned to death by crucifixion on the gates of Haifa. On receiving this information the British Prime Minister Lloyd George and Foreign Secretary Lord Balfour ordered Gen

Allenby to attempt to free him from captivity. Because it was filt that his release from capturitty by the Allies would immediately be welcomed by his followers and they would then transfer their whole hearted support to the Allies. Haifa with Mount Carmel in the centre was defended by a Turkish Brigade and supported by artillery and machine guns. With the Turks were several German and Austrian Officers who acted as advisors. The overall military Commander was German General Lyman von Sanders.

In spite of Turkish superiority in numbers and weapons the 15th Imperial Service Cavalry Brigade was tasked to achieve this almost impossible task. Some scholars and military historians believe that the task was given to the Indians as the Higher Command thought that it was an impossible task and doomed to failure. They did not want the stigma of defeat to be attributed to any of the famed English Cavalry Regiments that carried the honours from hundreds of battlefields across the globe on the regimental colours.

Also to be noted that while the British line regiments had conscripts and officers from the middle or lower classes the cavalry were officered entirely by scions of the nobility and only a stupid commander would have sent them on a suicidal mission much like the famed 'Charge of the Light Brigade' in the Crimea. Here it is appropriate to mention that one of the opposing army commanders was the much celebrated Gen Mustafa Kemal later known as Kemal Ataturk who had earlier given the Allies a bloody nose at Gallipoli and who after the armistice threw out the Greek, French-Armenian and other invading armies from Turkey. The British feared Kamal Ataturk and he is rightfully called the founder of the Turkish Republic. In fact the name Ataturk means father of the Turks a title which was bestowed on him by the Turkish Parliament.

At 2 pm supported by the Mysore Lancers who provided covering fire from a flank and cleared the enemy from the slopes of Mount Carmel the Jodhpurs went through a defile between the Mount Carmel and the river and took the Turks from an unexpected quarter. The Turks armed with modern machine guns and artillery and secure in their trenches faced a charge by 400 hundred lancers who at the point of their lances and the edge of their sabers completely routed the Turks. Taken by surprise the Turks could not believe what they saw emerging from the cloud of dust kicked up by the hoofs of the galloping horses and in their panic dropped their weapons and ran through the streets of Haifa where they were cut down or lanced. At the end of the day over a thousand and three hundred of the enemy including Germans and Austrians became prisoners of the Jodhpurs.

Also captured were dozens of machine guns and artillery pieces. Sadly this came at a price, Major Dalpat Singh was shot in the spine and killed, nineteen other sowars also lost their lives. Bahadur Singh lost his left eye and later when he became cinc Jodhpur State Forces was nicknamed the Kana General meaning the one-eyed general. But unlike Moshe Dyan he felt no need to hide the blind eye behind an eye patch but instead went around with a glass eye whose unblinking gaze sent shivers down the spine of many. For his services, Bahadur Singh received the IDSM (Indian Destiguished Service Medal).

For the loss of this eye he received a disability pension of Rs. 30 which was later increased to Rs. 60. Later he was also awarded the OBI for distinguished service.

Had Abdul Baha not been rescued it would have been the end of the Bahai Faith and there would have been no Lotus Temple in Delhi. The Lotus Temple is undoubtedly one of the world's most beautiful buildings and independent India's only great architectural achievement. It may come as a surprise to many that though Delhi has many great historical and architectural monuments the Lotus Temple receives the most number of visitors; in fact according to some it receives more visitors than rearly any other monument in the world. About the relative beauty of this monument as compared to other buildings in Delhi the people of India have voted with their feet overwhelmingly in favour of the Lotus temple.

An interesting incident occurred during the charge which shows the determination and grit of the men of the Jodhpur

Lancers. The British advisor to the Jodhpur State Forces a Colonel Holden seeing Major Dalpat Singh fall and fearing a repeat of the famous Charge of the Light Brigade at the Crimea ordered a halt to the charge and retreat was sounded by the bugler.

Taken by surprise the men reined in their horses, halted and turned around when a voice was heard calling them in Marwari "kathe bhag reha ho. Mundo kalo ho javelo" (where are you running? Your faces will be blackened) The Lancers turned around and took the Turkish positions and the town at a gallop annihilating all opposition at the point of their lances.

In the same battle, Col Hem Singh Bhati received the Military Cross. Col Bhati's own son Major Shaitan Singh was later to win an even greater name and fame for his heroic stand at Rezangla in the 1962 war against the Chinese where Shaitan Singh and his men fought the Chinese till the last of them fell. Major Shaitan Singh received the Param Vir Chakra posthumously. This feat is no less than that of the Spartans at Thermopylae.

Is it a coincidence or fate that brought three men, i.e. Sir Pratap, Abdul Baha and Kamal Ataturk to Mount Carmel at the same time and yet they never met. All three have had a huge and profound influence on their people and countries. Air Marshal Chandan Singh will say it is divine providence that brought them here to this Holy Mount to take back to their people a message of love, hope and unity of mankind and to discard old and outdated beliefs and rituals.

While the humanist legacy of Abdul Baha and Sir Pratap are being followed and celebrated the modernist legacy of Kemal Ataturk is being quietly buried by Endogen in Turkey, the country that exists today as it is, only because of Ataturk.

I personally am a believer in the sacredness of geography and recollect that moment in 1964 when serving with the UN in the same area I had the opportunity to fly in an Otter aircraft of the Royal Canadian Air Force over Mount Sinai and St Catherine's Monastery in the valley below.

I felt an indescribable sense of something special may be

even divine about the experience and a sense of profound peace and calmness descended upon me. For a moment I felt I was in a trance. I am very comfortable and very happy in my own faith and consider it to be the best but at that moment I could believe that this was the place where the Lord could have chosen to appear before Moses not once but twice. It is not without reason that the Muslims, Jews and Christians alike call it the Holy Land. Like the three great continents of Asia, Africa and Europe meet and clash here so do the three Semitic faiths have clashed with each other from the very time of their birth. The way events are playing out now it looks as if this may also be the final resting place of all Semitic traditions.

The next major engagements between the two antagonists was at Acre and Aleppo; though the Allies eventually prevailed they suffered very high casualties. The Jodhpur Lancers fortunately not only distinguished themselves again but also got off comparatively lightly. In November the war came to an end and the armistice was signed and punitive terms were imposed on Germany and Turkey.

Sir Pratap was unhappy at the humiliating terms that were imposed on the two countries and with great foresight warned the Allies that they should be prepared to fight another war with a rearmed Germany. This was not appreciated by the Great Powers and Sir Pratap was not included as the Indian representative at the subsequent Peace Conference. In his place was taken Maharajah Ganga Singh of Bikaner was made Indias' representative.

Sir Pratap's relations with Maharajah Ganga Singh had soured ever since Ganga Singh had taken over that part of Jodhpur State Railway which ran through Bikaner State and refused to pay compensation. This deprived Jodhpur not only of revenue but also a direct unfettered link to Punjab.

After the capture of Aleppo a simple stone column was erected eight miles north of the town at a place now known as Angrezi Kabristan. At its inauguration three Indian Lancers from Jodhpur, Hyderabad and Mysore stood around the column as an honour guard. The event was photographed and it is from this photograph that the Teen Murti Memorial in Delhi was modelled. It is now rightfully renamed as the Haifa Memorial.

The Jodhpur Lancers returned home in 1919 after an absence of five years. Not only had they distinguished themselves as no other unit had done but, more importantly, they had exploded the canard propagated by the British that Indian troops performed well only when commanded by British officers. The British had propagated this canard because they wanted to safeguard the interests of their own compatriots by providing them employment in the Indian Army.

All the great victories of the Jodhpur Lancers had been won under the command of Indian officers all of whom were from Jodhpur. The British government now had to concede that Indians were equal, if not more deserving of the King's Commission as their British counterparts. The future Field Marshal Cariappa and several others were beneficiaries of the change in policy when soon after the war they were granted the King's Commission.

The Prince of Wales Royal Indian Military College (now known as RIMC of which the author is a proud alumnus) was started at Dehra Dun with Sir Pratap as patron; the aim of the College was to prepare Indian boys for The Royal Military College at Sandhurst for eventual commissioning as officers for the Indian Army. Rightfully a portrait of Sir Pratap adorns the ante room of the cadets' mess today as it has from the time of its founding.

Gen K.S. Thimayya one of India's most celebrated geards was in the first of batch of cadets. This sowed the seed for the eventual Indianisation of the officer corps of our Army. Ten years later the Indian Military Academy was started, once again at Dehra Dun. Passing out with the first batch was Sam Manekshaw, and by the Second World War there were twelve thousand Indian officers.

When the freedom movement gained momentum, Lord Wavell the Viceroy informed the British Government that the loyalty of the Indian officers to the Crown could not be taken for granted and that His Majesty's Government should consider an early transfer of power to avoid a blood bath which the British would not only be unable to contain but would also entail an ignominious retreat by the British from India.

Historians of India's freedom movement need to study this aspect which has so far been neglected either on purpose or out of ignorance. Here it would of interest to mention that General K.S. Thimayya after a few years of his return to India on being commissioned as an officer from Sandhurst called upon Mahatma Gandhi accompanied by four other officers and offered to resign their commissions in the army if it would help the freedom movement. Mahatma Gandhi asked them not to resign their commissions, because after independence, India would need their services.

Gandhi, though a pacifist, but ever the pragmatist understood that an independent India would need an army to secure and preserve its freedom. When the Pakistanis invaded Kashmir in 1947, Gandhi asked to meet the newly appointed commander of the 161 Brigade Brig L.P. Sen later Lt Gen and Eastern Army Commander in 1962. The 161 Brigade was responsible for the defence of Srinager. Gandhi told him that he believed that all wars are futile. But at the moment, Brig Sen's duty was to use all the forces available to protect the land and people from the invaders and he must do everything possible to fulfil his duty. A lesson Nehru had failed to learn, at the time of independence he said that India has no enemies hence there was no need for an army and an armed police force was all that was required to maintain law and order. Nehru even went to the extent of supporting some members of the first elected Legislative Assembly who called the Indian Army an army of mercenaries.

This was strongly objected to by Maj Gen Himmat Singh, the nominated Military member of the Assembly in his speech to the Assembly in 1946. How wrong Nehru was, for within a few months of India becoming independent the Army was needed to fight the Pakistanis in Kashmir and to secure Hyderabad and Junagad.

Sir Pratap needs to be given due credit for initiating and sowing the seeds of independence. It is he along with Swami Dayanand Saraswati who had advocated the concept of swaraj and coined the term in 1880. They were also the first to use the term Harijan for the lower castes. Both these terms Swaraj and Harijan are wrongly attributed to Gandhi. A little known historic fact is that during the time Sir Pratap was the Maharajah of Idar in Gujarat. Mahatma Gandhi's father was at different times the Dewan of Rajkot, Porbandar and Wankaner States in Gujarat. All kinomen or fillow princes of Sir Pratap.

The Maharajah of Wankaner sponsored Mahatma Gandhi's studies in UK at about the same time Sir Pratap was sponsoring the education and cricket from his own pocket of Ranjit Sinhji, more famously known as the great cricketer Ranji who later became the Maharajah of Jamnagar. Both Sir Pratap and the Maharajahs of Bhavnagar and Wankaner interacted with each other and were related. There is also the fact that Mahatma Gandhi's mother belonged to the Pranami sect whose founder Jairathji was from Umarkot which was then a part of Jodhpur State. When people meet ideas are exchanged and have a way of turning up again unexpectedly in new places, in new forms and at different times. Nothing new, whether life or ideas are born without pathogenesis.

To Sir Pratap and Dayanand Saraswati, Swaraj meant a greater role for Indians in administration, army and industry which would enable India to become fully independent in the future and take its equal and rightful place among the great nations of the world. Swaraj they also said was the freedom to live our lives according to our own traditions which however had to be brought in line with modern thought. Indian society had to first change from within and only then can it and the country go forward. Blindly copying the West at the expense of the good in our own culture has cost us dear. Much of the woes that beset India today are attributable to Nehru's failure to grasp this maxim.

Here it would not be out of place to remind the sceptics and critics of the princely order that besides Swami Dayanand Saraswati who was patronised by the Jodhpurs, the Rajas of Khetri who were feudatories of Jaipur State and and also closely related to the Jodhpur family by marriage were patrons of Swami Vivekanand. It will surprise some even more to learn that it is the same Raja of Khetri who were also the patrons of Nandlal, the uncle of Motilal Nehru.

Motilal was born posthumously after the early death of his father Gangadhar and was brought up by Nandlal, the elder brother of Gangadhar. Nand Lal was an employee of the Raja of Khetri. The Raja of Khetri paid for Motilal's education. Kamla Nehru's father too was an employee of the Maharajas of Jaipur. Gratitude is a difficult thing to acknowledge and a vindictive Indira Gandhi repaid her family's debt by having the Rajmata of Jaipur Gayatri Devi and her son Col Maharajah Sawai Bhawani Singh MVC a war hero imprisoned on trumped up charges during the Emergency in 1975.

Had it not been for the patronage and support of the Khetris the Nehru line would have become another piece of flotsam and jetsam of the Mutiny of 1857 with residence in the Kanjar Mohalla of Agra where they lived after their move to Agra after they had to leave Delhi in 1857. The Kanjar Mohalla was and still is the red light district of Agra. After Agra the Nehru family moved to Lal Chowk in Meerpur Mohalla of Allahabad, another red light area.

On the return of Indian troops to India the process of demobilisation started in the British Indian army. Sir Pratap, on the other hand, started the modernisation of the Jodhpur State Forces, after having seen the Armies of Germany, US, France and England. He understood that valour and spirit were not the only qualities for success in war. He had also seen the use of aircraft and tanks in battle and talked about the necessity for Jodhpur to acquire them. Sir Pratap had already inducted armoured cars in the Jodhpur State Forces even before they were introduced in the British Indian Army. But death claimed him before all his wishes could be fulfilled.

However his successors undertook the task and made Jodhpur State into a pioneer of civil and military aviation in India. He was a firm believer in Plato's dictum "...only the dead have seen the end of war" so constantly warned against disarmament and warned the world that they should be prepared to face a rearmed and rejuvenated Germany in the not too distant future. Twenty years after the Peace Conference, Germany was ready to take on the world again.

Bahadur Singh, who five years earlier had been only a sowar (the lowest rank in a cavalry regiment), now returned home as a captain. He was now a man of high status and a social equal of the other officers who were all members of the landed nobility. Even without a private income his salary as an officer could help him to get married to a lady from a family of status. Proposals for marriage started pouring in and he agreed to the one received from the Thakur of Sanyari for his daughter Roop Kanwar whom he married in 1920. She lived all her life in their village Bagawas and in spite of suggestions from the Maharajah that she should join her husband in Jodhpur, she continued to live in the village.

Five children were born to them, two girls and three boys. Some time in the late 1930s Col Bahadur Singh on the insistence of another lady saint Gopalji Maharaj who stayed on the chabutra near Raj Ranchodji Ka Mandir met a holy man by the name Mukund Ji Maharaj who lived in a cave on Chittar Hill not far from the lines of the Jodhpur Lancers. Bahadur Singh became his devotee and on retirement when he moved back to his village requested Mukundji Maharaj to set up his abode in Bagawas and live a life devoted to spiritualism and meditation.

Mukundji was a Nath, an ascetic of the Goraknath Sampradaya which even today has several hermitages and shrines all over Rajasthan. They are the centres for religious and devotional activity for all classes and castes. It is not by accident that the great sixteenth century saint Meera Bai was born at Merta, a fiefdom in Marwar to a Rathore princely family. The tradition of renouncing family, wealth and position for a higher purpose is a deeply rooted tradition here.

Bahadur Singh was eventually appointed the Commanding Officer of the Jodhpur Lancers, a Regiment that he had first served as a line boy and a syce. The regiment was the only real home he had ever known. After his retirement he was appriated minister in the first democratically elected government of Jodhpur. Once the State of Rajasthan was formed with its capital at Jaipur its first Chief Minister Jayram Vyas offered Bahadur Singh a cabinet post in the cabinet of the newly formed state. But Bahadur Singh declined to move to Jaipur saying that he wished to spend his retirement years at his village in his beloved Marwar living close to his Guru Mukundji Maharaj. The Maharajas of Bikaner and Jaisalmer were regular visitors to Bagawas as were members of the Jodhpur royal family to pay their respects at the feet of Mukaundji Maharaj.

Till his end in 1969 at the age of 73 he would spend at least half an hour each day in deep meditation and prayer. Most people in Rajasthan are quite religious and abide by the customs and observances of their faith but I have noticed that among the Rajputs and particularly those Rajputs who have served in the armed forces, religious practice goes beyond mere adherence to rituals. They tend instead to become deeply spiritual and other worldly as they advance in years and so it is with Chandan Singh as was the ease with his father.

It is perhaps because of this that Rajasthan is the centre for many Bhakti, Shaivite, Shakta, Jain and Sufi movements. Interestingly though all these movements / sects have their own particular philosophy and ritual practices. The Rajputs tend to be quite catholic in their beliefs and find no contradiction in following and extending patronage to all of them.

With the old landed elites showing the way it is not uncommon to find commoner Hindus and Muslims alike sharing the same shrine. Religious strife is unknown in Rajasthan. Many of the professional singers of Hindu devotional songs are Muslims. In 1947 at the time of Partition there were no riots and killing of Muslims in Rajput states unlike what happened in British India. Most Muslims chose to stay on here and not migrate to Pakistan. The patronage to the deities and shrines of these sects over centuries has encouraged the development of devotional literature, poetry, music, dance and painting themed around the mahatmayas (stories of glory) of their particular deities. It is a paradox that there are more Sufi shrines and singers in Rajasthan than in the whole of Pakistan or elsewhere in the world.

The art forms of Rajasthan have today found their rightful place among the high arts of the world and when showcased occupy centre stage at the great art festivals all over the world. Rajasthani food, music and dance along with Jodhpur jackets, breeches, safas (nine metre long turbans) for bridegrooms and jewellery, lehangas, kurtis and odnis for brides have captured the entire spectrum at weddings and concerts in India. Even the wedding locations of choice for those who can afford it are the palaces and havelis of Rajasthan.

Event managers and owners of heritage properties have become rich catering to the demand for Rajasthan themed weddings. Another distinguishing feature of these art forms is that though their origins are lost in the hoary mist of time they have maintained an unbroken link to their origins, yet evolving with time and changing tastes, thus making them always relevant to the present. They are as popular at concerts and festivals at the Edinburgh festival and Madison Gardens as at the Mehrangarh Fort. A bridge between the past and present and between continents like no other art form elsewhere in the world.

There are many interesting anecdotes that show Bahadur's loyalty to his Maharajah. His Highness Maharajah Umaid Singh had personally requested Bahadur Singh to take charge and toughen Maharaj Kumar Hanuwant Singhji the Crown Prince as the latter was getting soft living at the palace and what better way to do that than be attached to the Lancers.

The next day, the Maharaj Kumar arrived in his chauffeur driven car in the morning. He was received by the Bahadur Singh himself, who saluted the 'MK' and asking him to change clothes, join the grooms and after having brushed the horses, to clean the stables. This was sacrilegious! A crown prince cleaning the stables! But a stunned 'MK' had no choice but to comply. After the Kana General returned to his office, a few of the groomsmen began to do the job for the MK but as soon as Bahadur Singh was informed of his orders not being followed, he rushed to the stables and fired the other grooms and stood there till the MK had cleaned the designated stables. After completing the duties, a very visibly fatigued MK changed clothes and was respectfully escorted to his car by the CO, who then informed the MK that the next day he had to arrive pre-dawn to complete the full load of work of a sowar or grooms.

This went on for many days and news of her son being treated as an ordinary groom reached Maharani Sahiba, who then asked for the CO to report to the Raika Bagh Palace. As ordered, Col Bahadur Singh reached the palace and stood before the Maharani Sahiba, who sat behind a purdah. She asked him if he knew who the Maharaj Kumar was and the CO replied that he did. She asked him that knowing who the MK was, why was he treating the MK like an ordinary sowar? Replying that he was only following the Maharajah's orders and that she might like to take up the matter with him directly, respectfully saluted, turned around and left the palace. Who knew that after twenty odd years her niece would be marrying the CO's son Chandan!

Col Bahadur Singh didn't spare even her brother Captain (later Colonel) Mohan Singh Bhati. The Captain, being the brother-in-law of the Maharajah had the habit of arriving late for the daily parade and inspection at the grounds, which did not set a good example to the younger officers and troops who had been therem since before dawn. He would also drive up to the grounds instead of walking after having his car parked. On both points the CO, whose anger was legendary, instructed Captain Mohan Singh to arrive on time and walk to the ground. Col Bahadur Singh told him twice, but the Captain didn't heed his words.

On the third day, while the entire force of the Lancers

mounted on horseback, Captain Mohan Singh arrived late and again drive directly to the parade ground. As Captain Mohan Singh walked up towards the squadrons, Col Bahadur Singh took off his belt and began thrashing the erring Captain in full view of all sowars and it took three officers a great deal of effort to pull the CO away from the cowering Captain who was on the ground covering his head. Captain Mohan Singh, who narrated this incident to Sajjan, was never ever late for parades and walked from the parking lot to the grounds. Another very interesting anecdote was that of the incident near the Lion's Rock. Lion's Rock is a small hillock near the village of Jhalamand which today touches the city of Jodhpur. However in the 1940s it was many kilometres away and had good flat grounds which were conducive for the horses.

It was a gruelling day of parades and manoeuvres on horseback. Col Bahadur Singh gave the orders for each officer rider to personally stable the horses after having removed the saddle, brushed off the sand and put water and feed and only then return to Jodhpur. While the officers and sowars returned to the stables, Col Bahadur Singh and a few other officers stayed back at the Lion's Rock and watched the troops dismount and stable the horses. Observing them through his binoculars he noticed that three officers had just handed over their horses and were preparing to leave without having personally stable their horses. This angered the CO, who cursing aloud grabbed his lance and ran down the hillock, mounted his horse and shouting at the top of his voice, charged towards the encampment and stables. The other officers realised what had happened and they too charged after their CO, knowing what he was capable of doing. By this time Bahadur Singh was nearing the camp and hearing the loud shouting and dust rising, officers and sowars realized what had happened and the three culprit officers ran into the stables for safety! Reaching the stables, Col Bahadur Singh, lance in hand, ran after the three officers. It took a great deal of persuasion by the other Indian and British officers to calm him down and more importantly take the lance from his hands.

The three defaulting officers were then brought before the CO. They were Maharaj Kumar Hunuwant Singh, Captain (later Colonel) Maharaj Prem Singh and a British officer. The three officers stood petrified and perspiring in front of the CO who being who he was had to punish the officers for not following his orders. The three of them were ordered to run around the parade ground three times carrying their saddles over their heads and in their boots and in front of the entire Jodhpur Lancers! The Kana General dismissed them after the third round was completed. Needless to say, his orders were never disobeyed again. (The above anecdote was narrated to Sajjan by Col Bahadur Singh's orderly, Risaldar Rawat Singh and also by world renowned polo player Col Maharaj Prem Singh, who was one of those at the receiving end of the punishment.)

Bahadur Singh was proud that whatever task the Lancers undertook they always succeeded be it in war or sports. The following incident took place in Risalpur and was narrated by Brig Hari Singh.

The Pathans from Afghanistan had assembled a large army and shown signs of invading India as the British fought in Europe. The Jodhpur Lancers, who were still undergoing conversion to armoured vehicles from horses, were deployed to defend against any attacks. They were joined by Sawai Maharajah Jai Singh of Jaipur and his Kachhwaha Horse.

Daily patrolling in the scorching heat was taking a toll on the morale of the troops and it was decided that a polo match would be organised to break the monotony. The rivalry between the two teams is well known and the troops of both armies were enthusiastic about the event.

Col Bahadur Singh gave the orders for the ground to be cleared and readied. The two teams were captained by the respective rulers. It was to be a one off "chakkar" and Maharajah Umaid Singh had in his team, Captain Prem Singh, Captain Mohan Singh and Risaldar Hanuwant Singh Sodha a big man whose job was to ride off the Jaipur ruler. Risaldar Hanuwant Singh Sodha was the maternal uncle of Sh. Jaswant

Singh MP, former Commerce and Defence Minister.

The chakkar started and as planned Risaldar Hanuwant Singh Sodha rode off Sawai Jai Singh each time the latter got hold of the ball. Needless to say, Jodhpur won, which pleased Col Bahadur Singh, who got up and went to the stables to congratulate the three players while the Maharajah proceeded to the refreshment stand.

Sitting down and having tea, Maharajah Umaid Singh was joined by the Jaipur ruler, who was red faced and cursing the tactics used by the Jodhpur team. Maharajah Umaid Singh being a kind hearted man and also brother in law to the Maharaja of Jaipur decided to have another chakkar but this time he replaced Risaldar Hanuwant Singh Sodha with the latter's brother-in-law Captain Sardar Singh, who was not as good a player as the Risaldar.

A tough match followed, in which the Jaipur team won and as the players, returned to their stables, a furious Col Bahadur Singh reached them and began to hit them with a polo whip cursing them loudly for losing to Jaipur! The three players had to run towards Maharajah Umaid Singh who had to placate the CO and told him that it was on his orders that the team composition was changed. Of course Sawai Jai Singh enjoyed the victory and the drama afterwards. Captain (later Major) Sardar Singh Jasol, a recipient of the lashings narrated the story to Sajjan at Jasol House.

The story of how Bahadur Singh became the CO is in itself very interesting and something today's generation might not believe. Major Bahadur Singh had been informed by Brig Duncan, Commander of the Jodhpur State Forces that he was not going to be promoted. The two never liked each other and had been at loggerheads ever since Duncan set foot in Jodhpur.

Having been given his orders, Major Bahadur Singh returned to his room at the Jodhpur Lancers' Mess (now Battle Axe Mess) to pack his bags. However, after a short while, while still wearing his uniform, he decided to pay his respects to Gopalji Maharaj, a lady saint on whom he had utmost faith, and whose abode was at the corner of the Raj Ranchoddasji Temple opposite the railway station. Alighting from his vehicle, he sat at the feet of this saint and said that he was retiring and leaving for his village. The saint thought for a while and said "Kurnel bansi" in her rustic way meaning that he would become Colonel. To this Bahadur Singh replied that it was too late as Thakur Prithvi Singh of Bera, a famous polo player, had been promoted to the rank of colonel and that he himself was informed by the State Forces Commander. The saint smiled and told Bahadur Sing to go to the 'Baiji Ka Talab', a water body within the old city, take a dip in the waters as he was, including his uniform and pith hat and then return to her. Without a word or questioning her instructions he followed them and a while later, still dripping with water returned to her.

"Now go", was all she said smiling and after paying his respects, he returned to his room to change and true to his nature he gave away his swords, saddles and boots and other items to various officers who had to come to see him off. At the end of the day and completing all formalities he left for his village.

It was a few days later while playing polo with His Highness that Col Prithvi Singh had a massive heart attack and collapsed on his horse and despite attempts to revive him, he could not be saved. His Highness the Maharajah ordered that news of the CO's passing away not leave the polo ground as he himself said "they will hang around me like vultures to be appointed CO". He then instructed Captain Mohan Singh to take a car and go to Bagawas and bring back Major Bahadur Singh who was the most capable of all the officers.

Retired Major Bahadur Singh had no inkling of what had transpired and was in his pajama kurta enjoying a retired life when Captain Mohan Singh arrived at his doorstep. He was informed that the Maharajah had summoned him to Jodhpur immediately, but did not tell him why.

Without changing, the Major and Captain got into the car and sped back to Jodhpur and straight to the palace.

The two were escorted to the Maharajah's personal office and after paying his respects, the Maharajah informed him of the situation and instructed him to take command of the Jodhpur Lancers immediately, before he was pressurised by relatives and hangers on and the British to change his mind and appoint someone else.

Major Bahadur Singh was promoted to the rank of Lieutenant Colonel and CO of the Jodhpur Lancers.

2
Childhood and Youth

"This boy strikes me as the tiny germ of mighty valour, that waits like a fiery spark for kindling, before it bursts into a blazing fire." Dushyant on seeing Bharat: by Kalidas in his play Shakuntala.

Chandan Singh was born on December 3, 1925, at the family's ancestral village of Bagawas where his mother continued to reside even when his father then Capt Bahadur Singh lived at Jodhpur, where his job as an officer of the Jodhpur Lancers required him to be. Capt Bahadur Singh was then commanding a 'Squadron' which had Mertia Rathores who were known as Rowdy Mertias because of their high spirited nature. The other squadrons were B sqn—Jodhas, C Sqn-Kaimkhanis and D sqn was mixed with Champawats forming the majority. Their house in Bagawas was a modest kuchha house which Bahadur Singh was to rebuild and renovate once his means allowed him to do so. Chandan was their first male child and another two sons were to follow. Two daughters had been born earlier.

According to Col Revat Singh also originally from the Jodhpur State Forces but about six years older than Chandan Singh, as a child Chandan was a very spirited boy who Col Bahadur Singh, a strict disciplinarian of the old school, found difficult to rein in. His early years were not spent in the village with his mother, instead Chandan's father like many Rajputs of his generation felt that a boy brought up in the zenana in the company of his mother and other ladies of the household would spoil him and make him soft.

So he was just one year and four months old when he

was sent to Gunawati near Makrana to live with the family of Capt Bir Singh, another Jodhpur Lancer veteran of Haifa who had boys of a similar age. He stayed with Capt Bir Singh's family for three and a half years. A few years later, Hari Singh, Chandan's younger brother, joined him in Gunawati. Bir Singh's family looked after Chandan Singh and Hari Singh as one of their own and even now ninety years later, Chandan Singh remembers and talks of them with great respect and affection.

He specially remembers the wife of Sardar Singh who was the elder brother of Bir Singh. Once while Chandan was playing in the fields he fell on a cactus bush and was badly injured. He had been pricked and scratched by hundreds of cactus thorns, a most painful experience and it was Sardar Singh's wife who treated him and nursed him for several days till he recovered.

To the readership of today's generation and even earlier ones this separating of young children, babies really from their mothers may appear odd but to me this does not, for even before I was weaned, I was taken away to live with my grandmother and sent to my mother only at feeding times. Once I was three or four my grandmother started staying with my uncle who was in the Army and from there when I was six I was sent to a boarding school and then except for one short meeting of about a week, I did not get to see my mother till I was fifteen and then only during school holidays.

When Chandan was five he was taken to Jodhpur by his father and placed with five other boys who included two of Capt Bir Singh's sons. They stayed in a dormitory near the Jodhpur Lancers' lines close to their officers' mess where Capt Bahadur Singh lived. The Lancers Officers' Mess was known as Shekhawat Rani Mahal, a small beautiful old palace of a dowager Maharani of Jodhpur which was built on the embankment of a small lake.

Close to their lodgings was a narrow gauge railway line which was to transport dressed sandstone for the construction of the Umaid Bhawan Palace which was going on at a frantic pace on the top of Chittar Hill. The boys would sometimes hitch a ride on to the tail end wagon when the train had to slow down to climb uphill. Here the boys were put in charge of orderlies and their education started. Their teacher was Moti Singh himself, a student in the local college who in his free time gave the boys their tuitions.

Even at this tender age all the boys were made to lead a Spartan life and attended school in an improvised classroom in the Lancers' Lines. The routine was to get up early, exercise, followed by prayers and religious rituals and sports. Their lessons would be in the mornings and evenings when Moti Singh returned from college. While here an incident occurred which was to shape his future life and profession.

In those days in Jodhpur like in most other towns water-borne sanitation was unknown and the toilets were manually cleaned, foul smells and flies were a fact of life and visit to a toilet was never a pleasant experience so if open space was available most people preferred to go to the open fields to answer the call of nature. Close to the Lancers' Lines was the Jodhpur airfield which was demarcated by an 'earthen doli' which is a rammed earth wall topped by thorny living or dead scrub, a common sight of the Rajasthani countryside. The dolis demarcate the field and also protect the crops from feral cattle and other animals. He had been warned not go across the 'doli' for the other side was frequented by a 'udan saanp' or flying snake in English.

But Chandan being Chandan even at this young age decided to see for himself what was on the other side and if possible see a 'udan saanp' for himself. He had just dropped his shorts and squatted when he heard a roaring sound which seemed to be getting louder and closer and lo and behold he saw the 'udan-saanp' flying straight towards him from the East silhouetted against the rising sun. A dramatic and frightening vision. Pulling up his shorts and picking up his lota he tried to hide behind a bush but to no avail, the flying snake still kept coming and so he ran to take shelter behind the trunk of a nearby acacia tree and just as he made it the flying snake was overhead and climbed over the tree blasting him with a strong gust of wind, sand and dead leaves.

Frightened as hell he ran towards his home vowing never to come there again. In the evening even though he feared admonishment from his father, he related the incident to him. Col Bahadur Singh explained to him that it was no flying snake but an aeroplane, a machine with wings and an engine like that in a motor car but with a fan fitted in the front that made it possible for the machine to fly.

This aroused his curiosity and whenever he got a chance he would go near the doli and see the aircraft landing and taking off. The aircraft fascinated him and it was then that he decided that one day he would fly them himself. The aircraft that he had seen and which were nicknamed 'udan saanp' were Hendley Page bombers of the RAF and Hendley Page passenger liners (developed from the design of the bombers) of the Imperial Airways both of which frequented Jodhpur.

Thanks to the interest in aviation and patronage of Maharajah Umaid Singhji had become a major civil and military aviation hub. The first Hendley Page passenger plane was a bomber converted into a passenger liner and they had inaugurated the regular flights from London to India via Paris, Rome, Athens, Istanbul, Baghdad, Masjid e Sulyman, Karachi Jodhpur and finally Delhi in 1920.

Both types of these Handley Page aeroplanes had a very long and thin fuselage which gave them an appearance of a snake with wings and hence the name 'udan saanp'. Maharajah Umaid Singhji had started the Flying Club in Jodhpur in 1931 and an English lady, a painter by profession, attended the inauguration and has described the event in her memoirs. She wrote that it appeared as if the whole city had congregated on the airfield to see this marvel. She also did a water colour painting of the Meherangarh Fort.

When Chandan was seven years old, Col Bahadur Singh decided that Chandan must receive a formal education. Before being packed off to school he was sent to his village to take leave of his mother, sisters and other female members of his family. On being asked to recognise his mother he could not do so for he had last seen her four years ago when he was only three years old and now he was seven.

Bahadur Singh's plan was to send them to Colonel Brown's School in Dehradun but on the advice of Madho Singh, a risaldar in Bahadur Singh's squadron who felt that this would alienate the boys from their roots, Chandan Singh was sent to the Rishikul School at Ratangarh in Churu District in Bikaner State which is both the hottest place in summer and coldest place in winter in the plains of India. The winter temperature falls to below zero at night and in summer the temperature at noon soars to over 50 degrees.

The school was run like an ashram with a very strict and Spartan regimen. At the Rishikul there was not much of a modern education and what was there, was confined to learning by heart Vedic hymns and the Upanishads. He learnt to recite them verbatim which even now he can do. One benefit of this type of traditional education is that it develops the power of memory to such a level that even today the Air Marshal can recall events, places and names of his associates of nearly ninety years ago. Not only can he recall the names of his associates but also the names of their spouses and children.

Even the great Greek philosophers like Socrates and Plato laid great emphasis on memory and the oral tradition, they were a bit contemptuous of the written word. Socrates was supposedly to have said, "You eat apples and not paintings of apples." Here it would not be out of place to record the dialogoue between Socrates and his friend Phaedrus as reported by Plato. Socrates repeating the words spoken several thousand years earlier by the Egyptian God King Ammon to Thoth the God of writing, "....This discovery of yours will create forgetfulness in the learners' souls, because they will not use their memories; they will trust to the external written characters and not remember themselves. The specific you have discovered is aid not to memory but to reminiscence, you have given your disciples not truth but semblance of truth. They will be readers of many things and will have learned nothing....They will be tiresome company, having a show of wisdom without the reality."

The medium of instruction was Sanskrit and great emphasis was placed on physical fitness and martial arts. A year later his brother Hari Singh joined him. The school uniform was a langot or loincloth as the British called it. The langot is a narrow T-shaped strip of cloth about three inches wide which is tied tightly around the loins and waist. There was no covering for the upper part of the body but in winter they were allowed to wear a vest. I recollect that when I was young, I too possessed a langot which was the common undergarment for all Indian males before the advent of knitted underwear. It could be worn as tight or as loose as one wanted and was supposed to prevent Hydrocele, which seemed to have been a common problem at that time but one hears nothing of it today.

At the National Defence Academy as cadets during our monthly medical examinations we were tested every month for Hydrocele and the method was to drop our pants and the doctor would place his hands under the testicles and ask us to cough which was one way the onset of this disease was detected. If one of the doctors on duty that day happened to be a lady doctor there used to be a rush to be examined by her.

Both the brothers, Chandan and Hari were spirited youngsters constantly up to something or another. When he was eleven years old he and a group of his friends produced a play based on the Ramayan. Chandan from the very beginning had a talent for the theatre, he was the writer, producer and star of the play. He would play the role of Ram and his brother Hari Singh the part of Lakshman. Chandan carried his love for theatrics till middle age as the photograph of him dressed as Charlie Chaplain at an Air Force party at Agra shows.

But the strict regimen of the school was now getting to be tiresome and he rebelled and organised a hartal (strike) by all the students protesting against the treatment being meted out to them by the teachers. The principal wrote to his father requesting that he be withdrawn as the teachers were finding him difficult to control and besides he had already learned all they had to teach. So Chandan Singh soon found himself at home, well versed in Sanskrit but with no knowledge of any other language including his native Marwari or even Hindi.

On the advice of his friends, Colonel Bahadur Singh decided to send him to Colonel Brown's School in Dehradun where it was thought that he would receive a modern education but at the last moment a close friend of his father intervened and suggested that as independence would soon come to India it would be better that Chandan was schooled in the Indian way and imbibe Indian traditions and ethos. So instead of Dehradun and a Westernised education he was sent to Benaras to study. He was admitted in the Central Hindu High School on the premises of the Benaras Hindu University. The standard of education was high and the faculty top rate, but the medium of instruction was Hindi and no English was taught.

Chandan Singh and the Quit India Movement

Some time in the early 1940s when under the leadership of Mahatma Gandhi the freedom movement was gathering momentum and the Congress Party Session was held in 1940 at Ramgarh then in Bihar now Jharkand. Patna became one of the major centres for the freedom struggle. At the conference the Congress Party was divided into two factions, one under Gandhi advocating a peaceful struggle and the other under Subhas Chandra Bose prepared to take up any means including an armed struggle to achieve their aims.

Benaras too was affected by the mood in Patna and slogan shouting, pasting of posters on walls and processions shouting pro-azadi slogans became common. Chandan too got caught up in the mood, he gathered his friends and led a procession through the narrow streets of the town shouting nationalistic slogans and singing patriotic songs. Being a born leader, Chandan was leading the procession holding the tricolour in his hand and shouting 'Inqalab Zindabad' when his march was rudely interrupted by a tight slap on the face. Chandan all ready to pick a fight and give a befitting response turned around to find that it was his brother-in-law Bane Singh, his eldest sister's husband who had slapped him. Bane Singh was several years his senior and was doing his masters at the BHU. Bane Singh on learning of what Chandan Singh and his friends were up to, had quickly mounted a bicycle and caught up with them and admonished him for doing things that would not only embarrass his father but could also put his career in jeopardy.

Col Bahadur Singh was at that time the Commanding Officer of the Jodhpur Lancers and was posted at Risalpur and involved in one of Britain's perpetual wars in the North West Frontier Province. The British would not have taken Chandan Singh's activities kindly and certainly the Maharajah of Jodhpur would have been displeased for the princely states had to maintain an amicable and diplomatic relationship with the British authorities who already having their hands full with the war, the Congress Party and Muslim League, did not want any further trouble in the Princely States.

Benaras and the Benaras Hindu University became the centre towards which all freedom fighters and many revolutionaries on the run from the police started gravitating, hoping to lose themselves in the floating population of pilgrims, students and visiting holy men. Many of them were from Bihar where the British Deputy Commissioner Mr. W.G. Archer Till ordered fire to be opened on a group of teenage school boys trying to hoist the national flag on the secretariat building, killing seven of them and wounding another thirty.

The first to be asked to open fire were policemen from the Bihar Armed Police and when they refused to do so the Army was called in but the troops who arrived were from the Rajput Regiment and they too refused to fire on the unarmed students and it was then that some Gurkha troops from Nepal who were unaffected by the nationalist movement were brought in and it is they who carried out the orders. A repeat of the Jallianwala Bagh affair. When Chandan Singh led the march of students in the streets of Benaras he was not only risking his father's career but his own very life. One good thing that Arthur Till and his wife had done while serving in Bihar was to bring to light and make famous the Madhubani style of painting. Till then it was an unknown folk tradition which the women followed to decorate the outer walls of their mud houses.

Soon afterwards, Jayaprakash Narayan and five of his accomplices escaped from Hazaribagh Prison where they were interned and came to Benaras seeking shelter and anonymity. One of this group earlier stayed in Chandan's room, unfortunately he does not remember who it was. JP was not a well known person then. Chandan after the berating he had received from his brother-in-law knew that he was taking a huge risk but so caught up was he in the prevalent mood of the country and the righteousness of the cause that he still went ahead and sheltered a fugitive from British law for over a month. If the end has been justified, Chandan has never shirked from risking his all and India needs to be thankful for it.

Those who know Benaras know, that it is not called the Eternal City in vain. It has always had an atmosphere of secular and spiritual inquiry and learning from time immemorial and so it was for Chandan Singh. His stay here with his keen sense of observation and assimilation, enriched his mind as no other place could have done. Benaras even today is a magnet that draws both voyeurs and those with inquiring minds from all over the world. The city can only be experienced but not described.

As predicted by Sir Pratap twenty years earlier a rearmed Germany rose from the ashes of the First World War and this time supported by Italy and Japan who had earlier been its antagonists. By 1939 it was ready to take on the Allies again. In a lightning campaign called the Blitzkrieg, Germany overran Poland and France forcing Britain into a humiliating retreat from Dunkirk.

As in the First World War, India being a British colony, found itself embroiled in the war and its forces were sent to the Middle East, North Africa, Abyssinia, Singapore, Malaysia and Burma. Later in the war they were deployed in Greece and Italy.

Jodhpur by now had become the centre of activity for the Royal Air Force and a flying club had also been started. The development into an aviation hub took place because of the initiative of Maharajah Umaid Singhji who himself was a graduate of the RAF Academy at Cranwell and a qualified pilot with the rank of an Honorary Air Marshal of the Royal Air Force.

More than J.R.D. Tata it is Maharajah Umaid Singh of Jodhpur who is the father of military, civil and recreational aviation in India. By 1930 Jodhpur was the most important aviation centre in India and on the map of international air travel.

After his matriculation, Chandan returned to Jodhpur. He was fifteen now and raring to join his father's regiment and take part in the war. The Jodhpur Lancers after shedding their horses in exchange for Daimler and Humber Armoured cars had moved to South India and were responsible for patrolling and guarding the coastline around Madras. But getting a commission was a problem, for one he was under age and second he knew no English, a prerequisite for an officer. So with great grit and determination he set about learning English but this was easier said than done because it was not easy getting an English tutor. To learn to speak English one also needs other English speakers to practise with and these too were hard to find.

Gopal Singh who became his tutor, did his best but it was not sufficient, so when he went for his first interview with a British Army Brig Duncan who was seconded to the Jodhpur State Forces, the outcome was a disaster. Chandan Singh mistook or misunderstood what the Colonel said and thinking that the major had been abusive, abused him right back in choicest Marwari resulting in a slanging match between the two. Brig Duncan did not hold a grouse against Chandan and put down his outburst to Chandan's high spiritedness, a quality which he considered essential for a cavalry officer and Chandan was called once again and this time he managed to clear the second interview. In the meantime, he had also acquired a working fluency in English.

After six months training as an officer cadet with a salary of Rs. 15 per month first at the States Officer Training School at Indore and then at OTS Bangalore, Chandan Singh received his commission as a Second Lieutenant in the British Indian Army and attached to the Jodhpur Lancers. He returned to Jodhpur and was attached to the Jodhpur State Forces Training Depot for three months where he was put through a horse riding course on completion of which he went to join his regiment which was located in Salem, a town in the state of Madras now Tamil Nadu.

The regiment's task was to guard the coast against raids by the Japanese. During his time here he was sent on several courses where either he received a Distinguished Instructors grading or flunked the course. There was no halfway performance.

After their tenure in Salem the regiment moved to Colaba Bombay where they received new Bren gun carriers and more Humber armoured cars in preparation for their move overseas to participate in the war.

He was all of seventeen years old. It was 1942 and events were moving fast in all theatres of the war. Today's generation will find it hard to understand the minds and feelings of both Chandan and his parents at that moment, to understand it just consider the fact that a boy of seventeen would today be in Class ten or eleven and here at this age, Chandan was going off to war with all its dangers and uncertainties. But for Chandan it was a challenge and an adventure which he grasped willingly and came out a winner. It may not be out of place to mention that two teenage Indian soldiers were recipients of the Victoria Cross during this war.

3

Second World War

The cauldron of war consumes both weak and bold
Leaving behind both the base and the purest gold
Former to forget, others to have their stories told
(author)

I have devoted many words in this chapter to the history and sociology of the Middle East and Persia where Chandan Singh served during the Second World War. When he arrived in the war theatre he was still in his teens, a stage in life when one's powers of observation and retention are at their peak. Being the intelligent and highly observant person that he is, what he saw, learnt and experienced made him into the person he was to eventually become. His father had also been in this war theatre during the First World War about three decades earlier when he was about the same age and stage in life as Chandan was now, in his teens.

I too have traversed the same ground in 1944-45 and then again later. But even though like them a soldier, I was not fighting a world war, but was instead a member of the United Nations Peace Keeping Forces trying to keep the Arabs and Israelites from each other's throats. The mutual animosity had its roots in the outcome of the two Great Wars and the countless earlier ones going back to the time of the stories of the Old Testament of the Bible.

Chandan was now a young man rearing for action, a keen observer of the human condition with a critical and slightly cynical view of the world. His character had been forged in Marwar but his mind and intellect sprouted and bloomed in

Mesopotamia, Persia and Egypt.

It is a paradox that the theatres of war where Indian troops were first sent to in the First War, Abyssinia, Eritrea, Persia, Iraq and Syria which saw some of the fiercest battles now in the Second Great War turned into relative backwaters, the real actions and fighting were to take place elsewhere after the first few months of the commencement of the Second World War. The peace in this area was mainly due to the presence of the PAI (Persia and Iraq Force) which was composed predominantly of Indian troops.

The Indian Divisions in these two areas after their initial victories took on the role of occupation forces and as a reserve to meet any contingency should the Germans break through the Caucasus or Tunisia. Chandan, the man of unrivalled action and achievement, was to find his true self and calling later but this is where he was forged. There could have been no better training ground, little risk of being killed but the danger, excitement and feel of battle was always present.

Southern Mesopotamia, the ancient name for present-day Iraq, was where the Jodhpur Lancers found themselves stationed during the war, it has three distinct geographical and anthropological divisions each of which is a fascinating study in contrasts and the adjacent parts or Persia where the Jodhpur lancers also operated formed other geographical and anthropological divisions distinct from the Mesopotamian ones.

Basra before 1914 had been the Ottoman capital of Southern Iraq and was captured from them by the Indian Army in just a few days in a brilliant campaign but were to later meet with strong resistance from the Turks and suffered very heavy casualties. Colonel Bahadur Singh, Chandan's father had served in Mesopotamia and Palestine during the First World War and from his accounts of his experiences, Chandan came to know about the geography, history and culture of the region which fired his imagination and enquiring mind.

Victories in the First World War against the Ottoman Empire in the Middle East were the result of the actions of the Indian, Australian and New Zealand troops however their role was never fully appreciated or recognised.

A BBC correspondent Fergal Keane visiting Basra reports about seeing a monument to the Indian War Dead from the First World War about thirty kilometres from Basra when he visited the site after the Gulf War in 2003. The monument was earlier located in Basra but when the port was being expanded it was shifted to its new location by Saddam Hussein who did so out of consideration for the Indian war dead and not for the British, New Zealanders and Australians whose graves lie alongside. Whereas all the British and Commonwealth graves have the names of their occupants engraved with details of regiment and date of death the Indian memorial has only this engraved "For Subedar Mahanga and 1770 Indian Soldiers". Our men were faceless nameless cannon fodder for the Empire not even deserving an individual headstone. But who are we to complain, for even seventy years after independence we have no National Memorial to our own war dead till the time of writing.

The Memorial is made of ochre coloured sandstone most likely carved and imported from Jodhpur itself or it may have come from Petra, the ancient capital of the Nabaeteans in present-day Jordan where one can find similar coloured stone. Keane has also mentioned the continuing existence even in the twenty-first century of the practice of kidnapping young girls for sale in other Arab countries in much the same way as it happened during the First and Second World Wars about which I have written later in this chapter. Some things never seem to change here.

On arrival in Mesopotamia, Chandan Singh took every opportunity to explore, read and learn about the region which is the cradle of human civilisation along with our own related and contemporary Indus and Saraswati Basin Civilisation. It is heir to about ten thousand years of recorded human history from the beginnings of agriculture, domestication of animals, the first cities and temples, metal working, the origin and development of writing, mathematics, weaving of cloth, organisation and founding of states and institution of kingship, the study of astronomy, measurement of time and the codification of laws, all of this and more started here as also overland and sea trade.

The land has been hotly contested by rival groups from the dawn of history and mutual bloodletting has been a constant occurrence. From a state of great civilisation to the present: what a fall! The reader will notice that the events taking place here today have an uncanny resemblance to what happened in the past.

That is why it is important to study history. Ignore it at your own peril as the Americans and their allies are now learning. Henry Ford may have been a great industrialist but when he said history is bunk and generations of Americans came to believe in it they condemned themselves to an era of self-inflicted and unnecessary problems leading to bloodletting in many parts of the globe including the cities at the heart of both the US and Europe. The West is fighting the symptoms of the disease rather than the disease itself.

Basra

The Headquarters of the British Forces known as the PAI Force for Persia and the Iraq Force was at Basra where the Jodhpur Lancers were quartered and tasked to protect and keep open the lines of communication to Tehran, the capital of Persia and to patrol the oil pipelines which terminated at Basra. In 1941 the British and Russian forces had occupied Persia to protect their strategic interests particularly oil assets. They replaced its pro-German King Reza Shah whom they themselves had installed earlier after the First World War and replaced him with his minor son Mohammad Reza Shah Pahlavi and installed a pro-Allied Powers man as Prime Minister. This was a repeat of what they had done twenty years earlier when the previous King the last of the Turkoman Qajar dynasty was removed by General Ironside the British Commander-in-Chief and Reza Shah appointed in his place after the First World War. It was through Persia that aid to Russia both civil and military under the Lend Lease agreement could be delivered. In all over ten million tons of warlike stores and an equal amount of food aid was delivered to the Russians via this route.

The Northern Sea route to Murmansk via the North Sea was very dangerous and difficult due to stormy weather, icebergs, German U Boats and aircraft. On the road from Basra and the Persian ports to Tehran and beyond to Azerbejan there was no interference from the Germans but tribesmen, bandits and Persian Army deserters would waylay the stragglers in the convoy looting the trucks and killing the occupants. Besides the convoys our troops had also to protect the oil fields, refineries, oil terminals and pipelines.

Just before the occupation of Persia and booting out of the Shah of Persia, Reza Khan, the British had done exactly the same in Iraq. They occupied Iraq in May 1941 and in a short and sharp war removed its pro-German dictator Rashid Ali who himself a month earlier had in a coup dethroned the eight-year-old boy King Feisal II and taken over the country. The British put Feisal back on the throne and put their own man to govern the country. Most of the actions against Rashid Ali's forces were undertaken by the Royal Air Force which was the first time in history that an Air Force achieved victory on its own.

The early operations in Iraq were controlled from GHQ in India and then from Cairo but this was not found satisfactory and the Persia and Iraq Force (PAI Force) with HQ at Basra was created. The majority of troops in the PAI Force were Indian. This Force was commanded by Gen Maitland-Smith and the ground troops by Gen William Slim who was to gain fame later as the Commander of the Fourteenth Army in India and Burma. Slim is considered by all military historians as the best of all the senior generals of the British Army and a general who appreciated the fighting qualities of Indian troops unlike other British Generals like Montgomery. Field Marshal Slim however was not one of Churchill's favourite generals but he was loved by troops of all nationalities who served under him. Basra was the most important port in the Persian Gulf, through it passed all the normal trade and war supplies to Iraq and Persia for further transport to Russia. The extraction of petroleum products from Iraq and Iran was done from the nearby terminals. It was therefore of great strategic importance for the Allied war effort.

But it was and still is a hell on earth. John Masters the well known novelist and former Gurkha officer who with his battalion was in the area at the same time has given an apt description, "the Persian Gulf is the arsehole of the world and Basra is eighty miles up it". The day temperature hovers around 45 degrees centigrade except when the hot summer sand storms from the north west and sometimes from the opposite south east lash the region bringing darkness at noon and sending the temperature soaring to over 50 degrees. The only redeeming feature of the land, are the rightfully famous Basra dates which are grown in plantations along the water channels of the Euphrates estuary and in the nearby oasis.

The rigours and monotony of a posting to this hellish backwater was almost unbearable for the British troops who were nearly all conscripts unlike their Indian counterparts who were one and all volunteers. The Tommies were an undisciplined lot and as was their custom, spent their time and relieved boredom in brawls, drink and visits to brothels which did a thriving business. Venereal Disease was common amongst them and the provision of PA Room(Personal Assistance Room) where water, soap and disinfectants were provided were established in all unit lines and troops encouraged to use them to wash their privies after a visit to the brothels.

A packet containing prophylactics was also made available to any soldier who wanted it. I do not know if it is still the practice but I do remember that till 1971 these were available in unit MI Rooms of the Indian Army. Antibiotics were still not available in this theatre. They only became available in 1943 and the absence of men from duty because of avoidable illness was a serious problem. But no amount of threats or cajoling by officers had any effect on the troops. Fortunately this problem was not faced by the men of Jodhpur Lancers whose sense of discipline, honour and self- respect kept them away from these temptations.

A sad fate for girls and young women, the flotsam and jetsam of the First World War and the break-up of the Ottoman Empire, some had been slaves but most were victims of poverty and war. Many of these girls at the start of their careers were pre-pubescent pre-teens much preferred by the Arabs because the Prophet had set the precedent by his own example in marrying Ayesha, daughter of Abu Bakr when she was six years old and consummating it when she became nine. After Mohammad's death, Abu Bakr became the first Caliph. This precedent is quoted as the authority by Muslim luminaries to legalise child marriage and its consummation in the Hadith.

These girls came from the Balkans, Colchis, Circassia, Armenia, Greece, Somalia, Baghdad and Damascus, The white slave traders were mainly Baghdadi Jews who had a monopoly of the trade in girls and eunuchs during the Ottoman rule. They first set up these girls in Istanbul, Beirut, Cairo, Damascus and Alexandria, catering to an international and Ottoman elite clientele. Some of these girls, eunuchs and boys also found themselves traded to clients in India particularly the princely states of Hyderabad and Junagad. The Nawab of Junagad preferred Africans, whereas for the Hyderabadi elite the first choice were fair skinned Caucasian slaves. Some communities of dark skinned people in Gujarat like the Siddhis and fair skinned Hyderabadis are descendants of these slaves.

Besides these people of slave origins even the slave trading Baghdadi Jews who were the principal slave traders of castrated boys, have left behind their progeny in India and are still to be found in Bombay, Calcutta and Pune. Gen Jacob like the Sasoons of Poona and Bombay was of Baghdadi Jew lineage.

The Portuguese colonies of Goa, Diu and Daman had Jewish settlers till the time of Saint Francis who started the inquisition in Goa and most Jews who could not escape were burnt at the stake like their co-religionists in Europe. On the abolishment of slavery in Europe and America these slave traders turned into jewel merchants and thanks to them Hyderabad still remains the centre for pearl trading in India. The money they had made in the slave trade was invested in gem stones and pearls for which the Indian princely order was an insatiable market.

The influx of Allied troops created a surge in demand for the services of these girls which was met by a further influx of girls from the countryside, poverty and unsettled conditions forcing their families to sell them to middlemen who then traded them at a profit to the brothels. No mention of their plight, leave alone any sympathy was offered to these forgotten victims of war, human avarice and lust. Like in the First World War venereal diseases became a problem amongst the troops but now with the availability of antibiotics and greater information about prophylactic practices it could be controlled.

Basra pearls are still the most prized of all pearls particularly in India but due to the disruption caused by the war, pearl fishing had come to a virtual stop as the demand for them had fallen and so had the price. Some of the senior Indian and British officers were able to pick up a fortune in pearls at throw away prices, but 2nd Lt Chandan Singh had neither any knowledge of pearls nor the money nor the inclination for this venture, otherwise on return to India he would have become a rich man.

Some British officers made a fortune from Jewish pearl traders as fees for providing them a safe passage to India. In the heart of Basra was the Indian Bazaar known as Amogaiz. It had shops selling textiles, spices and a few other manufactured goods. It was a popular market and its Gujarati, Bohra, Sindhi and Parsi shopkeepers were among the most affluent people in Basra. The Bohras were predominant in the pearl trade which they purchased here and shipped them to their kinsmen in India who were involved in the zardozi and moti ponah/patwa business.

The Bohras are known to be very honest and an enlightened community. However, the horrible practice of female genital mutilation was common amongst them. My friends and relatives from Udaipur which has a sizeable Bohra population and who themselves have many Bohra friends and are familiar with their customs tell me that this practice is still common. Though some voices from within the community are being raised against it. It is believed that the Bohras brought this practice with them from Yemen and Somalia when they migrated to India in the fourteenth century. Another community that prospered were the Parsis, who because of better education and greater familiarity with the British were able to corner lucrative contracts from the Anglo American Armies.

It is perhaps because of its location that Basra has been romanticised in literature and films. A 1924 Douglas Fairbanks starrer *Thief of Bagdad* was remade in 1940 starring an Indian actor named Sabu, who had starred in many other Hollywood films. This was screened for the troops and was a great hit with the Indian soldiers who never tired of seeing it repeatedly with an officer giving in Hindi a running live commentary of the dialogue and action.

For reading there was an H.G. Wells novel *Shape of Things to Come* in which Basra is made the new capital of the world after other cities have been destroyed by war, famine and pestilence. Then there was Sinbad Island from where Sinbad of the Thousand and One Nights stories set out on his voyage to the Indian Coast in the time of Harun al Rashid whose Wazir was a Barmakid of Indian origins.

The Barmakid family is acknowledged by all scholars including contemporary Arabs as being the founders and sustainers of the Golden Age of the Abbasid Caliphate. Soon after the assassination of the last Barmakid Prime Minister at the behest of Harun al Rashid the Abbasid dynasty came to an end and with them the rule and Golden Age of the Arabs. The subsequent caliphs where all of Mongol or Turkish descent. Their prime ministers, the Barmakids were of Indian descent and it is they who brought the knowledge Indian mathematics, medicine, philosophy and other arts to the court of the caliphs and the rest of the Arab world.

The Euphrates Marshes and the Madaan (Marsh Gypsies)

The Eupharates marshes are located south east of Basra and are peopled by the Marsh Gypsies who are known as the Madaan and they claim Indian descent which is accepted as a fact by all anthropologists and further confirmed by the record of their mitochondrial DNA which they share with people of Western India. For the sociologist and anthropologist the Madaan are a most interesting people.

Here it would be appropriate to give an English translation of the lyrics of a Marsh Gypsy song which not only confirms their Indian origin but also throws light on their adversarial relations with their Arab neighbours including the Caliphs in Baghdad and Damascus. It also confirms the importance of Basra dates in the lives of the Arab elites about which I have said much, later in this chapter.

O people of Baghdad-die. Your anger
Born from longing for fine dates cut off
By our blockade, long may it continue
It is we who beat you in broad day light
By force of arms and flayed you till you were powerless
You did not give thanks to God
For the bounties you received.
So call upon your slaves, brought from Egypt to break the dams
And your rich supporters who wear silk and gold
With sharp daggers fixed to their belts.
We, children of two migrations from India,
We will smash your heads,
We sail in decorated black ships made from the finest woods.
When you approach us in our canals and lakes,
Take care. We will hunt you down as hunters hunt birds,
There is no fighting like fighting the Zott.
It is not like eating and drinking at a banquet.
It is we who tasted war as babies.

Courageous both on land and water.
We shall attack you and please your enemies.
Cry then for you fine dates-
You will miss them at your holy feasts.
                    Quoted by Al Tabari, an early Arab historian of the
                                                        eighth century CE

One of the advantages of being with the Jodhpur Lancers was that the regiment it was equipped with Humber and Daimler armoured cars and tracked Bren Gun Carriers, so they had both transport and fuel unlike most other units which were mainly infantry. This enabled the officers to explore the area and go out on shikar, a favourite pastime of most officers.

While in Marwar when they were still horsed Cavalry the older officers had all taken part in pig sticking, a dangerous and exciting sport, but here in the marshes not only were there no horses even the sturdy armoured cars were of little use in the hunts but they came in handy to drive the hunting parties to villages located at the edge of the marsh, from here they would transfer to the taradas (canoes) paddled by local Madaan guides. Most of the hunting was done from these taradas at a time when the boar would swim across the water channels from one island to another on their feeding rounds.

The reed covered islands were home to wild boar the eating of which was taboo for the locals as they were Muslim, and hence the boar thrived in the area. The wild boar here, were of a different sub species and much bigger in size than the ones found in India. They were about six feet from nose to tail in length, three and a half feet in height and weighed about two hundred kilograms. They were dangerous beasts and killed and wounded several marsh people every year.

Not many urban people can imagine how dangerous a charging wild boar can be. The author however knows, I was mauled by one in 1974 at the Army's Field Firing Range near Reva in Madhya Pradesh where my Brigade was camping on its annual field firing and training exercises.

The Lancers were used to hunting boars from horseback

with a spear but hunting from boats was a novelty for them and though not as exhilarating as a chase on horseback it still provided a welcome change from the monotony of service in this backwater of war, and in its own way was quite exciting. In 1972 after the rest of the Indian Army had withdrawn from Bangladesh, my Battalion and I were located near Cox Bazaar on the coast of the Bay of Bengal where the conditions were similar to those in the marshes of Iraq and we too hunted wild boar in the same way from boats.

Abu our local guide and boatman in Cox Bazar would paddle our canoe silently through the creeks at high tide trying to listen to the sounds the boar made whilst feeding or splashing through shallow water and when we were close enough we would switch on the search light to spot the wild boar and shoot them as they crossed over from the islands to the mainland to escape the incoming tide.

The only difference between our method of hunting in Bangladesh and of the Jodhpur Lancers in Iraq was while they hunted during the day, we hunted at night, the headlights and batteries recovered from captured Pakistan Army vehicles serving the purpose of search lights to spot the wild boar. The rigors of heat and humidity during the boat ride were tempered with plenty of cold beer. Altogether a pleasant way to spend time and I am sure the Lancers too would have felt the same.

During the winter months the marshes were visited by large flocks of migratory ducks and geese which too were hunted by the Madaan and the Lancer officers. Shikar helped to supplement the otherwise frugal and insipid rations that were issued to the troops as almost no vegetables or dairy products were available locally.

To the Rajput officers and men of the Jodhpur Lancers this game meat was a heaven sent feast. The Rajputs love their wild boar even more than the comic book Gaul characters: Astrix, Oblix, Cacofonix and the rest of their Gaul gang do, and with whom the Rajputs also share a fondness for alcohol and warfare.

The Marsh Gypsies looked like people from Rajasthan and the women wore the same colourful clothes and jewellery as the women back home, but this is not surprising because their forefathers had migrated several hundreds of years earlier from India, in fact from exactly the same region and same time as the Rathores moved into Marwar.

Unlike their Bedouin neighbours the women did not cover their faces on which were displayed tattoo designs patterned like herring bones or garden rakes. Similar patterns were repeated on the chin and neck in a line running down to between the breasts and on their arms and hands exactly like those on Gujar, Meena, Banjara and Bheel women of Marwar and Kutch, and like those on their counterparts in India these tattoos disfigured the fine lines of their faces which in their youth before they were marked by tattoos would have been the envy of the most beautiful women anywhere.

The young girls were stunners but untouchable for they were all married very young while in their early teens, and they go as virgins to their marriage beds for the penalty for detected intercourse before that is no less than death, her brothers will slit her throat at the insistence of the Syeds. The seducer on the other hand, is held to be guiltless.

Even the buffalo, the mounds of dry buffalo dung cakes used as fuel for cooking, and the grass and reed huts had the look, feel and smell of home about them. But unlike Rajasthan which is a dry stony desert this area is entirely a marsh, small islands on which the people make a home for themselves and their buffaloes. These reed covered islands sometimes occupied by a single family while the bigger ones may house several and could be called villages, are separated from each other by waterways rich in fish and waterfowl. These waterways are the only means of communication to the outside world and also within the marsh.

In their excursions to the surrounding countryside the officers explored the Euphrates and Tigris deltas, where through the Shatt al Arab these rivers join the sea. Between Basra in the south to Kut El Amara in the north, and the

Persian border on the east is a vast marsh.

Scholars think this is the original Biblical Garden of Eden, for Eden in the ancient Sumerian language means grass land by the sea. At this time this area was unknown territory, the geography and people had not been studied for till about two decades ago it was a part of the Ottoman Empire and closed to foreigners.

The writ of the newly installed Hashemite King Abdullah was not accepted by the people of the Marsh who though outwardly Muslim did not have anything else in common with their Bedouin Arab neighbours whom they despised, the feelings being reciprocated by their Bedouin and town neighbours.

The Madaan looked up to their own clan chiefs for spiritual and social guidance and resolution of conflicts. They look different and are racially closer to Indians than Arabs. Some of the words of their language are the same or similar to their counterparts in the languages of Western/Central India. A few of them have traces of distinctly Mongolian features a reminder of the conquest and occupation of the area by Mongols under Hulagu, grandson of Changez Khan in 1258 AD.

After putting the last Abbasid Caliph Al-Musta'sin to death in a most cruel and gruesome way, Hulagu turned his attention to the common people and the country, and turned a once prosperous agricultural country into a desert wasteland by destroying the old canals and irrigation systems which had been developed over thousands of years. Millions were killed or uprooted, the Arab world has never recovered from this calamity till date.

The Madaan or Marsh Arabs as they are erroneously called have been in a state of perpetual war with the Arabs for over a thousand years, the terrain providing them shelter and protection from hostile armies. It took several centuries of warfare before the Caliphs at Baghdad were able to subjugate them and convert them to Islam. But their Islamic faith is like an outer garment worn for public display of allegiance to their new faith for inside the Madaan still observe the customs and rituals they have carried from India a thousand years ago.

They build no mosques and pay cursory obeisance to the itinerant Syeds who visit them to collect their tithes and preach that the rewards in heaven including the promised seventy-two eternally youthful virgin houries will be proportionate to the gifts offered to the Syeds all of whom claim descent from Mohammad. Some apologists explain away this by saying that the real Arabic meaning in old Arabic for virgins is raisins, if that be true than it is a poor reward for a boy who blows himself up in despair at not being able to find someone for fulfilment of his legitimate natural needs here on earth and has to be content with a promise of seventy-two raisins in the hereafter.

The elites being able to afford it have already harvested not only the best but almost the entire crop of young and desirable females, leaving nothing for the less privileged but the leftovers or castaways.

Over the years on the insistence of the Sayeds the Madaan have adopted the practice of circumcision of their male children. But being newcomers to the practice there are not many qualified professional circumcisers and the quacks tend to botch the operation inflicting great pain and infection on the victims. Because of the infection which takes months if not years to heal many teenage boys could be seen holding their dish-dashas (a loose outer garment worn by males) away from their bodies towards the front as their genitalia would be swollen with an infection of sepsis and contact with the garment was a very painful experience.

Modern medicines, antibiotics and qualified doctors were an unknown commodity then. With no medical facilities and utter lack of knowledge and practice of basic hygiene, diseases which had been controlled or easily curable elsewhere took a heavy toll on the populace.

Life expectancy was as low as forty years and only two or three children out of over dozen born to a woman reached the teens. With the Madaan unlike the Beduin monogamy was the rule rather than the exception. Wilfred Theisiger the famed explorer of the Empty Quarter of Arabia made a name for himself and acquired an iconic status amongst the Madaan by treating them with modern medicines and the knowledge he had in their use. But sadly while he was able to treat the men and boys, women and girls could not be seen by him and he could only diagnose and treat them from whatever their male escorts conveyed to him.

The ritual of circumcision is a major event for the family and village, and a feast is usually held to which friends and family are invited. Some officers were invited to one such event which was considered a great honour, bestowed on them probably because they had cleared the area surrounding the village of wild boar which were to the Madaan as much a menace as man eating tigers were to the people living in the jungles of India. More than sixty years later the details of one such event were described to me in vivid detail by General Ardeshar of the Army Medical Corps who was posted here during the war had been witness to one such ritual.

The village mudhifs (huts) were all decorated with multi-coloured bunting and there was an air of festivity in the entire village. About twelve boys in the age group of nine to nineteen lay side by side on the ground facing upwards, surrounded by the men, women and children of the village forming a wall of spectators. None of the boys expressed any embarrassment at having their genitals exposed in front of women and girls, for the marshmen while in the water are so often naked in the presence of women that no element of shame attaches to it. In addition to the Madaan the waterways were frequented by a fishing tribe called Berber (not to be mistaken for the Berbers of the Sahara) whose members of both sexes wear no clothes while fishing. Should a woman of this tribe when in this condition, chance upon a stranger her hands automatically go up and cover her mouth leaving the genitals and breasts exposed.

The wandering professional circumciser a particularly vile looking character moved from one boy to another, performing operations which should really be called mutilation. He used a knife that didn't appear to be either clean or sharp and then put the severed foreskins in a bag. He then went around and applied some sort of a grey powder on the operated part, the powder he said was the ashes of the burnt foreskins collected from earlier operations, the ash he claimed had miraculous curative powers! After collecting his professional fees he left by a tarada with no advice or prescription for post operative care.

None of the boys screamed or howled as this would have been considered a very shameful thing, but obviously it was a painful operation as was evident from their grimaces and tensed bodies. An onion pierced with a string was tied around the boy's waist to ward off pestering flies and insects from settling on the genitals. The Madan unlike some of their Semitic neighbours do not practise circumcision of females.

The boy's mother or sister would be sitting beside him keeping the flies away and as soon as the operation was completed would give vent to a weird cry of rejoicing that is described as ululating which to the locals is an expression of exhilaration and ecstacy (an onomatopoeic word, for the sound is simply "ululululululu" repeated in a high and rapid wail till breath gives out. As someone though not a scholar or an expert of the subject yet with a deep interest in anthropology and evolution of human speech my conjecture on the origins of ululating is that it started during the very early phase of evolution of early hominid species into homo sapiens while still in the original homeland in the African Rift Valley.

The sound has no meaning or syntax but similar sounds are often made by troops of baboons and apes when excited. Early humans have carried this practice to their new homelands for the practice is still to be found in very distant geographical locations. In Bengal and South and Central Africa it is a sign of celebration and jubilation. In the plains of North America the Red Indians do it for different purposes on different occasions. Sometimes the father would fire a celebratory shot or two from his rifle.

This was followed by a communal feast given by the families of the boys. The marshmen are very poor with few possessions or money, but yet go overboard in their hospitality. Several chickens and a sheep were slaughtered. The feast took place inside a large dimly lit mudhif about fifty feet long with the buffaloes tied at the rear end which space was shared by the women, darkness separating the sexes and the animals.

The walls and arched ceiling strengthened with bundles of reeds tied tightly together to stiffen them served the purpose of curved beams that supported the roof of the mudhif and had an uncanny resemblance to the insides of the Buddhist caves in Western Maharashtra where arched wooden beams have been substituted and represented by similarly shaped stone forms which have only a decorative function and have nothing to do with structural requirements.

The guests and hosts were seated on reed mats in two rows facing each other and piping hot black Arabian coffee in thimble-sized cups was served by a black African slave which they were expected to down in a single gulp. The food was then brought in, served on a large flat round dish almost four feet in diameter, it consisted of a mound of rice on which the mutton or chicken stew had been poured over, seven or eight people sat around and would dig their hands into the pile and help themselves, occasionally the host would pick up a morsel which in his consideration was a special delicacy, and pass it on to the guests to eat.

This is considered a special honour and favour and good manners required that this be eaten however dirty be the hands that picked up the morsel and passed it on. In fact, by the time the selected piece of meat had reached the guest it had been touched by ten hands. Except for salt and some dried dates used as garnishing there were no spices added to the food as the Madaan could not afford them, but even without any spices being used the food was delicious as it had been cooked over slow burning buffalo dung cakes and had acquired a smoky flavour much like the food at home. The Indians ate sparingly but the Madaan gorged themselves, as meat was a luxury rarely affordable. Their staple was rice or barley eaten with sour butter milk.

At the end of the meal marshmen, expressed their satisfaction over the meal with loud belches. This is considered to be the right way to express satisfaction and gratitude to the host for the quality and quantity of the food.

After the meal was over, a group of musicians trooped in and sat down beside the hosts. They carried drums, a string and a wind instrument both not dissimilar to those found in the villages of Rajasthan but what emerged were sounds and music quite unfamiliar and unpleasing to Indian ears, attuned as our ears are to highly developed and sophisticated courtly, classic and folk musical traditions.

Islam sadly does not encourage the performing arts. Hence ever since its conquest of the entire Middle East fifteen hundred years ago the arts except for calligraphy have atrophied and been lost.

The musicians were then joined by a young man and a boy in his mid teens who unlike the other men wore garments and make up which today would be called unisexual or bisexual. Their walk and gestures had something effeminate about them. They were professional dancers who travelled from one settlement to another to dance and entertain an entirely male clientele, something which in other places and societies would be performed by female performers.

The dance was a spoof on a theme very familiar to the Marshmen, an exploitation of the risqué possibilities inherent in the Muslim attitude in prayer where the forehead is pressed to the ground in supplication and the rump held high in the air.

The stage was then taken over by the teenager, he had long hair and in today's language would be termed a transvestite or lady boy. He was dressed appropriately and had the audience drooling. Like a trained courtesan, he captivated the audience with a shake and twirl of his hips and flutter of his eyelashes. His audience was captivated and ready to pay the going price, in fact some sort of bidding was going on. The dancer unfortunately came to a sad end a few days later. A Bedouin tribesman became besotted with him and followed him around from one performance to another but when he ran out of money the dancer ditched him for a new client with fuller pockets. When the Bedouin saw him go off with another man, in a fit of jealous rage he knifed the dancer, killing him.

What happened to the Bedouin is not known, the dancer's family probably claimed blood money and if that was not paid would then have executed him publicly by slitting his throat, watched by a cheering crowd consisting of both men and women as is the custom amongst the Bedouins and some Islamic countries even today.

In societies where the strict gender segregation is enforced it has become a practice to keep boys even though according to Islamic law homosexuality is banned. Keeping young boys aged between ten and eighteen is tolerated if they wear female attire and display feminine mannerisms then they come under the category of concubines with whom a temporary marriage can take place. According to the Sharia, concubines and slaves (gender not specified) are the property of the 'right hand' and a relationship is permitted. In other societies this would amount to pedophilia and would invite criminal prosecution and heavy punishment.

It is pertinent to note that many young suicide bombers are drawn from the ranks of the youth who have been abused and traumatised from an early age at the same time indoctrinated in the madrasas by mullahs who themselves are child abusers.

Some years ago in Delhi there was a parade by the lesbian and gay community who demanded legitimacy and acceptance for their sexual orientation stating that their sexual orientation should not be criminalised as they were hapless victims of their genes. Therefore what was considered as unnatural was natural to them. This subject was then a topic of drawing room discussion amongst the chatterrati and liberal class of Delhi. Staying with me at that time were my friends Dr. David Cove and his wife Anne. Dr. David Cove is one of the world's leading geneticists who has been the Secretary of the

World Genetics Society and Anne is an acclaimed painter. We are proud owners of one of her paintings gifted to us. It is a scene of a view of their beautiful and quaint twelfth century Norman cottage and garden in Leeds.

I posed the question of the same gender sex to David and his answer was that if it was only a question of genes then over thousands of years of human evolution this aberrant gene would have been eliminated from the human chromosome because homosexuals would not have mated with the opposite gender. Therefore they would not pass on this gene to the next generation. So it was more a matter of the social environment in which these people live their lives and was definitely an acquired trait.

The officers of the Jodhpur Lancers found this sort of behaviour repugnant because their tastes and aesthetics were based on their own cultural and social values. However the older officers could not help but notice that some of the dance movements and particularly the interlocking of the fingers of the two hands and then striking the middle finger of one in the depression between the knuckles of the other hand made a sound like, and as loud as the crack of a pistol. This feat was an exact replication of what the Kanjar dancing girls of Ghas Mandi in Jodhpur would do whenever they performed for the nobility during weddings or at a mujra for a social event. (Lakhi Bai, later known as Khursheed Begum, was Zulfikar Ali Bhutto's mother. Before her marriage to Shah Nawaz Bhutto, the father of Zulfikar, she was a Kanjar dancing girl from Ghas Mandi when at the age of twelve she was picked up by Bhutto's father).

Ever since the downfall of the Awadh feudal class, Jodhpur had become the most important centre and home of the best and classiest nautch girls in the country even better than the girls from Benaras and Lucknow, the other two nautch centres. They had in many cases been born into the families of professional entertainers and from a young age trained to sing and dance. Having to perform for discerning clientele at the royal courts or for the nobility they had perfected the art of refined speech, movements, facial expressions besides becoming accomplished singers and dancers.

They had perfected the art of being desired by all and making everyone feel special so that every man present felt that he alone was the centre of her attention yet these ladies belonged to no one. Many of these girls became famous names in the early years of Bollywood and some even went on to marry or became mistresses of the rich and famous. Even today the progeny of these early pioneers from the kotha to the kothi dominate the music and film industry.

There was nothing vulgar or cheap about them. It was an art form developed and perfected over centuries which now deprived of royal and cultured patronage is sadly lost. The private and intimate mehfils and temple performances by devdasis before discerning patrons of yesteryears have become vulgar stage and bar shows for drunks, philistines and boorish louts.

The author considers himself privileged to have attended the performances by some of the last generation of these great artistes in the late 1950s and early 60s. Alas it is all dead now and the present generation has to content itself with watching the Bombay bar girls and Katrina Kaif. For those nostalgic or curious about that era, watching Waheeda Rehman, Madhubala, Meena Kumari and Rekha in one of their classic movies like *Anarkali* and *Umrao Jaan* where they have played the role of a courtesan will give an idea of what I am talking about. But the silver screen is no substitute for the real experience. As Plato quoting Aristotle said, "You eat apples, not paintings of apples."

This was also a rare opportunity for Chandan to see the life of the Madaan from inside, a privilege and honour not shared by many, a parting gift of fifty rupees and a box of 12 bore shotgun cartridges was readily and happily accepted by the host. With fifty rupees he could buy a dozen sheep or one buffalo and the box of cartridges would help the family supplement their frugal larder with an occasional duck or goose.

The Southern Desert and the Ruins of UR and Babylon

The third region and historically the most important was the surrounding desert dotted with the ruins of ancient cities half as old as time itself and it was here that recorded history of the human race began. It is also here where the story of the Bible begins with the departure of Abraham and his family. But even before this, the King of Sumer Hamurabi had given to the world the first written law which is known as the Code of Hamurabi. It is in Sumer that the first division of time in multiples of six was developed as also the lunar calendar, the first example of writing.

Going back earlier to the age of myth, scholars are now unanimous that the marshes to the South are the proverbial Garden of Eden. In the ancient Mesopotamian language, Eden means grassland by the sea. It is also here that the Tower of Babel has been discovered and so have the ruins of the first urban settlements which developed into towns and cities.

But all that is history, the reality of today is that owing to human predations this land is now almost a wasteland. This area had also been of interest to archaeologists and philologists who had deciphered the ancient Sumerian/ Acadian scripts found inscribed on stones and clay tablets that the archaeologists had dug up. What surprised Chandan was that the names of many ancient Kings like Amar Sinh and Naram Sinh not only sounded familiar but on translation from Sumerian into English had the same meaning as in Sanskrit or Hindi. These names of kings were from dynasties who had ruled here before 2000 BC.

Some names of local places and kings which could not be deciphered before have now been shown to have their roots in our Dravidian languages indicating that the reach of both our Aryan and Dravidian civilisation extended far beyond the boundaries of present-day India. This should not be surprising because the ancient Kingdom of Elam which flourished at the time of the Old Kingdom in Egypt was adjacent to Baluchistan and their rule extended westwards towards what is now Iraq.

Their language was a Dravidian language closely related to Brahui which is still spoken in parts of Baluchistan. But more of Elam and its Indian connections later.

Persia

This ancient land home to a great Indo-Aryan civilisation and a melting pot of rival influences from India, Central Asia, Sumer and Greece had been the home of some of the greatest empires the world has ever known for thousands of years. There were periods of Persian domination of western regions of India including Afghanistan conversely Indian influence in all aspects of Persian life was pervasive. After all Zoroaster the founder of Zoroastrianism which was the official religion of Persia during its days of greatness was born in Balkh in Afghanistan which was then a part of the Indian civilisational world.

Balkih as it was known then was in its heyday, i.e. from about 700 BC to 1000 AD. It was considered the greatest city in the world where caravans from India, China, Greece, Anatolia and the Middle East would meet to rest and trade goods and, more importantly, to exchange ideas and even genes. Balkh like Nalanda and Vikramsheela was the home of a famous university where scholars, some of whom were Chinese princes, came to study.

So it is not surprising that all five religions/philosophies Hinduism, Buddhism, Confucian/Taoism, Greek and Zoroastrianism all share a common humanist and spiritual streak where the human condition and its interests and welfare occupy the central position in their thoughts and contemplation. They aim to find the divine through love and the pursuit of the aesthetic bliss.

Whereas in the Semitic tradition it is the fear of God, observance of rituals and blind faith in dogma that is paramount, leaving no scope to the individual to think for himself. As Kipling said of the people in the Middle East and West Asia, "the fear of death is the beginning of wisdom", in the Orient love and compassion is the path to wisdom

But Persia during the last few centuries after the death of Nadir Shah had entered into a spiral of diminishing influence and had been reduced to a pale shadow of its glorious past and become a plaything of the Great Powers particularly Russia, Britain and Turkey. Russia wanted an opening to the Indian Ocean, Britain to secure for its self oil supplies for the Royal Navy from the oil fields of the Middle East and the Ottomans of Turkey had always contested the ownership of lands from the Caspian Sea to the Persian Gulf on their eastern and south eastern frontiers with Persia.

Constant pressure and local civil wars had caused the downfall of the old dynasty and a Turkoman Qajar chieftain Muhammad Khan Qajar from the Caucuses Mountains proclaimed himself as the King towards the end of the eighteenth century after deposing Lotf Ali Khan of the Zand dynasty, and starting the reign of the Qajars which lasted for about a hundred and forty years and itself fell a victim to its own internal problems and the Great Game.

Replaced in 1921 this time by another non-Persian Turkic tribesman named Reza Shah who had started his career as a private soldier in the bodyguard of the Qajar Prince Shahzdeh.

The Prince's bodyguards were gifted some Maxim machine guns by the Germans and Reza Shah became a machine gunner because being a big and strong man he could lift and handle the machine gun singlehanded He acquired the nickname Reza Khan Maximi. He came to be King of Persia during the turbulent time following the end of the First World War when the old Qajar king fled to Paris in permanent exile leaving Persia with no government, Reza Khan by now an officer in the Persian Cossack Regiment was spotted by the British Commander-in-Chief General Ironside.

The General was impressed with his height and build. He was six feet three inches tall and muscularly built and thinking that maybe he could bring order in the country declared "he is my man" and appointed him Commander-in-Chief of the Persian Army. With three thousand of his men from the Persian Cossack Regiment (a kind of Praetorian Guard of the

Qajar Dynasty), which he now commanded and with some help from the British, Reza Shah marched into Tehran. Finding that the King had fled and there was a vacancy at the top, he declared himself the King with the title Reza Shah Pahlavi Shah en Shah of Persia.

Pahlavi was the name of an ancient Persian ruling dynasty which Reza Shah abrogated to himself to give some legitimacy to his own rule in the hope that the people of Persia would accept him and his heirs. But it was not to be so, for some years later he had to abdicate and was forced into exile and three decades later his son Mohammad Shah was kicked out of Iran by Ayatollah Khomeini.

The departure of Mohammad Reza Shah brought to an end the three thousand-years-old institution of Persian monarchy. Reza Shah's magnificent tomb in the heart of Tehran was torn down and the place converted into a public toilet by the new regime. A good lesson and example for all megalomaniac dictators and leaders.

But there can be no doubt that while they sat on the throne of Iran there was comparative peace and quiet in the country even though it was brought about in typical Mid-Eastern fashion by the liberal use of the hangman's rope or the firing squad cheered by the Western nations who forgetting their principles of liberal government drooled at the Shah's feet in hopes of getting cheap and secure oil.

After the Anglo-Russian invasion of Iran in 1941 the Russians occupied the northern part and the British the southern part. The PAI Force besides acting as a safeguard against a possible German breakthrough in the Caucasus, their Army Group South under Marshal Von Manstien had occupied the Crimean peninsula and could have turned southwards.

The PAI Force was also required to ensure the safety of the railway lines and roads over which thousands of tons of war time aid was shipped to Russia every month from the ports in the Persian Gulf right up to Azerbaijan and Baku. Camps were set up all along the rail and road lines and the Jodhpur

Lancers who were based at Masjed e Suleimaniya in south western Iran close to the Iraqi border escorted the convoys up to the Russian Border where they were then taken over by the Russians. In Iraq there is another town by the name of Suleimaniya. It is the largest town of Iraqi Kurdistan and is at an elevation of 3,500 feet and has historical connections with the Bahai faith.

Here during the winter months the men of Jodhpur Lancers saw snow for the first time. Some of the veterans from the First World War had of course seen it in France. Suleimaniya was once the capital of an independent Kurdish state and the Kurds who are inhabitants of the area are neither Iranian nor Arab but are an Indo-Aryan tribe whose language is related to Sanskrit. This theatre was in the backwaters of the war and no fighting took place but the troops had always to be on guard and escorting convoys over rough roads was not an easy task, particularly when there was a danger of ambushes by bandits.

The Jodhpur Lancers spent over two years in Iran. Their base was Masjid-e-Suleman and the nearby town of Haftekhel both in the Zagroz mountains in the petroleum producing areas of Iran. The modern Iran province of Khuzestan (Khurasan) where these towns are located is the ancient kingdom of Elam which finds mention in the Old Testament of the Bible.

Elamite the now dead language has no relationship with any known Middle Eastern or Iranian language. Its nearest relations are the Dravidian languages of India and the names of their kings and queens bear a close resemblance to Indian names. At one time, Elam ruled an empire that encompassed the whole of the Middle East and present-day Iran, Egypt and Northern Sudan. The Elamite Kingdom was not a Persian kingdom. The Persian Achaemenid dynasty came to rule after the final fall and disintegration of the Elamite Kingdom. The Persian Achaemenids were an Indo-Aryan tribe.

The chief town was Susa made famous because of the six month long feast organised by Xerxes whose queen was named Shasti in the seventh century BC; in the Bible she is called Esther. The name Susa is derived from Shusham which was the original and correct name of the capital city of Elam. The mass weddings were organised by Alexander the Great on his return journey from India at Susa where his Macedonians and other Greeks took on Persian and Indian wives.

Seleucus who later succeeded as the King of the Eastern Greek Empire married Aparma, an Indian Princess from Bakhtra (Balkh). It is from Seleucus and Aparma that the line of the great Indo-Greek kings of the Seleucid dynasty are descended and who came to rule an Empire which extended from the borders of India to the Mediterranean. Amongst the ruins of Susa and the nearby Ziggarauts have been found many pieces of stone sculpture and glazed brick works the designs which are now associated with Iranian works of the Achaemenian period and which were then imported into India during the time of Ashoka when he built his capital at Kumrahar, now a suburb of Patna.

Indian influence in Iran did not end with the fall of the Elamite Kingdom in 790 AD Al Fadl (766-809 AD), a Barmakid prince of Indian origin was appointed the viceroy of Khorasan (Elam). Earlier he had been the Viceroy of Tabaristan (Tapuria) which is the Iranian province in Northern Iran in an area south of the Caspian Sea where Tehran is located. Al Fadl and his father Yayha are considered as the founders of the Golden Age and Enlightenment of the Baghdad Caliphate. Without being overly chauvinist, one can safely state that Indian influence was present at Tehran and Susa, the modern and ancient capitals of Iran and also in Baghdad in ancient and medieval times.

Due to employment opportunities provided by the oil industry the people of these two towns, Haftkhel and Masjed e Sulyman were more prosperous than other places in Iran which at that time was undergoing a severe drought and famine for over two years. Several hundred thousand perished due to starvation and malnourishment. To make matters worse there was an outbreak of scrub typhus which took another heayy toll on the local population.

After meeting the needs of the Allied armies there was

little food or scrub typhus vaccine left to meet the needs of the local populations. Fearing an outbreak of rebellion the Allies shipped in wheat from India which itself was reeling from the Bengal famine which took the lives of millions.

For recreation Officers of the Allied Armies would visit the Anglo-Iranian Oil Company's club where they had a chance to interact with the families of the Oil Company's employees and also with prominent locals. It was here during these troubled times that Chandan came into contact with a local Zoroastrian family at the club in Haftekhel. The head of the family was Mr. Jahangir Cyrus who had one son Sia and two daughters Sisi and Zaleh, a fifteen year girl coming into bloom. Chandan was seventeen and it was love at first sight.

Mr. Cyrus encouraged the two teenagers, for after all Chandan was a cavalry officer and a handsome one to boot. India was the home of the largest Zoroastrian community in the world and perhaps Mr. Cyrus hoped that something would come out of the friendship of the two teenagers. Chandan on his part was able to supply the family with surplus rations and other goods from the overflowing stocks of the Allied Army which were either considered a luxury or were not available to the civilian population. He also used to pick up several Hollywood movies from the NAAFI stores which were then screened in the club and watched by both Zaleh and Chandan in the darkness of the club's theatre.

However, fate intended otherwise and the budding romance was nipped in the bud. Maj Bromilo, the Regiment's Second in Command, detected the affair and told Major Kalyan Singh who promptly wrote off to Chandan's father Col Bahadur Singh and before Chandan realised what was happening he received a movement order to proceed to Cairo. Leaving Hafte Khel and Zaleh behind, he was seventeen and she fifteen.

The Army Movement Control Organisation now took control of him and by air, road and train he journeyed to Cairo halting at Damascus, Baghdad, Haifa to an Army camp in the shadow of the Great Pyramids at Giza. Here a course on tactics in desert warfare was being conducted and both students and the instructors were housed in tents. Sharing his tent was a British officer Captain Henderson from Cardiff. He was a war time commissioned officer who before the war was a teacher by profession.

Henderson took kindly to Chandan and realising that Chandan's education was incomplete took him under his wing and during the next three months that they were together put him through a rigorous college education programme in both the sciences and humanities. At the end of three months, Chandan though without a formal degree was a thoroughly educated young man whose zest for further learning was now fired and insatiable.

From Henderson he also acquired the accent and manners of the upper English classes. Many years later when Chandan Singh was flying the monthly IAF courier to England he took time off to visit Wales to meet Henderson who was then teaching at the University of Wales at Cardiff. This is an example of what a good teacher can do to transform a raw youth to a man of the world in a short span of three months.

For recreation the students and the staff used to visit the bar and swimming pool of the Giza Mena House Hotel on the bank of the Nile close to the Pyramids. This hotel is now run by the Oberois. King Faroukh, the reigning monarch of Egypt, too was a frequent visitor along with a bevy of beauties from his harem. On one occasion when Chandan saw these ladies in Western style swim suits and Faroukh frolicking in the pool he perhaps got carried away. Capt Henderson promptly pushed him into the pool with an admonishment not to come out till he had cooled off.

After the tactics course he rejoined his regiment but was now posted to Masjed e Suleyman and never again got to visit Hafte Khel or see Zaleh Cyrus. During his tenure here Chandan got to see Tehran and many other towns but could not make it to Persepolis, the ancient capital of Persia which was destroyed by Alexander the Great after the battle of Gaugamela. Visits to the Iranian borders with Azerbaijan and

Turkmenia on duty while escorting supply columns over the Alborz and Zargoz Mountains gave him an opportunity to see the vastness of the Central Asian Steppe which extended five thousand miles from here to the borders of China in the East.

Then there was the Gorgon or as it is more popularly known the Alexander Wall which runs parallel to the northern border of Iran. The wall was a defence work consisting of a string of forts rather than a continuous wall which divided and protected the settled agricultural plains of Iran from the nomadic Turkic people of the Asian Steppe. It was sited on the northern slopes of the Alborz Mountains and was about two hundred miles from east to west ending on the shores of the Caspian Sea. Work was started on it during Alexander's time to protect his newly won dominions from raids from the north much the same reasons why the Chinese built their Great Wall.

Polish Refugees

The only thing that broke the routine and provided a break from the monotony was the unexpected arrival of ten thousand Polish refugees, mainly women and children. Churchill had agreed to take in Polish refugees in the expectation that they would be all men of military age and they would fill the ranks of the Free Polish Army which was based in UK. But the Russians kept the men behind to bolster their own army and sent the women and children who were a burden on them at a time when they themselves were suffering from severe food shortages.

On learning of this, Churchill wanted to have nothing to do with them and ordered they be returned to Russia. But by the time his orders were received these refugees had already been moved to the Persian Gulf ports in the empty motor transports of the supply convoys from where they were put on ships to India. When these refugees landed in India the British government would still have nothing to do with them.

Hearing of their plight and at the behest of the Maharajah of Jodhpur, the Maharajahs of Kolhapur, Jamnagar and Patiala took them and gave them refuge in their states. The Maharajah of Jodhpur wanted to put them in camps in Jodhpur but Marwar itself was in the grip of a famine. The descendants of these Polish refugees who are now spread all over the world acknowledge the humanitarian help of the people of India in their time of need and recently they organised a function in Delhi and publicly thanked India. Contemporary accounts of the refugees tell of the kindness with which they were received by Indian troops once they crossed over into Iran and their treatment in military hospitals run by Indians near Tehran.

The late Air Marshal Ardeshar, former Director of Air Force Medical Services, was at that time a Lt Col in the Indian Army Medical Corps in command of No 34 Commonwealth Army Field Hospital. In the early 1970s, I was posted in Poona and lived in rented accommodation in Koregaon Park close to General and Mrs Ardeshar whose daughter Meher was married to my friend and Regimental colleague Gus Deboo.

They lived nearby in Bund Gardens in a beautiful house overlooking the Mula River. Both my wife and I were frequent visitors to their house and it was Mrs. Ardesher who introduced Lakshmi to the delights of fermented juice of the fruit of the grape vine. Many long evenings were spent enjoying their hospitality, enlivened by the Air Marshal's war time stories of his time with the PAI Force in Persia.

As the Commanding Officer of the Commonwealth Army Field Hospital he had dual responsibility besides looking after the sick and wounded personnel from Commonwealth Armies he had to also look after the health of the thousands of Polish refugees who were housed in tents next to the hospital. These refugees mainly women, children and the old were in a pathetic condition. The lucky ones had come by boat across the Caspian or by train and road to the border.

But some had made a harrowing journey overland on foot from Siberia via Kazakhstan and other Central Asian Republics. They were sick, tired and emaciated. Dozens would die every day and they were buried in unmarked graves. The Indian medical doctors had to prioritise their treatment, the children were treated first, young women after that and if time and medicines permitted the very sick and aged were given attention.

An interesting story that he told me was about the German made Persian Army barracks which housed the Field Hospital. The barracks were newly constructed and modern but only a couple of weeks after occupation by the hospital the latrines started overflowing and no amount of acid and other chemicals could clear the choked drains. Long bamboo poles and iron rods were inserted into the drain pipes to clear the blockage to little avail. So when all else failed the supporting sanitary engineers were called and they dug out the pipes only to find the pipes choked with small stones leaving every one wondering as to what were stones doing inside the pipes. The mystery was solved by a British Warrant Officer, a veteran of the First World War who had served in Persia. He said that Iranians used pieces of stone to wipe themselves after defecation, toilet paper was unheard of and water was holy.

On arrival in India of the Polish refugees, the Maharajahs assumed personal responsibility for their care. At Jamnagar over five thousand Polish orphans were given shelter. The Maharajah would himself receive every freshly arrived batch and inform them, that now they were residents of Jamnagar and he was their Bapu (father). As such they should not consider themselves as orphans. In these camps the Maharajah started schools with Polish-speaking teachers, a church was built and life in the camp was organised to replicate life in a Polish village so that the children kept in touch with Polish culture and traditions.

On their first Christmas the Poles missed the snow and Christmas carols but were cheered when they heard the sound of a band playing the Polish National Anthem and saw a procession of three camels with the Maharajah in the lead carrying a sack full of gifts for the children reminding them of the story of the three Magi arriving with gifts for the new born Christ.

It is a moving experience to watch a documentary 'A little Poland in India' and see those one time pre-teen orphans now eighty-year-old grizzled veterans relate with tears in their eyes, the story of their time in India. Voices choking with emotion tell how the Maharajah and his family took them into their fold. Recently some of these onetime refugees visited India along with their families and met the Maharajah Digvijay Singh's daughter Princess Harshad Kumari and told her how much indebted to her father they are and for them India will always be their homeland.

At the time of departure all of them made long speeches thanking the Princess but she told them that in India brothers and sisters do not thank their siblings as it was their duty to look after them. As her father had adopted them seventy years ago they remain her brothers and sisters and she wished they would return home again. What surprised her, the most was that some of them could still converse in Hindi. Digvijay Singh was the adopted son and heir of the famous Ranji, the famous cricketer after whom the Ranji Trophy is named. Digvijay's younger brother was Duleep Sinhji after whom the Duleep Trophy is named. Here too Sir Pratap casts his long shadow, Ranjit Sinhji was his ward and it was Sir Pratap who sponsored his education and stay in England so that he could play cricket. It is only later that he came into jam when Sir Pratap manoeuvred to have him appointed as the Jam of Jamnagar! To honour Digvijay Singh the Poles have named a square in Warsaw as The Good Maharajah Square.

When the war ended in the middle of 1945, Chandan Singh was not quite twenty years old and he took the opportunity to explore the Middle East, Damascus, Baghdad, Cairo, Alexandria, Jerusalem, Babylon, Haifa, Acre, Amman, Nabataea and the Roman sites of Palmyra, Petra and Baalbek. With the very large numbers of Allied troops billeted or visiting the bigger towns there was a rip-roaring night life.

The bars and night clubs were open twenty-four hours and the memories of the war were drowned in whisky or the soft arms of the companion for the night. For the officers and men of the PAI Force not having been involved in any serious fighting after the first few weeks of the war had consequently suffered light casualties. Therefore there was not much for them to mourn, particularly when the good life was there to be enjoyed.

One of Chandan Singh's few regrets in life is that during his stay in Persia he did not visit the ancient city of Persepolis which was destroyed by Alexander and see the ruins of the Persian King's palace whose design was copied fifty years later by Ashoka when he built his palace at Kumrahar in Patliputra. The other place that he could not see was the Fire Temple at Baku which in Alexander's time was worshipped by both Zoroastrians and Hindus.

As soon as the war ended the Jodhpur Lancers were moved to Haifa in Palestine to keep the peace between the Arabs and the Jews who were migrating into Palestine from the war ravaged countries of Europe. Haifa was familiar to the Jodhpur Lancers for twenty-five years earlier as it was the site of their famous cavalry charge on September 23, 1918.

The orders of the Jodhpur Lancers were to patrol the sea coast around Haifa to prevent boats carrying Jewish refugees from Europe landing in Palestine. But having learnt the plight of the Jews the Jodhpur Lancers turned a blind eye and allowed the boats to land the refugees. Armed clashes between the two feuding factions were common and sometimes it involved the British and Indian troops. The Jews also indulged in acts of sabotage and terrorism.

The United Nations Ambassador to Palestine Prince Bernadotte, an uncle of the King of Sweden, was assassinated by a Jew. It was a thankless task but the work was not heavy and it gave the officers of the Lancers time to travel and see the world or at least as much as they could. They would also go driving to shoot in the Negev and Sinai deserts which abounded with gazelle much in the way they do western Rajasthan. For members of the victorious Allied Forces to travel to any part of the Middle East or any country in Europe no passports and visas were required to cross borders and a seat could always be managed in any Allied Air Force plane going to the desired destination. Accommodation and food was always available at the Allied Forces Camps in most places.

Dog River: UNESCO Inscriptions Monument World Heritage Site

Of all the places visited by Chandan Singh in the Middle East, with his keen feeling for history, none held more attraction for him with the exception of Haifa than the Inscriptions Monument Site at Dog River (Nahar al Kalb to the locals and Lycus to Romans). The reason for Chandan's interest in the inscriptions were many. But most of all it was because one inscription dated to just after the First War was about the feat of arms of the Indian Cavalry in which his father had served. Secondly an Australian sculpture was engraving another inscription dedicated to the Indian Army in the Second War in which he and the Jodhpur Lancers had participated much like his father two and a half decades earlier in the First War.

A memorial to Indian soldiers so far from home at such a historic site was a high honour indeed and he made detailed enquiries about all the inscriptions to which a fascinating story emerged, particularly its Indian connections.

The site being of such importance and yet no one in India knows anything about it so I have thought it fit to give a detailed account of the history and contents of the inscriptions. I myself became aware of them when I was visiting Lebanon in 1965. On an excursion outside Beirut, I stopped to look at the ruins of a very picturesque ancient Roman Bridge when I stumbled on the inscriptions. The ones in English I could understand, but the others I could not. So the next day I visited the offices of the Government Antiquities Department and met its director who told me the fascinating history of the site which I have included as an appendix at the end of this book.

One evening Chandan Singh was out pub crawling in Beirut which used to be called the Paris of the East before the civil war in Lebanon destroyed it. (I was lucky to spend a week in Beirut in the early 1960s as a member of the United

Nations and when one is barely out of one's teens it certainly was a place to be initiated to the good life.) Already having accounted for several bars and feeling on top of the world he entered another bar expecting to see the usual crowd of officers and bar girls but no sooner than his eyes got accustomed to the dim light he froze for sitting at the Bar was his master and patron the Maharajah of Jodhpur Umaid Singh and his younger brother, Maharaj Ajit Singh. Lt Chandan Singh wearing the uniform of the Jodhpur Lancers was spotted by Maharaj Ajit Singh who beckoned him to join them. They were both wearing Air Force uniforms as both held honorary ranks in the RIAF.

Chandan had no escape route and feared that he was in for a dressing down for being out so late at night. But he had no reason to fear for the Maharajah put him at ease immediately, asked him to sit next to him and inquired about him and the regiment. During the course of the evening the Maharajah told him that India was moving fast towards independence and the princely states would have to join the Indian Union so Chandan and other officers of the Jodhpur Lancers would have to make a choice about their future.

They would have to choose between transfer to the Indian Army or be demobilised and go home after the war. The Maharajah also offered a bounty of Rs. 10,000 to any one from Jodhpur willing to join the Air Force. Rs. 10,000 was a princely sum then equivalent to about Rs. 30 lakhs or more today. For Rs. 21,000 one could have purchased a bungalow in Lutyens' Delhi.

Chandan grasped at the opening that was offered by Maharajah Umaid Singh and requested the Maharajah that he would like to join the Royal Indian Air Force. The Maharajah who himself was a qualified pilot and held the honorary rank of Air Marshal was pleased to find another flying enthusiast and promised to help him. Soon enough, Chandan Singh received a call to appear for an Air Force Selection Board at Cairo. He also received a list of the subjects that he would be tested in and was therefore expected to study.

Among the group of officers appearing before the Selection Board was his friend Capt Akram who later chose to migrate to Pakistan and rose to become a General in the army. But the attractions of Cairo were too much of a temptation for a twenty-year-old leaving no time to study. He flunked the selection board. Fortunately for him and I would say for India too, Maharajah Umaid Singhji followed his progress or rather lack of it, arranged for him to appear for another selection board and this time for the Air Force in India at Dehra Dun.

But before returning to India, Chandan decided to take the opportunity to tour Europe. As an Allied Forces Officer travelling in uniform he could hitch a ride in any aircraft going to the destination of his choice and no passports, visas or other formalities while crossing national borders were required. Europe was a devastated land but many of the historic and beautiful buildings in Paris, Rome, Florence and London were undamaged but Germany was a ruin. In some towns not one building survived the ravages of war. The people were undernourished and the occupying forces who only a few months ago were trying to kill them were now occupied in feeding them.

The worst plight was of the Jewish survivors from the concentration camps. They were walking skeletons, but were still better off than the gypsy inmates of the concentration camps—not one survived. All that the Jews wanted was to get away and move to Palestine. He had met some Jews already who had managed to leave Europe earlier and settled in Palestine. In Palestine he had noticed that not many European troops were sympathetic to the plight of the Jews and he could sense under currents of anti-Semitism among the officers. On the other hand, Indian officers and men had cordial relations both with the refugees and the older Jewish residents.

The mood among the population in Europe fluctuated between the euphoric at the victorious outcome and total despondency at the trials and tribulations suffered during the war years. Even in England there was a shortage of food and other necessities but by and large the public was jubilant and they expressed their emotions openly. Hyde Park had turned into an open air love nest where returning soldiers and their girlfriends could be seen cosying up behind every bush and bench.

After his return to Palestine from Europe it was time for him to proceed to India to appear for the Air Force Selection Board. So in the latter half of 1946 he was on a Sunderland flying boat taking off from the Nile River at Cairo on the way to India. On the way they stopped at Jerusalem and stayed at the famous Shephard Hotel, from there to Lake Habbaniya North of Baghdad and then via the Shat Al Arab to Karachi. Here they transferred to a Dakota for the final leg of the journey to Jodhpur where the Dakota halted to refuel. At Jodhpur airport he was fortunate to meet his uncle Subedar Major Prem Singhji who took him home for lunch, the first home cooked meal after four years. Later in the afternoon they took off again and this time for Delhi Safdarjung airport and on landing proceeded to the Railway Station to board the night train to Dehra Dun.

After his failed attempt at Cairo, Chandan Singh ensured that he was not going to miss the second opportunity and so studied hard. The result was that he sailed through the selection board and went off first to Poona for a month and then for five months to Coimbatore for a course in ground subjects and thence to the RIAF Flying School at Jodhpur in January 1947 for flight training which was completed after a conversion course on Havards and Spitfires at Ambala.

As he was already an officer before joining the Air Force, he was commissioned as a Flying Officer with seniority from 1946 and as a bonus he received Rs. 19,000 as back pay. At the Flight School all the other trainees had been flight cadets but as the merger of states had not yet taken place he was still a captain in the Jodhpur Lancers and wearing their uniform, badges of rank and drawing a salary of a captain. This money he had received before joining the one month break after leaving Coimbatore and joining the Flight School at Jodhpur.

Earlier he had a serious difference of opinion with his

father. The father-son relationship was not at its best. So instead of spending the break at home he checked in to the Maidens Hotel Delhi with a pocket full of cash and added to that was his Clark Gable looks, a deadly combination which acted as a magnet for ladies both Indian and foreign. (The sobriquet Clark Gable was to stick to him during his tenure in the Air Force). When after a week or so, he got bored with Delhi he moved base to the Cecil's Hotel in Shimla leaving behind a bevy of heartbroken ladies in Delhi.

Not knowing any one in Shimla he went for a stroll on the Mall and having time on his hands when he noticed a pretty lady enter a door marked Music School, he followed her inside and decided to join the music school himself and bought himself a violin. The sudden interest in music was obviously not motivated or sustained because of any love for music but because the very pretty lady from the local well known Trehan family was also attending the music classes. It gave him the opportunity to spend time with her.

All his attempts to woo her got only as far as daily visits to the coffee house after the music lessons. Further progress became impossible when his leave ended and he had to proceed to the flight school first at Jodhpur and then at Coimbatore. At Coimbatore there was a camp housing Polish refugees of whom I have made a mention earlier. Chandan Singh befriended several of them including some pretty ladies. Deciding that flying was more important than pursuing an illusive muse, he hurled his violin at a tree trunk smashing it into smithereens, bringing to an end his dreams of evenings filled with music, wine and roses.

Romance always loses out to other emotions in men of action. In reality there is no such thing as a romantic hero however much women may want it to be otherwise. Novelists and poets sing praises to them. A real life hero has always other higher causes for pursuit.

Exceptional hand, eye and foot coordination had been honed and perfected during his horse riding days at Jodhpur before the departure of the Jodhpur Lancers to the Middle East.

His flying instructors soon found that like his horses before, he was able to control the aircraft as if it was an extension of his own limbs. From now onwards, Chandan and his aircraft were surely and firmly bonded into one indivisible homogeneous whole which nothing could asunder. Another chapter of his life started now with the heralding of independence, a pilot's wings and a row of medals on his chest.

4

Metamorphosis from Cavalier to Aviator

On returning home to Jodhpur, Chandan found that Jodhpur had become a major air base for the Allies and there were over half a dozen airfields which were being used regularly by the USAF, RAF and RIAF. In addition, the Maharajah had several private aircraft which he used, to tour the state often piloting the aircraft himself.

Besides Maharajah Umaid Singh, his son Yuvraj (crown prince) Hanuwant Singh too was a keen aviator. Maharajah Hanuwant Singh along with his friend Zubeida were unfortunately killed in an air crash a few years later. A highly dramatised version as is the way with Bollywood of their relationship was made into a film starring Karisma Kapoor and Manoj Vajpayee and released some years ago. Besides being a normal air base, Jodhpur because of its mainly clear weather for most of the year had also become a flying training school for the RIAF.

After his basic training at Jodhpur and advanced training at No. 1 Flight Training School at Coimbatore on Tiger Moth and Prentice trainers, Chandan was posted to a Spitfire Mk 14 Squadron at Ambala. These were exciting and heady days for everyone. There was the flush brought about by independence and the RIAF was fully involved in the Kashmir war where it played a stellar role in saving the valley from Pakistani raiders. But the Air Force did not let its preoccupation with the war to hinder its reorganisation and re-equipment plans.

The older Spitfire squadrons were given the latest models and some even the newer and better Tempests. New fighter, transport and bomber squadrons equipped with B-24s were raised and planning for the induction of jet fighters started and three De-Haviland Vampires the first of the batch of four hundred arrived to replace the old propeller driven fighters and for equipping the newly raised squadrons.

The IAF as it was now known after having dropped the Royal prefix was undergoing major expansion and re-equipment and was becoming one of the world's major air forces. Ambala was one of the main air bases for the protection of Delhi and also the Advanced Flying Training School was located here. The Spitfire was a proven aircraft and along with the Me 109 of the Luftwaffe, Mustang of the USAF and the Japanese Zero was considered to be the finest fighter aircraft to come out of the Second World War.

During the closing months of the war the Germans had introduced the jet powered Me 262 which could make circles around Allied aircraft. But it came too late into service to have any effect on the final outcome of the war. It was the Spitfire that had saved Britain during the Battle of Britain.

Chandan like every other fighter pilot was looking forward to conversion to the jets but fate was to deal him a different hand. One day in mid- November in 1949 he was returning to Base at Ambala in his Spitfire after a sortie near the border when his engine spluttered and failed. Fortunately he was at an altitude which allowed him to nurse his aircraft back to the airfield and after getting a clearance from control, lowered the under carriage and landed the Spitfire safely but from the opposite direction came another aircraft taxing on the runway at high speed preparatory to take off. Chandan had to pull hard to leave the runway and get on to the grass strip to avoid crashing into the approaching plane.

His speed was too high and his plane pitchforked and crashed. The plane was a write off and Chandan was severely injured, a crack in the spine and multiple other injuries including a fractured arm and broken ribs. The injuries were such that the doctors at Deolali and Poona where he was being treated for his injuries thought that not only his flying days but his future in the Air Force was finished. They even doubted whether he would ever be able to walk again. Chandan was only 24 years old, had come through the Second World War unscathed and in a moment all his dreams and aspirations had come to an end.

A lesser man would have accepted his fate but not Chandan. He was made of sterner stuff and miraculously recovered, went through painful physiotherapy sessions and in about a years' time was ready to fly again after a medical board declared him fit, but only for transports and bombers and not for the newly arrived jets. This was a big disappointment but these jets with their higher flying speeds would have subjected his spine to high G Forces which it may not have been able to withstand so soon after the accident.

He was sent to Agra for conversion training to transport aircraft. Later in his career he did get to fly high performance fighter- bombers. He still has a problem with acute pain in one foot and has to take regular treatment. After the completion of conversion training he was posted to a C47 Dakota Squadron and it is with transport aircraft that he performed miracles in the 1962, 1965 and 1971 wars. Strange indeed are the ways of fate that he as a transport pilot has had more combat experience than any fighter or bomber pilot in the Indian Air Force and his aircraft in 1962 and 1971 have been hit so many times by enemy fire that he has lost count.

By now he had completed the Flying Instructor's course in the UK and had become an instructor himself with a grading Master Green. For some time he was posted as an instructor at Jodhpur when one day he was flying a Havard trainer as a co-pilot to his flight commander when they hit a railway telegraph pole near Pali. The pilot was flying low to impress his fiancé who was travelling by train from Jodhpur to Bombay. Fortunately no one was seriously injured. During this time he had befriended Sqn Ldr David Boche the Squadron Commander of the jet engine Vampire Squadron who after a few dual sorties allowed Chandan to fly the Vampires solo.

In 1953 Chandan Singh along with a detachment of Dakotas from 43 sqn at Agra was temporarily based at

Bagdogra near Calcutta and in Jorhat Assam to support the Army. It was here while in supply dropping missions or landing at remote undeveloped air strips that Chandan learnt, evolved and perfected the technique of flying in the narrow but high Himalayan valleys which he was to put to great use later. In those days the border posts were manned by para-military troops and not the army but the IAF was responsible for their logistics support, Chandan Singh opened up for supply dropping the valleys leading to Zero, Machuka, Along, Keylong, Walong and other remote areas.

Also based at Jorhat was a detachment of Spitfire Fighters which was commanded by Flt Lt Bharat Singh an old friend who let him fly his Spitfires which Chandan loved to do because unlike the lumbering Transport planes he could perform aerobatics. His favourite place to do this was over the border town of Zero which always attracted a large crowd. On one such occasion his antics were witnessed by a lady who was the wife of an English ICS officer who was the Commissioner of Zero. As anyone who has served in the East knows that the Tea Planters Clubs are the centre of social life for not only the tea planters but also for the service officers posted nearby and other local gentry.

During the visit to Jorhat by Air Marshal Malse, the Air Officer Commanding-in-Chief Eastern Air Command, he was taken to the Planters Club where the Commissioner's wife was also present. She recounted the wonderful sight of a fighter pilot's aerobatics she had witnessed and how dexterous he was. Later Malse made his inquiries and Chandan Singh was hauled up for not only performing dangerous aerobatics but also flying a Spitfire which after his accident he was not authorised to do. But by now his reputation as a very skilful pilot and instructor was such that he got away without any admonishment. Malse felt that Chandan knew what he was doing and would always do the right thing.

Chandan had several brushes with law during his career which could have resulted in a court martial but his reputation as a thorough professional, one of the best the Air Force had always protected him. It was about this time that he appeared before the Air Examiner Board known as AEB from UK and was declared as Category A Examiner which meant that he was now qualified to test other instructors, even those senior in rank to him. During this time he flew several times with the Air Force courier to Nom Penh in support of the Army detachment located there and also to the United Kingdom on courier duty.

The Indian Air Force had a large number of leftover Dakotas from the Second World War which HAL and Air Force workshops reconditioned and made fit for service and these remained the mainstay of our transport fleet till the 1970s. Credit for maintenance of this and other old model aircraft whose production lines had closed has to be given to another maverick and ace, Air Vice Marshal Harjinder Singh who kept the Indian Air Forces planes flying even though spare parts were not available. He obtained the spares by cannibalising the war surplus aircraft left behind by the Allied forces after the war. An account of this feat appears in his biography, *Spitfire Singh* which has recently been released.

In 1948 when the Kashmir war was on and IAF Spitfires were carrying out offensive air support for the Army, Harjinder Singh even flew to Lahore in a Dakota and using his old connections, collected spares for IAF Spitfires from the Pakistan Air Force stores. However in 1954 the first batch of C-119s Fairchild Packets arrived and much of the heavier work was taken over by them. For operating from high altitude airfields in Ladakh extra jet engines were strapped onto its back which was a completely novel innovation which even its manufacturer the Lockheed Corporation had not visualised. But in a resource scarce country Jugaad comes to the rescue. The C-119s added greatly to the Air Forces lift capability which was needed to support our forward army posts.

By now Chandan had not only qualified on the C-119 and soon became a trainer for this type of aircraft and also started work on operating procedures for flying and dropping supplies in high and narrow Himalayan Valleys. With the

Chinese moving aggressively close to our borders new posts had to be established and with road communications being non-existent the only way to maintain our forward posts was by air.

National Defence Academy

From 1956 to 1958 Chandan Singh was posted to the National Defence Academy Kharakvasla near Poona. The Academy is one of the leading defence institutions of the world and was then and may still be the only academy where future officers of all three branches of the defence forces, i.e. the army, air force and navy are trained together. It was started at the behest of Lord Mountbatten when he was Viceroy. As a former Chief of Combined Operations he was responsible for planning for Operation Overlord that resulted in the Normandy landings on D Day in June 1944 during the Second World War.

He understood the importance of joint training, camaraderie and bonding between officers of the different services and this could only be brought about if in their formative years they had lived, trained and played together forming bonds of friendship and affection cutting across service boundaries. The best officers from the three services are posted here where their job is less of academic instruction which is performed by the civilian staff but more to inspire the cadets and gradually wean them to becoming service officers imbibed with the right leadership qualities.

To the cadets he taught Theory of Flight and trained them to fly gliders. To earn his flying bounty he used to go to Poona Air Base and fly whatever aircrafts that were available, including Canberra bombers which were based here.

From the letters received by me from his former cadets the readers can draw their own conclusions about what the Air Vice Marshal meant to the cadets and of the atmosphere in the Academy and the trepidation and fear in the minds of the teenage boys joining the academy for the first time. I would like to draw the reader's attention here to an earlier chapter of the book that covers the Second World War, when Chandan

Singh set out as an officer to join his regiment, the Jodhpur Lancers. He was exactly seventeen years old, the same age or even younger than boys joining college or the National Defence Academy today.

True leaders are those who make others into leaders, whose men in turn will willingly follow them to hell and back. Chandan Singh during his tenure at the National Defence Academy Kharakvasla was a man who made an entire generation of cadets who were really just teenage boys into not only men but also into leaders of men. These cadets of yore still worship him sixty years after both they and he left the Academy and I am going to tell this part of the story through them. I have also been to both NDA and IMA and had some great officers as my instructors and squadron/company commanders but I nor anyone I know, can think of anyone who was more inspiring and loved as Chandan Singh.

He was hero worshipped by all cadets who otherwise were a bunch of cynical and mischievous teenage rogues, always ready to put their officers in embarrassing situations. The cadets loved his flamboyance, his swashbuckling style, cowboy hats, colourful scarves and his two seater open MG sports car. The men of Jodhpur have always been fashion icons and trendsetters.

It is no accident that for nearly a century the Jodhpur breeches and jackets have been the standard wear for all equestrian events the world over and they combined with the Jodhpuri safa are the clothes of choice for bridegrooms all over India. Raghvendra Rathore has capitalised on his inheritance to become India's most well known designer for men's wear. It may surprise many to learn that the style of turban worn by Swami Vivekanand was inspired and adopted by him at the suggestion of Raja Devi Singh of Khetri, Rajasthan and he acknowledges this in his memoirs when he states that he met Sir Pratap of Jodhpur at Khetri and he and Devi Singh told him to wear the turban to protect his head from the burning sun in Rajaasthan.

I will now let his former cadets speak for themselves. These former cadets are now hard bitten former warriors in their late seventies who have seen several wars but turn sentimental to the point of tears when they speak of him.

Col D.S. Sandhanwalia, Kumaon Regiment

"Though difficult to believe ever since we graduated from NDA the earth has gone round the sun more than sixty times. When some of us are together memories go back to the wonderful days of our mid to late teens in the 1950s. Nothing in the world can match that feeling of ecstasy in remembering and recounting of those bygone days. We have played our innings and we believe played it well. For the future generations the trials and tribulations are many but they cannot afford to lose our core values while coping with them. Ultimately it is the NDA credo of "service before self" that will guarantee the safety and integrity of the nation.

I am very proud of my family's military heritage. My father served as an officer with 2/14 Punjab Regiment in the First World War in Egypt and Mesopotamia much as Chandan Singh's father Col Bahadur Singh had done. Both also received the OBI/OBE for gallantry. My father died in 1948 when I was ten years old. Before my father's time many of my other ancestors had served in Hodsons Horse. It was therefore natural for me to follow in their footsteps. So I felt very proud to have been selected for the National Defence Academy. Even before joining I acquired that superior air of joining the company of elites. This sentiment was further reinforced when I travelled to Kirkee Railway Station in a First Class Compartment with slabs of ice on the floor to keep me cool. There was no air conditioning in trains then. When I got down at the station, I discovered much to my dismay that there were more "elites" like me than coolies on the platform.

Any residual feeling of superiority and euphoria soon evaporated when we found ourselves with our steel trunks on our shoulders and jogging to the three ton trucks waiting to take us to the Academy. We learnt our first lesson quickly— ours was 'not to reason why' for the next three years. Subedar

Harnam Singh of the Guards who had come to receive us was shouting something which I did not understand. However seeing others crawling on the wet platform, I too joined in and this was followed by front rolls.

As we headed for the Academy huddled in the back of three tonners we tried to seek comfort in the company of each other to prepare ourselves for the impending calamity. All of us were feverishly hoping that the truck would never stop for by now we were certain of what awaited us on the Academy soil. Perhaps NDA wanted to disinfect us post-haste so that it could instil in us an attitudinal change befitting a future officer's mental makeup. Before we got out of the trucks, Sub Harnam Singh warned us that he wanted proper military style motions as he was not happy with our sloppy civilian style movement and motions.

Fortunately I adapted to NDA's demanding routine quickly. I was assigned to King Squadron which was soon to have the new commander Sqn Ldr Chandan Singh. Before joining NDA, I used to cycle ten miles every day to school with my sister sitting behind on the carrier. This prepared me well for the King Squadron cross country team. I found that my other course mates like Ajit Virdi, Ghuman and Paramjit Pammi more than matched my running skills and resoluteness. Sure enough we continued to wrest the Academy Cross Country running trophy as long as we were at the Academy. I won my half blue in my second term. We even won the cutter rowing trophy on Khadakwasla Lake. While Jigs Ratnaparkhi shouted 'In and Out, In and Out'. Just a few inches from the finish line we overheard the crew of the leading cutter say, "these bloody Surds from King Squadron again". I suppose an inch is an inch when things are hot.

By then I no longer had a problem with spoken English, thanks to Raja Menon (later Rear Admiral and TV commentator and husband of painter Anjoli Ela Menon). In our first term, Raja Menon would do the talking and I would listen, that did me a lot of good. In the third term, our Squadron Commander, Sqn Ldr Chandan Singh organised an essay writing competition which I won.

Sqn Ldr Chandan Singh, the ruler of our hearts and minds in King Sqn inspired and galvanised us in a manner that enabled us to win inter squadron competitions more often than I can remember. In fact there was a time when we never competed for the second position or below. He steered us through the rough and tumble of life at the Academy with consummate vision, adroitness and perseverance. That spirit imbibed by all of us in full measure was passed on to future generations.

The Duke of Wellington once said that the Battle of Waterloo was won on the playing fields of Eton. This applies equally to NDA as well. You had to see Chhotu Bhandari in the boxing ring to see the effect of Chandan Singh's motivation. The 'Atomic Kid' used to beat the daylights out of his opponent. Many years later, Jigs Ratnaparkhi commanding an MIG squadron at Tezpur took me to the blue yonder for a really great time. He fulfilled my ardent, long cherished dream to soar above the clouds and feel the effect of 8G. I must also confess that the protective wings of Chandan Singh gave me self-belief bordering on arrogance.

During the Golden Jubilee Celebrations of my course at NDA in December 1999 the atmosphere in the King Sqn ante room was so surcharged that as I got up to speak the nostalgia of the scene of Chandan Singh coming to take over the squadron in his open MG two seater sports car, dressed in a cowboy outfit simply overwhelmed me and after speaking for just twenty seconds I broke down. Four ladies whom I had never met before were also in tears as also my wife. That was my spontaneous and unplanned tribute to my Alma Mater NDA and my squadron Commander of yore, Squadron Leader Chandan Singh".

Col Paramjit Pammi

"I am from the 17th Course NDA King Squadron and was a first termer when Sqn Ldr Chandan Singh was our Squadron Commander and Flt Lt La Fontain later Air Chief was our

Divisional Officer. Chandu's very presence in the training area gave solace and courage to scared and lost boys like me who had landed up straight from the villages to a strange and seemingly cruel place. More than half a century later, I remember him with admiration and affection even though after leaving the Academy, I never met him again.

We were blessed to have the gallant Sqn Ldr Chandan Singh as our Squadron Commander. I have yet to know of a more inspiring leader of men than our Chandu. We worshipped the ground he walked on and even today when we ourselves are in our late seventies, we love and hold him in high esteem. Last year two of my course mates drove all the way from Delhi to Jodhpur to see the Air Marshal and I am happy to say that the old warrior is well and alive.

Bangladesh would not have been liberated as soon as it did had it not been for Chandan Singh's contribution to the war effort. With only fifteen helicopters he airlifted two infantry brigades with supporting artillery to Dacca which resulted in the surrender of the Pakistan Army. Even in 1962 he made the impossible possible by transporting AMX-13 tanks to Ladakh and stopping the Chinese advance. Here too he flew the first sortie.

Air Marshal Bharat Kumar

"Air Vice Marshal Chandan Singh was a Divisional Officer for a short while at the NDA and then took over King Squadron in 1956. Maitland and LaFontain were also posted as divisional officers. Two of them used to be ragged by the cadets and could not control the combined classes but with Chandan Singh it was an entirely different story. There used to be pin drop silence and everybody would be wide awake. He believed that cadets could be trained to have Officer Like Qualities (OLQ) and within a year there was not one cadet in King Squadron who was under warning for lacking OLQ.

In my book *Unknown and Unsung*, I have described his activities in the 1962 war, how he cleared the AN-12 aircraft for operations in Ladakh, his actual sortie on October 20, 1962 when his aircraft was fired upon and received nineteen hits. I have mentioned his stint in 43 Sqn and how he and Wing Commander Lazaro went about finding the safest routes through the narrow valleys and the standard operating procedures drawn up by Chandan Singh then are still operative today six decades later".

Air Marshal Nanda Cariappa

"What can I say about Chandan Singh? He has always been my role model".

On completion of his tenure at the NDA in 1958 he was posted back to 43 Squadron at Calcutta which had a detachment at Srinagar transport squadron where he completed the work on Standard Operating Procedures for supply dropping at each and every high altitude post located in the narrow valleys and was also appointed as the chief inspector and trainer for all transport aircraft. For his path breaking work he was awarded the Ati Vishisht Seva Medal. As a squadron leader he remains the junior most officer to have ever received this award which is normally reserved for Major Generals and above and equivalent ranks in the air force and navy.

The Station Commander in Srinagar was Group Captain Anant Narayanan who wanted Chandan to carry out a detailed reconnaissance of the whole of Kashmir particularly the Ladakh region. He flew into the Shyok and Nubra Valleys and chartered the routes for other aircraft to follow. He landed at Thoise, Haji Langar and Daulat Begoldi at the foot of Karakoram Pass and reported the existence of the road cutting through the Aksai Chin plateau which caused panic in Delhi and a police party was sent on foot to confirm the sighting. Once over Leh his aircraft had an engine failure but he managed to return to base and land it safely at Srinagar.

For his outstanding work not only was he awarded a AVSM but also given a very good report by Gp Capt Narayanan which resulted in his being earmarked to go to Russia. Feeling the necessity to have even bigger transport aircraft, negotiations were started with Russia to acquire AN-12s. Chandan Singh was selected to proceed to Russia along with several other pilots and airmen to train on AN-12s and bring them back to India. The AN-12 was not only bigger than the C119 and Dakotas but was capable of operating from high altitude air fields with full loads without the aid of an additional strapped on booster engine.

Chandan was then posted to 43 Squadron at then based in Kolkatta. At that time 43 Squadron maintained a detachment at Srinagar for the purpose of troop deployment and supplies north of Ladakh range in addition to landings at Chushul.

Mountain flying entails genuine hazardous operations where one had to understand limitations of the aircraft at high altitude descending to low altitude keeping in mind the physical features of the jagged edged mountainous features and valleys.

There were 11 DZs which could be supplied by aircraft only that were flying at low altitude as there were no parachutes available at that time and were pushed out by the air crews physically. Correct flying over the DZs had to be properly planned so that aircraft dropping could fly as low as possible to the DZ ensuring that there was least damage to the supply material.

It is for this purpose that a through and detailed study of SOP had to be laid down before screening the pilots of the detachment. Final approach and getaway approach was normally carried out by experts only. Chandan was not only detachment commander for 2 years but also screening and tranining all pilots without causing damage to the aircraft and survival of all flight crew members.

He laid down the SOPs for all 11 DZs in the territories of the Nubra and Siyok Valleys and are pretty much followed till this day even after over 60 years.

Russia

About fifty officers and men compromising both pilots and engineers proceeded to Moscow. Amongst the pilots besides Chandan Singh there was Wing Cmdr Gadiok, Sqn Ldr Tom

Anderson, Sqn Ldr Jaggu Shaw and Sqn Ldr Basu. After a short stay in Moscow for briefing and issue of cold weather clothing they were taken to an air base at Shishlanskya some distance away. Besides the conversion training they also had classes in Russian and in a month or so most had acquired a smattering of the language to be able to get around without an interpreter.

The four engine AN-12 despite its size and weight was a dream to fly and as most of the pilots were experienced with thousands of hours of flying time the changeover was smooth. However for some reason, Wing Commander Gadiok who was the senior amongst them and other pilots except for Chandan Singh were dissatisfied and wrote to Air HQ that the AN-12 was not suitable for the IAF and was only fit for courier service. The Indian Air Attaché in Moscow, Group Capt. Lodhi came to see things for himself and spoke to all the pilots and again all of whom except Chandan declared the aircraft unfit. On being questioned as to why he differed, Chandan declared that he was prepared to fly the aircraft and show Gp Capt Lodhi that the AN-12 met all our requirements plus some more and this Chandan promptly did.

Earlier he had put the AN-12 into manoeuvres which even his Russian instructors thought not possible. Chandan Singh while working on the standard operating procedure for supply dropping missions to army posts located in the high and narrow Himalayan valleys had mastered the art of putting the aircraft into a steep bank to turn around the aircraft at the same time gaining altitude. He had practised this with AN-12s too surprising his Russian instructors who because they had no need to do so in their own environment and therefore had not even thought about doing this manoeuvre. Lodhi reported this to Air Marshal Pinto who was very pleased with Chandan's response and on ascertaining from the Russians that Chandan was fully qualified had him along with his co-pilot Flt Lt Vashist recalled to India a month before the other pilots to start training a fresh batch of IAF pilots on the AN-12 in Chandigarh.

In the meantime, a signal arrived from the Russians that Chandan Singh had passed the conversion course and was appointed as instructor on AN-12. Such was his skill as a pilot and his standing with his superiors that even before the course had ended he had been graded not only qualified but also appointed as an instructor for which a separate course is required.

The Russians had told Air Marshal Pinto that Chandan had become so proficient that their own pilots could learn a thing or two from him. On arrival in Delhi, Air Marshal Pinto asked Chandan Singh whether he could land the AN-12 at Chushul which even the Russian instructor already in Delhi had said was not possible but Chandan offered to take Air Marshal Pinto along to prove the Russian wrong. Much against the Russian's advice, Chandan along with Vashist took the Air Marshal and the Russian not only to Chushul but also to Leh and to drive home the point further he did two additional landings and take offs all of which were perfect.

While in Russia nearly all the pilots and ground crew had became fluent in the language and also made friends and visited the homes of their hosts. They found the Russians to be good and simple people but noticed that there was definitely some class distinction amongst the majority European/Slavic Russians and the other ethnic groups. Though most Russians were poor and their food simple, they were very hospitable and drank vodka prodigiously. It was difficult to get away from them at the end of a party.

When the training was over and it was time to return the Indians gifted all their cold weather clothing which was of a better quality than the standard Russian issue to their Russian counterparts. These were received with gratitude.

On return to India with the AN-12s they were posted to No. 44 Squadron at Chandigarh and immediately got down to conversion training of new pilots, supply dropping and ferrying of troops to Ladakh and other forward army posts. This also gave him time and experience to give the finishing touches to the draft of the Standard Operating Procedure for high altitude supply dropping. This SOP is now used by all air forces of the world when operating in similar conditions.

When the rest of the pilots and ground crew returned from Russia along with additional AN-12s they started flying missions to Ladakh. The AN-12s were based in Chandigarh which had a runway only 900 metres long so they would first take off without loads and pick up the loads from Ambala or Pathankot and then return to Chandigarh after dropping loads wherever they were required. The station commander was Gp Capt Murat, another very fine officer who had implicit trust in Chandan Singh's ability as a go-getter and doer.

At Chandigarh Chandan Singh stayed in a separate bungalow normally allotted to married officers. He was over thirty years of age and wanting to get married. A deep and close friendship developed between him and a lady doctor who was single and worked at the Chandigarh Postgraduate Institute of Medical Science. They visited the gurudwara together every Sunday and all their friends thought that something would develop from this friendship.

She moved in with him and Chandan wished to make the relationship permanent. However for reasons of her own, she desired otherwise. The relationship ended when Chandan Singh was posted out of Chandigarh to proceed to the USA for training with the Central Intelligence Agency. His tenure at Chandigarh had been one of the most satisfying and fulfilling one so far in his life.

Professionally he was recognised as an ace pilot flying several long hours a day an aircraft he loved and had mastered. He made several friends and at a personal level his friendship with the lady doctor was a source of great happiness and satisfaction. But life is never static and moves on particularly for those whose professions demand total dedication even if it is at the expense of other commitments as is the case of people whose calling is the military or medicine.

The late 1950s and early 60s were demanding times for the Army and Air Force. The Chinese dragon was breathing fire, the Dalai Lama had crossed over to India to find refuge and solicit aid. In Tibet he was unable to bear the suffering of his people but the Government of India seemed somnolent. Some even suspected that the Defence Minister Krishna Menon a known communist sympathiser, was a Chinese agent. Nehru not only turned a blind eye to his shenanigans but actively supported him. With the Dalai Lama given refuge in India the Chinese decided to raise the ante and ambushed a party of CRPF at a place called Hot Springs, killing ten and taking the rest prisoner. The border in those days used to be manned by armed police detachments from the states or CRPF.

5
Indo-China War 1962

It is not my intention to write the full story of the China-India War of 1962 and I intend to confine myself only to the role of Chandan Singh during this war. Chandan Singh's contribution to the defence of Ladakh before and during the war is immense and if the Indian Army fared better here than in NEFA (Arunachal), credit to a large measure has to be Chandans. Even in NEFA and other sectors of the border Chandan Singh's indirect influence prevailed amongst the aircrew flying in support of the Army.

Even before the completion of his tenure at the National Defence Academy, he was posted to 43 Squadron. He was appointed Chief Inspector of Transport Aircraft which meant that he was the chief trainer and examiner of all transport pilots. At the same time he perfected the operating procedure for flying transport aircraft through narrow mountain valleys to drop supplies to army posts. The trick was to first fly high over the valley and then circle over it and gradually descending to lower altitudes all the while familiarising oneself with all the physical features around till one had descended low enough to accurately drop supplies. If when required several aircraft where to operate in the same valley at the same time as happened quite often because only three to four hours of operating time was available in the morning before fog made flying impossible.

Chandan devised operating procedures for this type of flying which are still followed and have become Standard Operating Procedures not only in the IAF but also in all the air forces of the world operating in similar conditions.

After his stint at the National Defence Academy, Chandan Singh was posted to 43 Squadron at Chandigarh as a flight commander. Chandan Singh opened up the valley routes for operations to Kargill, Leh, Thoise, Fukchey and Chushul airstrips and many other DZs and border posts, some of which like Sultan Chushku were so remote that even in summer they had to be supplied by air. For this initiative and development of operating procedures he was awarded the Ati Vishisht Seva Medal. This medal is usually awarded to officers of the rank of major generals and equivalent ranks of the other services and Chandan became the junior most and youngest officer to have ever received this medal. In those days even general officers only received this rarely and that too for having rendered exceptional service in war and peace.

Now however these awards are given as a matter of routine for keeping their political, bureaucratic and military superiors happy rather than for any real distinguished service as was the practice in the past. Besides the Vishisht Seva Medal, Ati Vishisht Seva Medal and Param Vishisht Seva Medal. A new series of Medals such as Yudh Seva Medal, Uttam Yudh Seva Medal and Param Yudh Seva Medals has been instituted. To old timers it is laughable to see brass hats who have not heard a shot fired in anger strutting around with a chest full of medals. They have begun to look like comic book Ruritanian characters with the left side of their uniform shirts weighed down with medals and sagging to below their waistline. I am reminded of a remark by a young officer to another during the visit of a portly Vice Chief of the Army Staff to his unit which I overheard: "Damn! It is not his paunch, it is his breasts that his belt has to support."

Earlier the Russians were asked to fly the AN-12s to Chushul and Leh, to assess the suitability of these airfields. The Russian pilots did a few approach runs at Leh and Chushul but refused to land stating that it was too dangerous. On return the Russians declared both airfields unsuitable for AN-12s. Sqn Ldr Chandan Singh was then asked by Air Marshal Pinto whether he would undertake the mission. Without hesitation he agreed and along with Vashist took off from Palam and flew and landed at Chushul and Leh.

Both sorties were with perfect landings and take offs. This amazed both the Russian test pilots and the IAF brass. Thereafter the training of more pilots for AN-12s started at Chandigarh at a frenetic pace and Chandan Singh certified all the new captains and co-pilots on the AN-12s.

During this period an interesting incident occurred. A newly acquired MI-4 helicopter was to be flown to Chushul to test it. Chandan Singh had flown to Chushul in a C-119 Packet earlier that day with an American civilian. On learning of the presence of the MI-4 Chandan decided to stay and see the MI-4 for himself. The American flying with Chandan Singh was a Lokheed Martin technician who was helping the IAF to install mounts to attach turbo jet engines on top of the fuselage of the C-119s. The extra thrust from this engine helped the aircraft to operate with full loads from high altitude airfields in Ladakh.

By the time the MI-4 did a few take offs and landings several hours had elapsed and when Chandan decided to return he found that the batteries of his Dakota were dead due to the cold and try as they could to hand rotate the propellers they would not move. So they had to spend the night in sub-zero temperature at Chushul. Wing Commander Lazaro, the 43 Squadron Commander, was worried about the safety of his aircraft as the Chinese were not too far from Chushul. He ordered his Chief Maintenance Officer Sqn Ldr, Sandanwalia and some mechanics to proceed to Chushul to get the C-119 back into operation.

On arrival when the Maintenance Chief tried to revive the engines he too failed. To examine the engines and see what was wrong he had the cowlings opened and saw that the lubricating mixture had frozen solid in the cold and it looked more like axle grease than lubricating oil. It took them another day to think of a solution and eventually an Army Engineer Officer Major Trilok Singh came to their rescue. He produced some oil burning stoves called bukharis (heaters) which were lit and placed under the engine cowlings and this did the trick. They managed to raise the cylinder head temperature to 130 degrees first of one engine and then of the other while Chandan Singh kept sitting in the cockpit apparently oblivious of fire hazards.

After about four hours the lubricating oil became fluid again and with assistance the engines were restarted. Chandan Singh along with the maintenance team and the American civilian who was probably a CIA man were airborne again and returned to Chandigarh.

Air Commodore J. Thomas who was then a young Pilot Officer and flying in the same area as Chandan has written that on 19th October during a sortie he received word that Chandan's AN-12 had been fired upon by the Chinese and had received nineteen hits and all aircraft were ordered to return to base. Air Marshal Pinto AOC in C Western Air Command accompanied by Air Vice Marshal Mulgaokar came and inspected the aircraft and recorded the nineteen hits. The balloon was finally up. When the AOC in C returned to his Headquarters, Chandan too went home for some much needed rest and for the rest of the story of some of his finest hours I can do no better than to relate the story in his own words.

"Passage of time by more than half a century has dimmed the memories of this octogenarian cavalryman, soldier and pilot. Names and events have become hazy, thought process waning, however one event comes back crystal clear is the airlift of AMX-13 tanks to Chushul.

A number of writers and historians have written about the events of 1962 with varying interpretations. My story is about the very brave troops of the Indian Army positioned in Ladakh and the air crew of the transport aircraft of the Indian Air Force who maintained them. The Division equipped with outdated First World War and Second World War vintage weapons faced an army five times in number with state-of-the-art weaponry and excellent lines of communications. Our troops on the border were entirely dependent for maintenance on air supply and mules or human porters.

In Ladakh the border posts were manned by contingents of the Police and Paramilitary forces. It is no wonder then that the entire border was overwhelmed in a period of eight days. Many of the posts were wiped out to the last man. Some of these policemen belonging to the Rajasthan Armed Police were from my home district and I know their families.

It was during this period that I had a show down with Krishna Menon, the Defence Minister. He had come to Srinagar on a visit and was scheduled to return to Delhi. Being qualified to fly VIPs, I was detailed to fly him. However the weather packed up and the Station Commander informed Menon who was staying in a hotel that due to the weather it was unlikely that any aircraft would be able to operate from Srinagar that day. But Menon was insistent on flying immediately and came to the airport. Here the station commander and the OC Flying tried to explain the situation to him but to no avail and in their helpless state turned to me.

Turning to Menon, I told him that irrespective of rank and appointment, I as the captain of the aircraft had the final authority and under no circumstances would I put the aircraft and the life of the crew in danger as my first duty was to them. I also told him that he could see for himself that the weather was so bad that not a bird was in the air. Finding me not obliging, Menon glowered at me and the station commander and stomped out and returned to his hotel without saying another word.

The following day I flew him back to Delhi but not wanting to have another face off, I did not meet and greet him at the foot of the boarding ladder when he boarded the aircraft and when he disembarked at Delhi as is customary for captains of aircraft when flying a VIP to do. In Delhi Menon complained about me to the Air Chief. An explanation was called for but fortunately my higher commanders supported me and the matter ended there.

Chushul airfield in South Ladakh now became an objective for the Chinese Army. Chushul was defended by 114 Brigade commanded by Brig T.N. Raina MVC (later General)

One of the approaches to Chushul was through the Rezang La Pass which was defended by a company of 13 Kumaon commanded by Major Shaitan Singh PVC (posthumous). Major Shaitan Singh and I were both from Marwar and were of the same age. Like me, he had been commissioned in the Jodhpur State Forces at the same time as myself. We therefore knew each other well and as my duties involved supply drops and ferrying of troops to the forward area, I was in close touch with most of the Army units and Shaitan and I saw each other quite often.

At the forward air bases, messing arrangements were quite inadequate, Shaitan who was fond of cooking thoughtfully would have a fiery mutton curry which he cooked himself in our native Marwari style ready for me if he knew I was scheduled to land and he was around. When flying in the troops I and the other pilots including Thomas and Vashist observed how unprepared the Army was. The newly inducted troops did not have proper winter clothing, were shod in canvas shoes and did not even have proper tents to house them. What they had were canvas tents used by the army in the plains. The tents were not windproof and those living inside them would literally freeze at night. Is it a wonder then that there were more casualties from frost bite and high altitude sickness than from enemy bullets?

Another Jodhpur State Forces Officer in the area was Lt Col Revat Singh CO of 13 Dogra. This battalion was deployed along the road from Leh to Chushul to protect the bridges. Revat Singh was several years older than myself and had served with the Jodhpur State Forces when my father was the CO of the Jodhpur Lancers.

My relationship with Shaitan Singh went back to the time of our fathers. His father, Lt Col Hem Singh Bhati OBI and my father had served together in the Jodhpur Lancers during the First World War and were both present in the trenches in France and later at the Battle of Haifa. My father had lost an eye at Haifa and Hem Singh had received the Order of British India for gallantry.

The lack of proper equipment, particularly cold weather clothing and modern weapons did not speak highly of the government's commitment to defend this remote area of India.

One day while flying a supply sortie to Leh, I received a message from Shaitan Singh that he was sick and admitted in the Military Hospital at Leh and that he wanted to see me urgently. The hospital was located close to the airfield so I walked down to meet him, and found Maj Shaitan Singh in bed looking very weak and dejected. He told me that for the last fortnight he had been suffering from dysentery which the doctors had not been able to control. (Dysentery is a common ailment in the mountains where most of the water sources are contaminated due to open defecation practised by the locals. At this time no facilities for filtration or chlorination of drinking water was available at outposts). A few days before Maj Gen Grewal, the newly appointed Commander of the third division had visited the Field Hospital, the GOC remarked that while his troops were battling the Chinese, he Shaitan Singh was lying in bed, implying that he, i.e., Shaitan Singh was evading combat. Gen Grewal was a fine commander but was under tremendous pressure as he was handicapped due to shortage of troops and material. He was trying to marshal all his resources at Chushul to face the imminent Chinese attack and had made the remark without knowing Shaitan Singh's character.

Major Shaitan Singh, a proud Rajput could not stomach this seeming aspersion on his courage and told the GOC that even if he had to be carried on a stretcher he would join his men. The GOC instead felt offended at the reply and left in a huff without saying anything else and neither gave instructions nor made any arrangements for him to return to his unit.

Gen Grewal who had done the best that anyone could have done under the circumstances and his division had put up a good fight when they were attacked by the Chinese. Gen Grewal was tragically killed in a helicopter accident in 1964 when flying to Srinagar from Leh. Maj Shaitan Singh invoking Rajput honour, friendship and clan fidelity pleaded with me to somehow get him to his company, even though he was very weak and not in a condition for any duty, leave alone combat or even to undertake the two weeks long foot trek over high mountain passes to reach his post. I had no option but to respect his feelings, and against the advice of the Officer Commanding of the Hospital, I promised to fly him to his company post at Rezang La in a helicopter the next day.

So the next day I flew him in a MI-4 helicopter to Rezang La. From the air I could see the build up of the Chinese Forces and anticipated that the attack would come any day soon.

The attack came the very next day and by the evening, Maj Shaitan Singh and all his men were dead having expended their last ammunition but not their honour and not before they had made the Chinese pay a heavy price. Of the 120 men with Shaitan Singh, 114 were killed, the remaining six were wounded and taken prisoner and it says something about their grit and determination that although all six were wounded, they all managed to escape a few days later and rejoined the brigade at Chushul.

In dying the men of 13 Kumaon extracted a heavy price from the enemy, according to the official Chinese account of the battle the Chinese suffered several hundred casualties which slowed down their further operations. This gave respite to the beleaguered brigade and an opportunity for tanks to be flown to reinforce them to face further attacks by the Chinese Army. The bodies of the dead including that of Shaitan Singh were recovered by Col Revat Singh Commanding Officer of 13 Dogras. The next year in April the snow started thawing.

His body and the bodies of a hundred and twenty of his men who had died fighting the enemy to the last man and last bullet were buried under several feet of snow frozen stiff in the position that they had breathed their last. Col Revat Singh too was a common friend from our days together in the Jodhpur State Forces. It was perhaps a coincidence or providence that found Shaitan Singh, Revat Singh and myself all veterans of the Jodhpur State Forces from the Second World War again fighting together almost twenty years later. However this time the enemy was the Chinese and not the Axis Powers.

Col Revat Singh and I were again to find ourselves together during the 1971 Bangladesh Liberation War. While I as Station Commander Jorhat was the senior IAF Officer operating with IV Corps, Col Revat Singh was operating in the Chittagong Hill tracts with a force of Tibetans fighting alongside with us. The Tibetans were a part of an organisation called Est 22 which was the Army counterpart of ARC. Both functioned directly under the Cabinet Secretariat. Revat Singh's Tibetans did a magnificent job in 1971 liberating most of the Chittagong Hill Tracts from the Pakistan Army.

At the time of independence the State Forces were merged into the Indian Army. There was a certain unfair bias against them for it was felt that they were not adequately trained or qualified. Many were discharged from service and others had to put up with the loss of several years of seniority and rank when they transferred to the Indian Army. This was grossly unfair for when called upon to perform it was these State Forces officers and units which delivered the results whether it was in Kashmir in 1948, the Goa operations in 1961, 1962, 1965 and the 1971 wars.

For this action Maj Shaitan Singh was posthumously awarded the Param Vir Chakra. The man responsible for the sorry state of the Indian Army and countless deaths, loss of national honour and land, the Defence Minister Krishna Menon has been rewarded with a statue installed in front of Army Headquarters at the behest of our political masters as symbol of their superiority and subservience of the military leadership. A road leading to South Block has also been named after him.

Till date no memorial or even a plaque acknowledging the heroism of these troops has been installed in Delhi. Their heroism was no less than that of the Spartans under Leonidas at Thermopylae (given a choice I would like Menon's statue to be melted and the metal used to make sanitary fittings in public toilets. Mahatma Gandhi would I am sure approve of this and whoever was responsible for initiating and giving permission for installing the statue must also join him in the hall of shame. The present Iranian government has had public toilets built over the memorial and grave of Reza Shah, the late Shah of Iran's father)

In a matter of eight days all our frontier posts from Haji Langar in the North of Ladakh to Walong in Eastern India were overrun by the Chinese and the plains of Assam lay open to attack, In Ladakh Chushul air field located at 15,000 feet now became their objective. Raina's Brigade defending Chushul depended mainly on air supply. With a number of enemy medium machine guns located on the north and north west of the airfield each sortie to Chushul was fraught with danger. Every day sorties were returning with dents or holes on the fuselage caused by small arms and machine gun fire. Circuit flight patterns were being altered on a daily basis. Intelligence reports indicated imminent attack".

A Cabinet meeting was called by Pandit Nehru who was visibly shaken and almost panic-stricken at the reverses suffered by the Army in the Eastern Sector due to which his favourite general, a fellow Kashmiri Pandit and kinsman Lt Gen B.M. Kaul had to be removed from command. In fact he had feigned illness and had left his headquarters at Tezpur feigning illness and flown to Delhi where he was admitted to the Military Hospital leaving the IV Corps headless. In any other army or country he would have been tried by a court martial and sentenced to death by a firing squad for cowardice in the face of the enemy.

Lt Gen Kaul had been appointed to command IV Corps by Nehru and Menon and tasked to throw the Chinese Army out. The Chinese army was the world's most battle hardened Army and appointing Kaul, a supply corps officer, to command the Corps to evict the Chinese was considered by many as the most astonishing thing since Caligula's appointment of his horse as Consul. In fact if one were to go through the list of those in key positions at the time it reads like the roll of the whole of Caligula's cavalry regiment.

One had Moraji Desai, the urine drinker as the Finance

Minister, Menon, a thorough scoundrel, as Defence Minister and Gen Thapar, an incompetent and spineless man, as the Army Chief. Not wanting another fellow Kashmiri kinsman Pandit Brig T.N. Raina to suffer the same fate as Kaul, Nehru pleaded with Army Headquarters to do something. Army Headquarters always willing to oblige the Prime Minister and without examining whether it was feasible or not but probably inspired by a similar action taken by Gen Thimayya at Zozila during the Kashmir War came to the conclusion that tanks could probably be used to stop the Chinese Army in Ladakh and NEFA.

On the orders of the COAS, Gen P.N. Thapar whose family was related by marriage to Nayantara Sehgal, the daughter of Nehru's favourite sister Vijaylaksmi Pandit, it was decided to airlift tanks to Chushul even though the AMX tanks were beyond the carrying capacity of AN-12s.

There was great hesitancy on the part of Air Headquarters to undertake this mission because they did not think it was possible to do so. They conveyed their opinion to the Prime Minister. Here it would not be out of place to mention that Gen Thapar's father had supported the Jallianwala Bagh massacre and as the head of the Golden Temple Managing Committee had presented a Siropa to Brig Dyer for his resolute action. This single treacherous act caused a rift between the Hindus and the Sikhs which has not fully healed to date and is being exploited by powers inimical to our interests.

Indira Gandhi and the Indian nation have and continue to pay the price. As for Gen Kaul he was so close to Nehru that according to Lt Gen S.K. Sinha, the much respected former Vice Army Chief, Gen Kaul used to address Nehru as Jawahar Bhai. Gen Sinha said this while addressin a seminar organised by the Centre for Land Warfare Studies some years ago.

But such was the pressure on the Army that promptly six AMX-13 tanks of 20 Lancers arrived overnight at the Chandigarh Air Force Base, the operating base of 44 Squadron (AN-12 aircraft) and a hurried attempt was made to load one tank on to an aircraft with the expected disastrous result. Brig

Raina bypassing his immediate superior, General Grewal GOC 3 Div, Raina had been sending frenetic messages to Army Headquarters creating a panic like situation. So Army Headquarters had asked AMX-13 tanks to move to Chandigarh from Ambala even before getting a clearance from Air Headquarters.

Raina was later awarded the Mahavir Chakra for the defence of Chushul but many present during the battle questioned the propriety of the award. They felt that as the Brigade Commander at best it should have been a Vishisht Seva Medal for leadership. The Maha Vir Chakra is next only to the PVC for acts of personal gallantry beyond the call of duty in the face of the enemy. At no time did Raina personally ever come under fire or face to face with a Chinese soldier. Even Chushul Airfield where the Brigade Headquarters was located never came under effective enemy shelling.

Shaitan Singh and his company were however so located that not only did they come under intense shelling and ground attack from the enemy but were beyond the range of supporting fire of our own artillery guns which were pre- First World War 3.7 Mountain Howitzers with a range of only about five thousand yards. Gen Jacob in his book *Surrender at Dacca* has scathingly criticised Raina's competence and leadership. The official history of the Pakistan Army describing the events of the 1971 War states that the actions of II Corps which Raina commanded were at best pedestrian.

Even Raina's elevation to the Army Chief's post reeks of nepotism. It was manipulated by bypassing Gen P.S. Bhagat VC, the most competent and charismatic general India has ever had with the exception of Gen Thimayya, Gen Hanut Singh and Gen Sagat Singh. Gen Thapar himself would never have become the Chief if Gen Rajendra Singh's tenure as Chief had not been cut short by one year to accommodate Gen Shrinagesh which further resulted in making Gen Thorat ineligible to take over as Chief after Gen Thimayya relinquished command.

Gen Thorat was another respected and competent general who as Eastern Army Commander had been continually warning the government of the danger posed by the Chinese. In Delhi there were several Kashmiri kinsmen and friends of the Nehru family in positions of authority and influence. This clique continued to wield power till the time of Indira Gandhi and Rajiv Gandhi.

Nepotism did not start with the Lalus and Mulayams. It was started by Nehru and his father. If we have to have hereditary heads of government we would have been better off with the maharajahs. They at least had class and a sense of belonging to the land of their birth. The tragedy is we learn nothing from history and the mistakes committed in the past. The present sorry state of affairs leading to litigation in civil courts by senior ranks of the Army has been the result of similar planning during Manmohan Singh's tenure to position favourites in favoured appointments so that when the time comes the favoured ones can take over the top posts.

The elevation of Gen Rawat to the post of COAS over the heads of two officers who were slightly senior to him was a much needed correction of the wilful misdeeds and mistakes of the past and thank God for it. Facing a two-front war and internal insurgency, India needs the most competent person at the top. Gen Rawat has fully lived up to the expectations and trust reposed in him. After a long time the Army has a Chief who is not afraid to speak his mind to the public and the ruling class.

AVM Chandan Singh continues: "Having flown three sorties the previous day and having nineteen machine gun bullet holes in the fuselage of my aircraft while flying over Chip Chap to drop supplies, I was unaware of the developments, and was off duty that morning and fast asleep at my Sector 16 Chandigarh home when I was woken up by a telephone call. Group Captain Murat Singh, the Station Commander, asked me to come immediately to the airfield 6 kilometres away.

On the way I picked up Sandy Sandhanwalia (later Air Marshal), our Chief Technical Officer. A kilometre short of the airfield, we came across a strange and unfamiliar sight. There was this weird and odd looking object next to the control tower, and of almost the same height. As we drove in Sandy exclaimed, "by God it is an AN-12, but why on earth is the nose facing the sky?"

"I drove to the spot and to our dismay we noticed that while loading a AMX tank, the ramp had collapsed, the tank was stuck at the threshold and the fuselage of the aircraft was at the vertical. The Commanding Officer of 20 Lancers along with three of his officers all very smart, eager and determined and the officiating Commander of 44 Squadron who had supervised the loading met me on the tarmac. Hopelessness and disbelief were writ large on his face. The CO of 20 Lancers, Lt Col Gurcharan Singh, popularly known as Butch, spoke to me that we must not fail or words to this effect. Bestowed with anticipatory IQ, Sandy's positive and pragmatic mind was already in motion, working out causes and solutions to overcome the problem."

"I realised that this dismal sight must be the reason for my urgent summons and this was to be the mission for the squadron. While taking stock of the situation, I observed affirmative optimism on Sandy's expressive face prior to being marched into the Station Commander's office."

"Apparently the Station Commander had been awake the whole night and in contact with the Chief of the Air Staff and the Air Officer Commanding in Chief Western Air Command, trying to organise the loading and airlift of the tanks. Now after admonishing me for having been asleep, he gave me the gist of events and reactions, the Officer Commanding the Squadron Wing, Commander Ghaoliok was now in hospital after having been hurt in the mishap.

I was received by the OC Flying, Officiating OC of the squadron and the Russian representative. The last dignitary gave an emphatic "Nyet" to the airlift based on two factors, one the tank weighed eleven tons more than the permissible weight the AN-12 could carry and the non-alignment of the centre of gravity would create an uncontrollable wobble. The other three also gave thumbs down on the same plus two other factors. The general consensus was that this was an impossible task. The Air Officer Commanding in Chief, A.M. Pinto was on the line and wanted to speak to me and asked, "Is it possible or not possible?" to which I replied, "Sir we can try and we should try."

He spoke of the importance of the operation and asked whether I would undertake the mission. Fortunately Sandy and I had already discussed the problem and ways to solve it. So I was able to answer in the affirmative and volunteered to take the first flight. The AOC in C was extremely pleased that after being told by everyone that the task was impossible my reaction was positive. He asked me to get on with it and told me that time was of great essence." (Another celebrated and senior Air Force officer who was Chandan's contemporary, once said that for Chandan every challenge was an opportunity which he converted into a success.)

"Back on the tarmac near the horrible apparition, Sandy, the officers of 20 Lancers and I got into a huddle. In fact while I was with the Station Commander, these four had more or less worked out the framework and were waiting for my considered consent. Instead of a single point jack under the threshold member there would be two additional semi-arc-shaped jacks and the floor bed to be covered with wooden sheets to distribute the weight.

Ramps were to be reinforced with jacks and spreaders, both winches would be utilised, etc. My main concern was centre of gravity alignment. Sandy, myself and the Lancers' team, after due deliberation and calculations, found a simple solution, that with the gun facing backwards, the tank's centre of gravity would coincide with that of the aircraft. This was possible because unlike other tanks which have the gun turret mounted at the centre of the hull in the AMX the gun turret is mounted well to the rear and by turning the gun backwards the tank's centre of gravity would shift in the same direction."

"Col Gurbachan Singh (not to be mistaken for Lt Col Gurcharan Singh CO of 20 Lancers) was the Chief Engineer at Ambala had been called urgently and asked to join the team. He was given the task to manufacture/produce jacks, spreaders, mooring points, stopper blocks, etc. for six aircraft. Our team of 44 Squadron and 20 Lancers worked with the Engineers from Ambala and by 1600 hours that very day five AMX tanks had been winched on to the spreaders and firmly and safely secured, fine-tuned to perfection. One by one we inspected each aircraft critically ensuring safety and security against all contingencies."

"Offloading at Chushul was to be managed with all turbo prop engines running, kicking up clouds of dust. Capt Chiky Dewan, the commander of the 20 Lancers Contingent, was everywhere. His drive, keenness and enthusiasm were exemplary and contagious. He trained each member of all the tank crew in execution of safe and efficient offloading procedures devised by himself and conducted a number of dry runs so as to accomplish the task in 10 minutes flat."

"By 1700 hours, I was satisfied and ready to brief the assembled aircrew and the ground staff. This extraordinary, first time ever attempt, against the advice of the Russians themselves and our own experienced experts had to be handled with utmost diligence and caution. Fortunately, the crew members, i.e. the pilots, navigators, signallers and gunners were all experienced and professionally highly competent.

Having been the Air Force Examiner on Transport Aircraft for the preceding four years, it had been my honour and privilege to test each one of them for grading. Zeal and enthusiasm generated by the 20 Lancers crew had percolated into their psyche as well."

"In my briefing all aspects including emergencies and likely contingencies arising out of G effect, inertia, wobble and other abnormalities at various stages of take off, climb, cruise, final approach, and touchdown were covered. Equally important offloading and quick turn round under persistent enemy threat from Rezang La and Mugger Hill ridges were discussed threadbare in all details, ensuring no glitches or goblins of any hue and colour.

We had observed from the previous days' sorties to Chushul that shelling was getting closer and closer to the runway, albeit not yet posing any worrisome threat. In a separate briefing to the flying crew, I laid stress on direct final approach, thus avoiding presenting an easy target for enemy machine guns at Rezang La and Mugger Hill. Direct approach was feasible by delicate manipulation of controls, high degree of airmanship while aiming to touch down within the first fifty metres of the runway as gently as possible and use the full length of the runway (1,800 metres only) with least ham handedness whilst applying reverse thrust."

"Chushul airfield is situated in a bowl-shaped valley at 14,000 feet, is 1,800 metres long and covered with interlocking steel plates. Bitumen patch up was carried out on a daily basis by Army Engineers. One bad landing could disintegrate a part or even a large portion of the air strip. We were ready, confident and I had total confidence in all the Captains of our aircraft for I knew them well and had certified them. Our plan was simple and obvious in that, the first aircraft (myself) was to land at the break of dawn, transmit only if experiencing any abnormalities, turn round period of fifteen minutes each, for all the four aircraft."

"As per plan we took off at an hour before dawn, with others to follow at varying intervals of time only after I had given the all clear after landing and offloading the first tank at Chushul. After reaching the cruise level, on reflection, I concluded that after all the hullaballoo, this for me was a routine everyday sortie. I recalled my first sortie to Chushul almost nineteen months to the day back to prove the capability of this wonderfully versatile aircraft against the advice of Russian advisors and also some of our own sceptics, with the present AOC in C Air Marshal Pinto on board. And now the curtain was to be raised over Chushul and its final defence.

This time, however I had been bestowed the honour of having a genuine VIP on board a tank and its crew including the force commander Capt Chiky Dewan himself. Four of the remaining aircraft commanded by the best Captains and air crew, followed, offloading their precious cargo of an AMX tank at regular intervals. We had taken off from Chandigarh in darkness at about 4.30 am and by 7.30 the last of the five tanks had been offloaded at Chushul."

"To conclude, for us the operation was over and for the tank crew it was now to commence. They had to emerge out of the pressurised cabin on to a high altitude (14,600 feet) airfield and that too without any acclimatisation, get into heavy duty performance, i.e., offload tanks under thick dusty conditions generated by four huge turbo prop engines.

They had to undo the mooring rings, untie safety chains, remove stopper blocks before and after, haul out the heavy weight jacks, place them under the threshold frame, place the supporting jacks under the ramps, cover the ramps with wooden spreaders, crank out the AMX tank manually and put back everything, leaving no debris behind, mount the tanks and finally drive out within time into the Spangur Gap. Seated safely in my pressurised cabin, I witnessed this marvellous display of human activity by the new generation of men from my old regiment."

"I remained hovering in the air at a safe altitude for around eighty minutes and observed the offloading of the remaining tanks with a copy book display of precision. For the Captains and the Air Crew of 44 Squadron including myself this was a job well done. It was over... thank God it was over, Halleluiah. My final sighting of these gutsy, intrepid and courageous cavaliers was their tank formation moving well past the perimeter, clear off the mine field, heading straight towards the enemy canon and build up. David was about to challenge Goliath."

"For me this was personally both a very proud and poignant moment. Twenty Lancers was a successor regiment of the Jodhpur Lancers in which my father the late Lt Col Bahadur Singh OBI had served in the First World War and later commanded. I too was commissioned into the Jodhpur Lancers and served with them in the Second World War, I transferred to the Royal Indian Air Force after the war, how this came about has been told in an earlier chapter."

"Initial success of the operation was palpably evident to us at Chandigarh when forty hours later we were informed that normal circuit flights over Chushul could now be resumed. However another message received later placed the airfield out of bounds on grounds of political/military strategic considerations .It remained closed for decades afterwards. Two days later the Chinese declared a cease fire and withdrawal to the Line of Actual Control."

For his actions in the 1962 war he was awarded the VrC (Vir Chakra), his second award for gallantry and distinguished service.

It is fortunate that the Chinese did not have air bases in Tibet or Sinkiang at the time. So could not use their fighter air craft against our transports, whereas all our own areas could be covered by our own fighter bombers and Canberra Bombers. Why we did not use our Air Force in an offensive role is a question that has never been answered. If our unarmed transport could operate in this theatre as the Chinese had nothing to counter them, I see no reason why our combat aircraft did not do so.

In this barren treeless terrain where there is no cover to hide they would have extracted a heavy cost and perhaps even driven the Chinese out of Aksai Chin. Perhaps it had had to do with the mind set of Gp Capt Devan the Director Offensive Air Operations at Air HQ who was overly cautious and advised the Air Chief against it. Nehru fearing that use of offensive air support would invite retaliation on Delhi, accepted Devan's assessment.

Later in 1971 when he was AOC in C Eastern Air Command during the Bangladesh Liberation War he displayed the same qualities and both Chandan Singh who served under him and General Sagat Singh GOC IV Corps had problems dealing with him. But when things turned right he would jump in and claim credit.

Devan also displayed a streak of meanness, Sagat as Corps Commander was responsible for a border with China, Burma and East Pakistan. This border was several thousand kilometres long with very poor surface communication facilities. The only way he could tour his command and keep track of the developing situation was by moving around in a helicopter and this he did. Sagat had a forceful personality and a proven track record in war, so was a much respected and admired leader.

Devan as AOC in C was technically in a superior position to Sagat, but Devan compared to Sagat was was an unknown and colourless entity and both military personnel and civilians tended to ignore him. He resented this and he made every effort before and during the war to place obstacles in Sagat's path. The first thing he did to obstruct Sagat was to withdraw the IAF helicopter allotted to him but fortunately Sagat had at his disposal an Army Air OP flight of Chetaks, one of which he commandeered and in its pilot Capt Sihota later Lt Gen and Army Commander, he had a man who would take him where ever he wanted to go. Once they even landed in an enemy mine field with the Army Commander Gen Aurora on board.

In 1962 the Chinese did not anticipate that we would use tanks and hence did not carry their anti-tank weapons in this theatre. The threat of facing tanks perhaps made the Chinese rethink about assaulting and capturing Chushul. It is not an exaggeration to state that South Ladakh was saved because a few brave and innovative men at the risk of their lives and reputations managed to get the tanks to Chusul in spite of all the odds and scepticism. They made possible the impossible.

With the arrival of tanks and other reinforcements, Raina could have easily cleared the Chinese from their forward positions but as was his character he played safe with the result that the Chinese today dominate the heights and Chusul air strip can no longer be used by the IAF. Again in 1971 he was to show lack of initiative and leadership as stated by Gen Jacob in his autobiography and also in the official *History of the Pakistan Army* where it is stated that the actions of his corps were pedestrian. He was rewarded by promotions first as army commander and later as Chief of Army Staff, whereas Lt Gen Sagat Singh who had repeatedly shown great initiative, leadership and courage was denied promotions.

Raina also showed lack of moral fibre when he as COAS acquiesced to the imposition of the Emergency in 1975 by Indira Gandhi. He had been informed forty-eight hours in advance and after consulting the Military Operations Branch of the Army Headquarters where my former commanding officer then Brig later Lt Gen C.N. Somanna was the Deputy Director General Military Operations, Raina informed Indira Gandhi that the Army could control any law and order problem arising out of the constitutionally and morally illegal imposition of the Emergency.

It was only after receiving this assurance from Raina that Indira Gandhi imposed the Emergency on the nation. At this time I was serving on the staff of a brigade at Kanpur when we received orders to standby to take action should the need arise.

The story of the helicopter and transport pilots of the IAF who in spite of all odds, performed heroically, well beyond the call of duty and what could legitimately have been expected of them needs to be recorded. Unlike the fighter pilots their feats often go unrecognised. Like their counterparts in Ladakh the helicopter pilots in the Eastern Sector like Williams and Sehgal too performed heroically in supplying the army and evacuating casualties sometimes at the cost of their own lives.

Moraji Desai as a Finance Minister was responsible for denying funds to the Defence Forces keeping the forces starved for equipment and resources. His ignorance of security considerations and strategic issues costed the country and the world dearly. In 1978 when he was the Prime Minister of the Janata Party government he refused permission to the Israelis for the use of Jamnagar Air Base to carry out a strike on Kahuta where Pakistan's nuclear research establishment was located.

If he had acceded to the Israeli request there would have been no Pakistani Atomic Bomb and nor would the North Koreans have one, for it has now been revealed that the Korean Bomb is actually a Pakistani Bomb. Just imagine how much safer India and the world would be if these two rogue states were without nuclear bombs. This lack of knowledge of security and strategic issues amongst the political class and civil service continues to bedevil our country even today.

For his actions in Ladakh he was awarded the Vir Chakra but the citation makes no mention of the high point of his achievements and leadership in the operation—the taking of the AMX tanks to Chushul. This is however credited to another pilot who had no part in the ferrying of the tanks to Chushul. Such is the accuracy of citations written by some commanders. I have seen a repeat of this during the 1971 Bangladesh War when several undeserving officers received high honours and many of the truly deserving were left out.

6

History of Tibet and Its Betrayal

One of the canards spread by the Chinese is that Tibet was always a part of China which in reality it never was; of course they had diplomatic, religious and trade relations which are but natural among neighbouring nations. In fact the reality is the other way around, for substantial parts of its history large areas of China were under Tibetan suzerainty. Chinese claims on Tibet are premised on the fact that during the reign of the Mongol Emperor Ghenghiz Khan and his heirs particularly Kublai Khan when Marco Polo visited China, Tibetan representatives were seen in the Court at Peking.

At that time China itself was a part of the Mongolian Empire and Tibet and Mongolia have always had close relations which continue even till today and the relationship between Mongolia and Tibet was never between master and vassal, in fact it was possibly the very opposite. The Mongolians always acknowledged the Tibetans as their superiors and so if the same logic was to be applied, the Tibetans can claim to be masters of China.

Much of Chinese claims are based on the Anglo-Chinese conventions of 1890 and 1893, some details of which were kept hidden from the public by the British authorities at the time and which even our present-day scholars are unaware of. The facts of these conventions are that Durrand who represented British India was not negotiating directly with the Chinese. He was instead negotiating with another Englishman who represented the Imperial Chinese Customs Department.

The British were keen to obtain further trading privileges in Hong Kong and Shanghai for opium and other goods.

They were also demanding that the New Territories be added to Kowloon in Hong Kong. To obtain these very lucrative concessions Britain acknowledged China's non-existent limited suzerainty over Tibet which was of no economic value to them.

The Chinese claim that diplomatic gifts received by them from neighbouring nations was tribute by a subject people is a canard. On the contrary, the Chinese paid such huge sums as tribute to Tibet and Tibetan monasteries that they ran out of gold and silver and were forced to introduce paper currency and made payments in bolts of silk cloth for their imports. The price of a horse was twenty bolts of silk cloth and that of a young and beautiful slave girl fifteen bolts! As recently as the installation of the present Dalai Lama the KMT Government of China under Chaing Kai-shek paid a tribute of 400,000 pieces of silver to Tibet.

Masters do not pay tribute, only vassals do. The Chinese have always complained that the nation was bankrupted by the payment of tribute to Tibet and sometimes when the opportunity arose particularly during the long period of the minority years of newly installed Dalai Lamas which followed his installation while still a child when Tibet would be ruled by a regency council, they sent out expeditions to plunder some of the monasteries located in the eastern border provinces of Tibet, namely Kham and Amdo. Some of these expeditions resulted in disastrous defeats of the Chinese Armies.

The system of succession of the Dalai Lamas was unique to Tibet where the death of a Dalai would be followed by several years of rule by a regency council. This system was a great weakness for it sometimes led to anarchy that was taken advantage of by the opponents of Tibet.

Nehru's knowledge of Indian history was somewhat sketchy for he had studied in England and even later when he may have read something about Indian History it was through books written by Englishmen as textbooks for Indian students. These textbooks as everybody knows are written and prescribed to further the agenda of the ruling establishment of the time. (His book *The Discovery of India* is a cut and paste job which is more remarkable for what it leaves out than what is included. It is definitely not suitable as a textbook even for school students).

His admiration of socialism and the Stalinist model of government and development and his desire to play a preeminent role in the newly emerging Asia and the world stage made him accept the Chinese canard and in the process sacrificed for ever Tibet and India's interests. An unforgivable act which has resulted in the near extinction of an ancient civilisation and people, and also created an insoluble problem for India. A heavy price for the present and future generations to pay to satisfy his personal ego and ambitions.

Morally and legally the Hanification of the Tibetan population is genocide by another name. Linguistically, racially, culturally, and genetically the Tibetans are a different race from the Han Chinese and so are the Mongols, Manchurians, and many other ethnic minority groups. Millions of these minority races have been killed in the process of Hanification and yet the apologists of the Chinese amongst the Indian left and intelligentsia completely ignore this genocide and hold up the Maoist doctrine of governance and development as the only role model for the people of India to follow.

Few people know that prior to the adoption of Buddhism as a state religion and its emphasis on ahimsa as a guiding principle for state policy and individual conduct the Tibetans were the most powerful and warlike people who dominated an immense swathe of land starting from Western China, including Central Asia and right up to the Middle East. There were times when other armies entered Tibet but the cold and rarefied air of the high plateau of Central Tibet combined with the stubborn resistance by Tibetans forced them into ignominious retreat leaving behind their horses and their dead.

When the Chinese Army invaded Tibet in 1950 they found themselves short of food even after having ransacked the countryside of all food supplies. They would have starved to death like the earlier invaders had not Nehru agreed to supply huge quantities of rice from India via Jalep La Pass in Sikkim. This at a time when India itself was suffering from food shortage. He did this all because he wanted to earn the gratitude of Mao who he hoped would then support him to fulfil his ambition to present himself as the leading light of Asia if not the world. A legitimate ambition for a politician but definitely not one to be achieved by throwing overboard the interests of one's own country.

What a price India and Tibet have had to pay for him to pander to his ego. But Nehru was wanting a role for himself on a bigger stage and to achieve it he moved closer to the Chinese Communist leadership. In 1952 he agreed to downgrade India's representation in Tibet to consul-general, implicitly conceding that Tibet's foreign relations were controlled by China. Two years later he agreed to withdraw the Indian military posts and trade representative from the Chumbi Valley that had been established by Younghusband.

During the hasty and ill planned withdrawal from Yatung several lives were lost including that of the Company Commander of the 2nd Battalion Jat Regiment Major Nagal the father of my friend Lt Gen B.S. Nagal the present Director of the Centre for Land Warfare Studies, the Indian army's premier think tank. With great difficulty and persuasion was a team from 1 Maratha Light Infantry under 2 Lt Bulbul Brar allowed to proceed to Yatung and recover the bodies. (Gen Brar was later given the thankless task to clear the Golden Temple of terrorists) Nehru also had the telegraphic link to Lhasa and other facilities handed over to China.

By all these actions he effectively not only gave up all Indian claims in Tibet but also surrendered Tibet's rights to have independent relations with the outside world. Our trade representatives at Kashgar, Gartok, Yatung and Gyantse were withdrawn cutting off our centuries-old links to Tibet. The following year at the Bandung Conference whatever residual interests and rights that we had in Tibet were signed away on a piece of paper called the Panchsheel agreement. Shades and shades of Chamberlain!

But more shameful than all this is an act that has been kept hidden from the Indian public. In 1951 just after the relics of the Buddha's disciples which had been returned by UK had been exhibited in Gangtok and Kalimpong and are now housed at Sanchi. India not only facilitated the journey to Lhasa but played host to the newly appointed Chinese Military Governor of Tibet, General Chang Chin Wu even after having received reports of atrocities being committed by the first batch of Chinese invaders led by General Liu Po Cheng.

At this point in time access to Tibet from China was very difficult, so much so that the Chinese Military Governor of Tibet had to proceed to Lhasa via Calcutta and Sikkim like Younghusband before him. If one Chinaman found it difficult to go to Lhasa directly how much more difficult it would have been to move an entire army and then support it. To compound the error he permitted thousands of tons of rice to be transported from India to feed the Chinese troops in Tibet at a time when India itself was short of food grains. What a wasted opportunity!

The real bombshell amounting nothing to less than treason is refusing to accept membership to the United Nations Security Council which was offered to India on a platter and not stopping at this but passing it on to the Chinese! The second is the refusal of President Kennedy's help which he offered in 1962 to build and test a nuclear bomb.(Swagato Ganguli quoting former Foreign Secretary M.K. Rasgotra in the editorial of *Times of India* on June 15, 2016) If any one of these actions were taken we would not have suffered the humiliation of 1962 nor the thousand cuts inflicted on us by Pakistan every day. A question that needs to be asked is why did Nehru do all this? Was it out of a sense of idealism, an attempt at image building of himself as a world leader or was there something else? After giving it a serious thought and discussing the subject with people whose views and judgements I respect, all of us came to the conclusion that we can rule out the first option, i.e. idealism.

If it was a sense of idealism that motivated him then he would not have promoted the interests of his daughter to succeed him. She had no qualification except a ruthless streak to eliminate her opponents that that would qualify her to hold high office. Nehru's actions smell of nepotism to his family and his caste after independence nearly seventy-five per cent of central ministers, chief ministers of states and senior civil servants were from his caste. A backlash was bound to occur and it did with a vengeance. The Mandal Commission and the indefinite extension of reservations at the expense of merit is the result besides a continuation of caste conflicts and divisiveness of society. The inescapable conclusion is, that those of Nehru's actions that were patently against India's national interests, were motivated by less than altruistic factors and more by nepotism and egotistic image building exercise and a probable third factor which has now been introduced that needs to be examined and to be spoken about, which I will do in the next paragraphs.

It is a well known fact that honey traps and blackmail have been tools of diplomacy and war since time immemorial. The point to consider here is was Nehru a willing or forced victim of the ploys by nations and agencies inimical to India and its interests? Personal sexual orientation as long as they are in consonance with the law of the land are nobody else's business, but for people in public life who allow it to affect their functioning and decision-making it is very much a matter of public interest. I therefore put the facts as are known before the reading public, for them to come to their own conclusions.

Nehru, his libido and his affairs have been a matter of discussion for ages. There is a great deal of speculation and rumour mongering in these accounts but some stories do seem to have some basis in fact. Some of his political heirs and loyalists of his dynasty have been quite smug if not proud of his purported affair with Lady Mountbatten because they feel that an affair with the Vicereine adds to his stature. Those who have seen Lady Mountbatten and have described her looks called her ugly with a prematurely wrinkled and thick leathery skin. Her own daughter Pamela Mountbatten has described her as "My mother the maneater."

Two persons, both my kinsmen who were on Mountbatten's staff during his tenure in Delhi, Colonel Govind Singh as Commander of his Bodyguard and Maharajah Narendra Singh Sarila as his ADC have confirmed this to me. Both also denied existence of any affair between Nehru and Edwina. Of Nehru's other affairs whether with Shradha Mata, Padmaja Naidu and others, Nehru's apologists are in a vehemently denial mode and accusations of character assassination are made. However even a person like Khushwant Singh, otherwise a sycophant of the Nehru-Feroze Gandhi clan, has written about Nehru's peccadilloes.

Excessive libido seems to be the character trait of people in power for as they say power is the ultimate aphrodisiac. In India of late thanks to hidden cameras and sting operations we have seen enough of them from the chambers of the Supreme Court to bedrooms of Raj Bhavans. The greatness of Mahatma Gandhi among other qualities is in the fact that not only did he not deny the existence in him of what is natural but wrote about how he tried to control it so that others too could follow his example and learn to control what our scriptures speak of as the beast within.

Nehru who projected himself as Gandhi's natural heir however went to extremes to hide them. This opened him to manipulation by people and agencies in the know. The Communists and Pakistan have been past masters of this art and so have the CIA and MI-5. As General Zia ul-Haq revealed in his plan "Operation Topac" for subverting India in his address to the Pakistan Inter Service Intelligence Agency in April 1988, the first phase had always been subverting and compromising the Indian establishment and leaders. Our leaders with cupboards full of skeletons were and still are often willing victims of their designs.

Two men with whom Nehru interacted with on a regular basis and who influenced his decisions for a ceasefire in Kashmir and turning a blind eye to Chinese incursions, Lord

Mountbatten and Chou en Lai were known for their same gender preferences even though like Nehru they were married. By the time Nehru had become prime minister he had been a widower for several years and stories about his disturbed marital life were rife even when Kamala Nehru was alive. Should Nehru have decided to get married again to any one of the innumerable, well educated and beautiful women who had become a part of the freedom movement and moved in close proximity of its leaders, I am sure Gandhiji would have approved and given his blessings.

So what is it that made Nehru so circumspect and secretive? the answer seems to lie in what Prof. Stanley Wolpert has written in his excellent biography *Nehru: A Tryst with Destiny*. The book hit the mark when it mentioned facts about his sexual orientation. As was to be expected the book was banned in India at the behest of Nehru's loyalists. Banning the book was the easiest and safest course of action open to them. But the proper right course would have been to take the author and publisher to court for libel and defamation but this would have drawn attention to aspects of Nehru's life which they did not want to have revealed and they would have found it impossible to refute the facts brought to light by Prof. Wolpert who is not a writer of pulp fiction but a well known authority and professor of South Asian History at the University of California Los Angeles and author of several books and biographies on the subcontinent.

I have been fortunate to have spent three days in his company and in the company of the Maharajah of Sarila discussing this and other issues at Orchha in Madhya Pradesh as guests of the Maharajah of Orchha, Madhukar Shah who is a former student of Prof Wolpert. Like Wolpert, Sarila has written an excellent book on India's independence. Prof. Wolpert's biography of Jinnah is banned in Pakistan for it portrays him as a pork-eating Scotch-guzzling man. Wolpert's book on Nehru is banned in India.

He knew that this was his vulnerability and the Chinese and Pakistanis exploited this fully. In order to protect his reputation and position he was left with no choice but to give in to their blackmail. The sacrifice of India's national interest to safeguard his own was the price he paid to keep his secret from being exposed. In order to put a stop to whispers doing the rounds within the circle of his party about his orientation and private life and to present himself as a champion and upholder of 'moral values'.

The well known scholar and writer Devdutt Patnaik has written that some elements of the Congress Party of which Nehru was the leader went to the other extreme and started a campaign to destroy all representation of the sensual and erotic in carvings and paintings in Hindu temples, hoping that by these actions all discussion on the subject would end.

Had Gurudev Rabindranath Tagore not interceded with Gandhiji to put a stop to this mad plan there would have been no Khajuraho, Konarak and hundreds of other temples today. Nehru's lack of aesthetic sense is reflected in the designs of all buildings constructed by the government during his stewardship which any one can see when looking down the vista of Rajpath from Rashtrapati Bhawan. These Nehruvian shoe boxes in their shabby ugliness spoil one of the most beautiful urban vistas in the world.

Even that great man of the arts and President De Gaulle's Minister of Culture, Andre Malraux has commented on Nehru's lack of aesthetic sense in his memoirs, in other words calling him a moron. It is ironic that the Government of India under Congress rule awarded Malraux the Nehru Peace Prize an unimaginative Babu copying the citation word for word from the commendation cited on the back dust cover of Malraux's autobiography titled oddly *Anti Memoirs*.

7

Clandestine Operations in Tibet

The early years of the Chinese occupation of Tibet is an important chapter in the history of the US Central Intelligence Agency and India's support for the freedom fighters of Tibet. In Tibet the CIA introduced new types of equipment and aircraft-like the U2 and Helios, and new parachutes were combat tested in the most extreme conditions. For many of the case officers, Indians and CIA alike the Tibet campaign was a defining moment. Second the country from where most of these programmes were staged was India.

In earlier accounts, India's role barely gets a mention if at all. In reality Tibet led Washington and New Delhi to become secret partners over the course of several administrations in both countries. At the abject pleading of Nehru which even B.K. Nehru who was his cousin and the then Indian ambassador to Washington found humiliating, President John Kennedy had put the US firmly behind India to help it face the Chinese threat. He also prevented Ayub Khan, the Pakistani dictator from intervening to take advantage of the situation.

Even when relations between the two countries appeared to be severely strained during the Nixon-Kissinger era there remained discrete intelligence cooperation. (The CIA's Secret War in Tibet).... This cooperation started during Nehru's time and continued even under Shashtri and Indira Gandhi notwithstanding Indian politicians' propensity of seeing the CIA's hand in everything that went wrong in India from too much salt served in the subsidised food in the Parliament's canteen to a cabinet minister's wife eloping with his security guard.

Another thing that must be understood is that for reasons best known to himself, Nehru kept the Indian army completely in the dark about what was happening inside Tibet, so much so that it was the police forces operating under the Home Ministry who were responsible for the Indo-Tibet border, the Defence Ministry having no role whatsoever in this regard. Was it because knowing that he had blundered in accepting Chinese suzerainty over Tibet in 1950 and not trusting the army general staff to keep his monumental blunder under wraps, whereas the police could be expected to play ball and not stir the hornets' nest or was it because Nehru did not trust the Army and was overly dependent on the intelligence Bureau Chief Mullik who was playing his own games to protect and enlarge his own turf as is the want of intelligence chiefs the world over?

He pandered to Nehru's insecurity and fears of military coups and also kept him informed about his political colleagues, friends and foes alike. The recent disclosures on the snooping on the family members of Subhas Chandra Bose is a telling indictment about the misplaced priorities of the IB and Nehru.

Nehru and his intelligence chief Mullik knew exactly what was happening inside Tibet for the Chogyal of Sikkim's two sisters, Princess Pema Tseudun (Coocoola) and Princess Pema Choki (Kula) who were both married to high ranking members of Tibetan nobility and government officials were keeping India informed. It is not as if the Indian Army was totally unaware of the Chinese build up but could do nothing to correct the situation for want of political direction.

However, a few courageous generals like Gen Thimayya, Gen Nathu Singh, Gen Sheodat Singh and Gen Thorat tried their best to correct the situation but all four had to pay a price for highlighting the issue. Gen Thimayya used several unorthodox channels to collect information and warned the government on several occasions of Chinese plans and build up. It is now revealed that Gen Thimayya had planted agents amongst the mountaineering teams that were on climbing expeditions to peaks like Gurlamandata and Kailash and they reported back about Chinese road building activities inside areas that were on the Indian side of the border.

The border was not however the Army's responsibility. It was manned entirely by armed civil police personnel who rarely if ever ventured out or forward of their bases situated in some cases over a hundred kilometres from the border. Blaming the police rank and file for this would be incorrect. The fact is that there were no police officers present with the men to give orders and manage the borders.

Getting no response from the PM or Defence Minister and to add insult to injury compliant generals from the logistics branches of the army were being promoted and urged to command fighting formations. Gen Thimayya resigned, but Nehru the consummate politician that he was outwitted him. Lt Gen S.P.S. Thorat as GOC in C Eastern Command had produced an excellent report on the subject. For his efforts he was shunted out to Southern Command which had no operational responsibility.

Before him Maj Gen Maharaj Himmat Singh who as Deputy Defence Minister had prepared another report and he too was relieved of his post and given an unimportant sinecure as the Lt Governor of the newly formed Himachal Pradesh and chairman of a public sector undertakings. It would have been the easiest thing to have sent a few photo reconnaissance aircraft over Tibet to monitor Chinese activities but the airforce was no longer under the control of the Commander-in-Chief of India, a post that was abolished at the end of General Rajendra Singh's tenure and to which change Gen Shrinagesh, the next COAS acquiesced and there was no way that the army could now ask the air force to carry out the recce flights and obtain the required information.

Till the mid-1950s the chief of the Indian Air Force was a British officer who following instructions received from Washington and London did not want to do anything to provoke the Chinese as the Korean war was still on and even the Allied Air Forces had instructions not to violate Chinese air space even though Chinese MIG-15 fighters operating from inside China were locked in air combat with allied planes over Korea. Gen MacArthur was sacked by Truman when he protested against these restrictions.

As far as the public in India including most research scholars are concerned the war with China was limited to the operations in the latter part of 1962. Chandan Singh of course played an important and gallant role in these operations but what is not known is that he was also involved in clandestine operations against the Chinese for the greater part of the 1960s.

It is necessary here to give a brief historical background of India's role during this period. This account will help the reader to understand the Tibet problem with which we will have to live with forever. For much of the information in the succeeding paragraphs I have relied mainly on the recently declassified files of the CIA, a paper published by the IDSA, Maj Gen Maharaj Himmat Singh's Report (his daughter Ratna was married to my uncle the late Col Kishan Singh Rathor MVC and I have seen his private papers), Air Vice Marshal Chandan Singh's own account and my recollections of conversations I had with members of the Sikkim royal family in the 1960s when I met them socially on several occasions in Calcutta at Tripura House on Alipur Road.

The Rajmata of Tripura was from Panna, my home town and related to me. So whenever I passed through Calcutta, I would drop in to see her and her family. I also got some information from other sources most importantly from Brig K.P. Singhdeo the Maharajah of Dhenkanal and former Minister of State for Defence with both Indira Gandhi and Rajiv Gandhi. Brig K.P. Singhdeo and I have many common relations and are also good friends. The Sikkim royal family had been long-term tenants of Dhenkanal House on Gokhale Road Calcutta.

Dhenkanal is also only about thirty kilometres away from Charbatia which became the principal base for the ARC of which Chandan was the first Station Commander. ARC was established with the assistance of the CIA at Charbatia at the behest of Biju Patnaik the then Chief Minister of Orissa whose state capital was then at Cuttack only ten miles away. The Maharajah of Dhenkanal the father of Brig K.P. Singhdeo also had a house in Cuttack close to Charbatia and was friendly with Biju Patnaik. He became an important link between the Sikkimese royal family and the IB and the ARC base.

Chandan Singh and the Maharajah became good friends and the fact that the Maharajah's sister-in-law came from Bera, a small town close to Bagawas Chandan's home in Rajasthan, helped to bond their friendship. It also helped that her father had commanded Jodhpur Lancers and Chandan's father had taken over command from him. The reader may think it was unlikely that clandestine operations would be the subject of social conversations but both Tripura House and Dhenkanal House were frequented by the American consular officials and other diplomats who we now know from the CIA papers were actually undercover operatives and as often happens they in the company of beautiful princesses and good wine would let slip bits of information even in my presence for after all I was related to their hosts with whom they were doing business.

But I think that by the time I met them the Sikkim royal family had outlived their usefulness to the CIA who by now must have developed other sources and in any case the princesses were not too keen on the armed part of the struggle which they said was bound to fail and had already caused great suffering to the Tibetans. They were now more concerned about the welfare of the refugees and their resettlement in India.

They were also very involved with the preservation of Tibetan culture and promoting the Tibetan cause in world forums, something that they were very good at. In spite of their emotional bonds with Tibet, they considered India home and their loyalties were very much with Sikkim and India.

The Americans and other Europeans particularly the British loved associating with Indian royalty and they would frequently turn up uninvited, assured that they would be hospitably received. In our private conversations we joked about their cockney origins and carpetbagging ways. It was a tradition among the princes to have an open house and they took full advantage.

Another favourite meeting ground was the polo ground in the Maidan and relationships were established by the white ladies with the players, the best of whom were from Jaipur and Jodhpur in Rajasthan. Maharani Gayatri Devi's brother, the Maharajah of Cooch Behar in North Bengal was also a good polo player and handsome to boot. Beside his string of polo ponies he was always trailed by a string of European socialites.

Rarely did the whites ever reciprocate the hospitality. There wasn't much that the people whom we now know to have been CIA operatives gave away but now that the CIA papers are in the public domain, I can join the dots and dashes. The Sikkim princesses were however quite free with information about happenings inside Tibet and as they were both married into leading families of Tibet some of whose members had stayed behind, they remained the most reliable source of information.

But as the CIA papers reveal the CIA was completely mistaken in thinking that the princesses were their agents. They were just too smart for them. Instead it was the princesses who used the CIA contacts to push their own pro-Tibetan freedom struggle agenda and get the Americans involved in the struggle by the Tibetans against the Chinese.

The CIA papers also reveal that the princesses did not receive any payments from them as the princesses were not such people. There may be slight inaccuracies in this account which relies so much on memory and also the CIA papers which are probably not wholly accurate and are also self-serving but nonetheless important for they throw light on the Indian Intelligence services and other principal players, including Chandan Singh and the Dalai Lama's brothers. It is at one of these soirees that they planted Hope Cooke on the Crown Prince, later Chogyal of Sikkim and a lady called Mary, a friend of the famous actress Shirley MacLaine on Lhendup Dorjee.

Mary was later to marry Lhendup Dorjee. He was the brother of the Bhutanese Prime Minister Jigme Dorjee whose mother Rani Choki was another Sikkimese princess, an aunt of princesses Coocoola and Kula. Both the Sikkim princesses were married to high ranking Tibetan aristocrats and officials. The Crown Prince was a widower having lost his beautiful Tibetan wife some years ago and Lhendup was a graduate of an American College and became Prime Minister after the assassination of Jigme Dorjee but had to flee Bhutan later as he too got involved in a palace plot. Jigme Dorje's sister was the Queen of Bhutan. These relationships bring out how closely related were the Bhutanese, Sikhimese and Tibetan aristocracy.

In 1950 when the Chinese invaded Tibet it was Princess Pema Tsedeun*, popularly known as Coocoola whose husband was the Governor of Gyantse in South Tibet and related to the family of an earlier Dalai Lama. Coocoola kept the Government of India in Delhi informed by wireless from Lhasa of the happenings inside Tibet.

Coocoda was our only source. She risked everything her freedom, her property, her family and her very life to save her beloved Tibet and this was only the beginning of a lifelong battle she waged for the Tibetan cause till her death at the age of eighty-four in Gangtok in 2008.

After the Dalai Lama no one has done more to bring to centre stage in world forums the Tibetan problem and the humanitarian crisis in Tibet than she and her younger sister Princess Pema Cheoki (Kula). They understood that in the modern world the battle for the hearts and minds of the public was just as important as other battles and this battle they won hands down.

The Chinese are still chafing at their defeat in the theatre of public opinion. I have digressed enough from the subject of this biography and now return to Air Vice Marshal Chandan Singh. For those who wish to know more about these remarkable ladies, they can see the notes at the end of the book. According to the Dalai Lama himself in one of his interviews the resettlement and welfare of Tibetan refugees and the expenses of the Tibetan government in exile was greatly facilitated because he had available to him a large reserve of gold which starting from the early 1950s the Tibetan government had moved to India.

This gold was first stored with the Sikkim royal family and then invested with bankers in Calcutta. It is from the interest received from these investments that the Tibetan government meets most of its expenses even today. Princesses Coocoola and Kula not only facilitated this operation but played an active and leading part in the safekeeping and investment of the treasure.

Without the availability of these funds the Tibetan government in exile would not have been able to carry out its activities. This was a hazardous operation carried out under the very nose of the occupying Chinese Army. But a huge quantity of gold was still left behind in the monasteries and other places in the Kham and Amdo regions of Eastern Tibetan where the writ of the Tibetan government did not fully run as local clan chieftains and war lords while acknowledging the suzerainty of the central government tended to run their own show in their fiefdoms.

The natives of Kham known as Khampas who never acknowledged Chinese sovereignty had broken out in open armed rebellion against the Chinese and for some time the Chinese had no control or presence in large parts of the province.

Chandan Singh was later involved in clandestine operations in support of the Khampas and some reports even indicate that ARC and the CIA were involved in flying out to India the left behind golden horde and other treasures after their planes had dropped the men and supplies to the rebels in Kham. By now it had become too dangerous to fly bigger aircraft into Tibet, land them there with fighters and supplies and then fly back to India. So the CIA provided ARC with a special aircraft called the Helois.

This is a Stol-short takeoff and landing aircraft which was capable of landing and taking off from any piece of hard ground barely forty or fifty metres long. Nehru was astounded at its performance when it was demonstrated to him during his visit to Charbatia. The Helios was normally a single engine aircraft but for operations in Tibet in order to cope with rarefied air it was modified to a twin engine version.

When the Dalai Lama escaped from Tibet and sought refuge in India the armed struggle in Tibet flared up and the CIA started air dropping arms supplies from Thailand and Kurmitola, Tezgaon and later Sylhit airfields. All of them were in East Pakistan but physical contact with Tibetan freedom fighters was mainly at Darjeeling and Kalimpong where large numbers of refugees had settled. Calcutta was another venue because both the Tibetan leadership and the CIA found this a more suitable location for covert meetings as there was a sizeable expat crowd and their meetings did not draw unwanted attention.

The Indian Intelligence agencies were aware of these meetings and being sympathetic chose to turn a blind eye with Nehru's tacit approval. But immediately after the 1962 war our IB and the CIA started collaborating in not only information gathering but also in covertly supporting the armed struggle inside Tibet and it is now that India's man for all seasons cavalier and aviator Chandan Singh takes centre stage once again.

The humiliation suffered by India at the hands of the Chinese compelled Nehru to seek American help. President Kennedy was more than sympathetic and offered both weapons and intelligence support. It is with the intelligence gathering part of the operation that Chandan Singh was deeply involved. The clandestine war in Tibet and the raising, arming and training of Tibetan volunteers was carried out by another outstanding Officer Brig Obhan later promoted Major General. Obhan raised Establishment 22 at Chakrata with the first batch of volunteers from the Tibetan refugees. The number 22 was given to the organisation by Obhan because that was the number of the Artillery regiment he had commanded.

Chandan Singh helped to set up the Aviation Research

Centre at Charbatia and became its first Commanding Officer. Charbatia was chosen as the base for ARC because it had earlier been the main operations and maintenance base for the now defunct Kalinga Airways, a brainchild and baby of Biju Patnaik the Chief Minister of Orissa. Patnaik was a maverick, a pilot himself who had supported the Indonesian rebels in their freedom struggle against the Dutch, carried out several arms supply drops and ferried the rebel leadership to different parts of the country.

He then became a politician, a businessman and advisor to Nehru on defence matters in the nation's hour of crisis and it was he who made available Charbatia as the operations base for ARC. The necessity for setting up ARC was felt because one of the prime reasons for the humiliating defeat in 1962 was the total lack of intelligence about the Chinese military and logistics build up in Tibet.

This lack of knowledge of Chinese actions was surprising for in the treeless Tibetan plateau there is no cover to conceal anything. However, Nehru's disinclination to do anything that would displease the Chinese kept the IAF from carrying out photo and visual reconnaissance flights over Tibet, even though in the Canberra we had an excellent aircraft for this type of mission to which the Chinese had no counter measures. In the Nehru era the army had been grossly neglected but the Air Force had managed to acquire the latest aircraft and in sufficient numbers.

Training with the CIA and Setting Up the Aviation Research Centre at Charbatia

Once the decision to set up ARC was taken, eight pilots, Lulu Grewal, Chandan Singh, Navej, Charlie Jai Singh, Subramunium a police officer, Sqn Ldr Anand, a paratrooper Srivastav and another civilian both from the private aviation sector were selected and sent to the United States for training with the CIA. Out of these six came back to India and only two were found suitable for advanced training.

The two were Squadron Leaders Lulu Grewal and

Chandan Singh. From Delhi all the selected pilots were flown to Washington DC and the aircraft parked in a dark unrecognisable part of the airport. From there they were taken in a van with darkened windows to some other place, probably Langley, the CIA headquarters for an interview and initial briefing and from there they were again transferred to another secret location where their training started.

It was only years later that they learnt that this location was the secret CIA base Camp Peary. After four weeks of training in low level night flying in different types of aircraft but mainly C-46, six of the trainees were returned to India as they were considered unsuitable for this type of flying leaving behind only Lulu Grewal and Chandan Singh.

They were now moved to another location in the Midwest and introduced to a type of specialised night time very low level flying called horizon flying. This entailed flying at tree top level barely 30 to 40 feet above the ground in total darkness and without any navigational aids. It was according to Chandan Singh the scariest thing he had undertaken so far.

Out of the two only Chandan Singh qualified and he then had to do conversion training from the slower and older propeller-driven C-46 which was a larger version of the more famous DC-47 popularly known as the Dakota to B-49 the faster, jet-powered US version of the Canberra bomber.

On return to India, Chandan took command of the newly established ARC base at Charbatia and Lulu Grewal became in charge of clandestine air operations at ARC HQ New Delhi. During his stay he managed to fly the still top secret two seater version of the U-2 as a co-pilot. The Americans did not permit him to fly the U-2 solo.

Once at Charbatia his work was cut out for him. Not only did he have the administrative burden of setting up the base from scratch but almost immediately they had to be prepared to receive and launch CIA intelligence flights over Tibet and Central Asia. Just two weeks into Charbatia four twin engine Helios VSTOL (very short landing and takeoff) aircraft arrived as a gift from the CIA.

These planes were to be used to induct Tibetan freedom fighters and their supplies into Tibet and on occasion bring out gold and other treasures from monasteries which had still not been occupied by the Chinese. Once during Nehru's visit to Charbatia, Chandan Singh gave a demonstration of a Helios landing in under a hundred yards and dropping a passenger and taking off once again in less than a minute. This happened in close proximity of where Nehru was seated leaving him gasping and he commented on what happened.

At the same time C-46 and U-2 with electronic radio monitoring equipment started arriving and used Charbatia as a staging post. The planes would arrive from Bangkok and then fly close to our border over Tibet. These planes were fitted with electronic surveillance devices. On return to Charbatia the pods containing the surveillance devices and data would be flown back to Bangkok and no one in India heard anything more about them.

For deep penetration and long distance flights over West China and Central Asia U-2s were used. These would be brought with their wings dismantled in a transport aircraft from Bangkok and taken inside a large hanger where the wings would be bolted on to the fuselage and the planes would then take off for their mission at night under the cover of darkness. They did not land back in India and generally flew to some base in Turkey or Germany.

On three such missions, Chandan flew with the CIA over Tibet and several times more independently. Sadly none of the intelligence gathered was passed down to the Defence Forces on the pretext that such intelligence was of strategic value and for the Prime Minister's eyes only. This I believe is true even today. If it were not so, Kargil would not have happened and in 1971 we would have had detailed information of Pakistani Army dispositions.

Gen Jacob has observed in his biography how his requests for photo reconnaissance flights over East Pakistan were stonewalled. The tendency of Indian officialdom to treat their departments as private jagirs is so pervasive that not only do they brook no interference but also refuse to share information with user agencies who need the information in real time to evaluate and incorporate it into their planning. This leads to unfortunate results as happened in Pathankot in 2015.

While at Charbatia, Chandan Singh became one of the very few foreign pilots to get to fly the C-46 along with the Americans over Tibet. He did three missions over Tibet. But none of the intelligence gathered was handed over to India. On completion of the missions the electronic pods would be detached from the aircraft and flown to the US for processing of information.

The Chinese are still resentful of the fact that we had provided assistance to the Tibetans and allowed the US to run clandestine operations from India.

Note: Nehru had met Princess Coocoola several times both in Delhi and Gangtok. He, like many others, including the then US Ambassador to India John Kenneth Galbraith was infatuated by her, which was resented by Indira Gandhi. Indira was also envious of the beauty and sophistication of Gayatri Devi, the Maharani of Jaipur. Being vindictive by nature, she had Gayatri Devi imprisoned and all the privileges and powers of the Chogyal, the brother of Coocoola taken away in spite of the family's services to India.

8

Indo-Pak 1965 War

For the history and background to the 1965 war I am indebted to my friend Maj Gen Dhruv Katoch VSM, SM from whose excellent book on this war, *Honour Redeemed* published by the Indian War Veterans Association, I have with his permission lifted full paragraphs and reproduced them.

History and Background

In the middle of the previous century, a series of unrelated events took place, that were to propel India and Pakistan to their second war in less than two decades since gaining independence. This was a time when the cold war was at its peak and the rivalry between the US and Soviet Russia was at its all time high. Pakistan astutely sided with the West, joining the Central Treaty Organisation and South East Asia Treaty Organisation.

The appeal in joining these organisations was to receive economic and military aid from the US and other Western nations ostensibly to fight communism but covertly to be used against India. Pakistan was aware of its importance to the Western Powers as a frontline state in support of US plans to contain communism. It played its cards with great panache and managed to bolster its military capability and economy.

During this time, India was hampered by a slow growth rate and hamstrung military, a fall out of Nehruvian policies and socialism. The debacle suffered at the hands of the Chinese in 1962 had left deep scars in the national psyche and consequently India in the mid-1960s was arguably at its lowest ebb, economically and militarily. India's perceived weakness was seen by Pakistan as an opportunity to wrest Kashmir from India by force.

However India was slowly but steadily augmenting its military capability post-1962 and the morale of the Army had fully recovered. Policy makers in Pakistan veered to the view that this window of opportunity was limited and having missed the chance to capture Kashmir in October 1962, it now focused on keeping the Kashmir issue centre stage at all international fora and using all means available to grab Kashmir by force.

Another factor which may have encouraged Pakistan to mistakenly adopt a policy of aggression was the outward personality of Lal Bahadur Shastri, the Indian Prime Minister who had assumed office only a year earlier after Nehru's death. He was short, of a small build and mild mannered but within his small frame he hid the heart and spirit of a lion. The Pakistanis were to learn this at their cost.

The Pakistan plan to take Kashmir by force consisted of two components. The first code named Operation Gibraltar envisaged the infiltration of thousands of regular and irregular troops dressed as Kashmiri guerrillas into Jammu and Kashmir, to create an uprising in the state and to tie down Indian Forces.

This was to be followed by Operation Grand Slam, an armoured thrust across the Chhamb Sector to capture Akhnoor and threaten Jammu. Grand Slam was to deliver the coup de grace by exploiting the success achieved by OP Gibraltar. But for a series of chance events, Pakistan very nearly succeeded in its nefarious designs.

It is now revealed that the Pakistan Army Chief Gen Musa opposed these plans of Ayub Khan for he felt that this could lead to a general war on all fronts for which Pakistan was not prepared. But he was overruled by Ayub who after the adventures of the Pakistan Army in Kutch in early 1965 felt that India was a walkover and the world community would not intervene.

In many ways the short conflict in Kutch was the harbinger

of what was to follow in the latter part of 1965. The operations in Kutch were limited in scale with India deploying only an Infantry Brigade group in the early stages of the conflict and thereafter bolstering it with additional forces.

Offensive air power or armour was not used by India. Pakistan however had no hesitation in using tanks and other aided equipment which it was treaty bound not to use against India. This transgression of the terms of the treaties was ignored by the US and its allies and contributed to the confidence in the Pakistani leadership that not only would they get away with it but that the US would support it.

After the ceasefire the case went for arbitration where it gained what it could not militarily. Its main offensive led by tanks had been beaten back by a company of the Central Reserve Police repeatedly. At the intervention of the United Kingdom, Pakistan was awarded 780 square kilometres of territory out of 9,100 sq kms claimed by it.

Pakistan launched Operation Gibraltar on 1st August, with the infiltration of thousands of regular and irregular troops across the ceasefire line. These forces moved to their pre-designated areas from where they were tasked to launch their operations on 7th August. As usual our Intelligence agencies failed us and we remained blissfully unaware of what was happening. It was only by chance that the infiltrators were discovered which gave us time to take counter measures and for the Army to retrieve the situation.

19 Infantry Division by a series of heroic actions stabilised the situation and had the infiltrators on the run. The capture of Haji Pir Pass by the Paras led by Maj later Lt Gen Ranjit Dayal, was a key component of the offensive operations of the Indian Army which cut off the supply routes of the infiltrators.

On 1st September the Pakistanis launched the second part of their plan Operation Grand Slam in the Chhamb Sector. Here a plucky defence by the heavily outnumbered and out gunned 191 Brigade imposed a vital delay on the Pakistani offensive which gave India time to redeploy its forces and take counter measures.

In terms of numbers the two sides were equally matched but in equipment, particularly armour and artillery guns, Pakistan had a tremendous advantage. Not only were they the latest models available but in numbers too they were superior to India. The Indian Army was still having to make do with Second World War vintage weaponry including .303 First World War rifles. The only modern weapon in the Indian Army's inventory were the Centurian tanks which equipped four-armoured regiments compared to the ten regiments of M-48 Patton tanks of the Pakistan Army.

The launch of OP Grand Slam left India with no choice but to extend the area of confilict across the international border. India's XI Corps crossed the border and advanced towards Lahore but the initial success and surprise was not fully exploited partly because we did not have the means to cross the Ichhogil Canal in strength and attention being diverted to the Ferozepur area where the Pakistan 1 Armoured Division had crossed the border and was poised to strike deep into Indian territory. This attempt was however foiled by a gallant defence put up by our Army which in spite of inferiority in numbers and quality of armaments annihilated the entire Pakistani Armoured Division at Khem Karan which came to be known as the Patton graveyard.

Our I Corps led by 1 Armoured Division crossed the border and moved towards Chawinda and Sialkot. This caught the Pakistani leadership by surprise and some initial gains were made but however they were not fully exploited because the infantry which was mounted on wheeled three ton trucks could not keep pace with the cross country movements of our tanks and secondly because some senior commanders were overly cautious which gave the Pakistanis time to bring in reinforcements. However the Pakistani armour was once again bested and some territorial gains were made.

Lack of modern weaponry was a severe limitation faced by Indian troops. We were outnumbered in tanks and artillery, both qualitatively and quantitatively. Overall the outcome of the war was in India's favour. All Pakistani plans were foiled and Ayub Khan was soon to lose his job for having failed to achieve his aims and the severe losses suffered by his army and air force.

On our side besides the lack of modern weaponry, we were severely handicapped by very poor if not total lack of intelligence of enemy plans and movements. This weakness still plagues us as was revealed in the Kargil War.

The Indian Air Force though equipped with the more modern Hawker Hunters, Mysteres and Gnats still had a large inventory of the 1940s vintage Vampires and Toofanis which were no match for the Pakistani F-86 Sabres and we lost many of them. However the Hunters and the Gnats performed very creditably and achieved a very good kill ratio as compared to the PAF. The Gnats in particular did a splendid job their small size and manoeuvrability made them more than a match for the F-86 Sabres and they came to be known as the Sabre Killers.

One part of the story of the IAF's action that has till today not been told is the use by the IAF of AN-12 transport aircraft for offensive missions over Pakistan during the war. These missions were led by Wing Commander Chandan Singh, the Air Force's man for all seasons. He had earlier received an AVSM and a VrC and was later to receive a MVC in 1971 making him the highest decorated officer in the Defence Forces.

The AN-12 is an unarmed and slow moving transport not designed for offensive use and was an easy target for Pakistani aircraft and anti-aircraft guns. However it had the advantage of range and ability to carry great loads. Chandan Singh exploited these qualities with devastating effect.

At the time these missions of the AN-12s were classified as Top Secret. Hence neither Chandan Singh nor any of his crew received any recognition or awards for these unprecedented and heroic actions.

Chandan Singh's insistence on the suitability of AN-12 transport aircraft for the IAF had already paid dividends during the 1962 war when they transported the AMX-13 tanks of 20 Lancers to Chushul and once again they proved their weight in gold in 1965. Their use as heavy bombers was something that even its manufacturers the Russians had not envisaged.

The IAF higher command realising their potential as bombers decided to assign this additional role to the AN-12 Squadrons to fill the gap in their bomber fleet. Chandan Singh was asked to train more pilots in the new role assigned for this aircraft. This training and reassignment of roles was put to devastating effect on the Pakistanis in the 1971 war in the Western Sector.

Several night bombing missions involving the dropping of hundreds of bombs over strategic targets were carried out by AN-12s including one on Sui Gas Plant and Skardu airfield. Although several aircraft were hit by anti air-craft fire not one was lost, proving once again the suitability and sturdiness of this aircraft.

The Years Between Two Wars

After the 1965 war, Chandan Singh was posted at Chandigarh when he received an offer from Biju Patnaik, the Chief Minister of Orissa and owner of Kalinga Airways to join his airline as Chief Operations Officer. As COO he would be based in Delhi. Biju was a qualified pilot and keen aviator himself and he knew Chandan Singh from his Charbatia days. It was a tempting offer made all the more attractive by the salary which would be several times more than what he got as an Air Force Officer which was not something to be scoffed at.

He was married and had two children to maintain. In the meantime, he received another offer this time from Air India to join as a pilot on its newly acquired Boing 707s. These were very tempting offers hard to resist. But the offers to join civil aviation were not the first he had received. Earlier he had been offered a job with the now defunct Khambata Airways which too at the insistence of his superior officers he declined.

The Air Force is oriented towards combat flying by fighter and bomber aircraft and primacy is given to the fighter pilots. The role of transport and helicopter wings are considered secondary to their main task of achieving air supremacy. Consequently the fighter and bomber pilots enjoy an advantage over the transport and helicopter pilots when it comes to promotion to higher ranks

Soon after the 1965 war, Chandan Singh was promoted to Group Captain and posted lo HQ Western Air Command as AIR2, a job which made him responsible for all transport aircraft in the Command. His friend Group Capt later Air Marshal M.M. Singh was Air 1 responsible for fighters. For a while he was officiating SASO and authorised himself with the permission of Air Marshal Shivdev Singh to fly Hunters, dual at Hindon and solo at Jamnagar. Flying a high performance jet was an exhilarating experience which he enjoyed very much but he did have a frightening moment when he thought he was lost and had to ask the ground controller indirectly to guide him back to base. Shivdev was of an adventurous type and he asked Chandan to fly across Rohtang Pass into Lahaul and Spiti Valley in an Aluette helicopter which tested the performance of the aircraft to its limits.

In 1968 Chandan Singh decided to quit the Air Force and accept one of the two assignments offered to him. So he put in his papers for release from the Air Force. When the papers landed on the desk of Air Chief Marshal Lal, he sent for Chandan Singh and told him that he had examined his record of service and it was outstanding and nothing could stop him from rising to the highest ranks of the service. The Air Chief refused flatly to release Chandan from the service telling him the Air Force needed him and that he had a most challenging job for him in mind, a job for which no one else was more suitable.

Chandan Singh was to go as Station Commander to Air Force Station Jorhat. Hitherto Jorhat was considered a punishment posting. It was a Second Word War air base not much changed from then but had a heavy load of flying of transport aircraft and helicopters in support of the Army and it also had a couple of flights of fighter-bombers.

But it was low in the priority of the Air Force and no resources had been released to upgrade the facilities. The earlier Station Commanders considering this as a punishment posting had always managed to move to greener pastures before completing even half of their regulation tenures as such had taken little or no action to improve either the operational or administrative facilities.

The Air Chief wanted Chandan to make Jorhat into a model Air Station which would be an example to the others. This was a challenge which Chandan could not resist and he withdrew his papers requesting release from the Air Force.

By now Chandan Singh was wanting to settle down and get married So he inserted an advertisement in the matrimonial column of the *Times of India* much in the manner Gen Sagat Singh had done earlier. It is surprising how close and parallel are the lives these greats of the 1971 and other wars. One of the first responses he got was from a family very close to the father of Jaswant Singh, former cabinet minister in Vajpayee's Government. Jaswant had been a cadet during Chandan's tenure at the NDA.

Jaswant's father, Major Sardar Singh of Jasol had been Chandan's squadron commander in Jodhpur Lancers. The proposal therefore had to be taken seriously. Chandan flew in an air force plane to Jodhpur and was met by the family of the proposed lady and Sardar Singh and Jaswant Singh. On seeing the lady, Chandan was taken aback, she was undoubtedly very pretty but she was only in her mid teens. Too young for him for he was nearing forty.

He walked out very unhappy with the turn of events. On the way to the air force station Jodhpur to fly back to Delhi Jaswant accompanied him in the jeep and asked him not to leave but Chandan would have none of it till Jaswant pulled out a photograph from his pocket and showed it to him. The photograph was of a lady who was the paternal aunt and cousin of Jaswant Singh's wife and twenty-six years of age. Chandan Singh accepted the proposal there and then and the marriage was fixed for a date a few months later.

However there was a problem, having lived the good life as a single person, Chandan was bankrupt and his friends had to pass the hat around among themselves to raise funds for the marriage.

At this point I would like to write more about Chandan's family in brief. His eldest sister was married to Thakur Bane Singhji, an ICS officer from Galthani village, near Sumerpur and elder sister married to the Thakur of Nanan near Pipar. His two younger brothers were themselves decorated officers.

Hari Singh joined the Royal Bodyguard later named Durga Horse and on merger with India joined the 2/9 Gorkha Rifles. An outstanding sportsman while in Chopasni School in which he participated in hockey, football, and athletics among others and was declared the best sportsman in the Jodhpur State Forces when he got commissioned.

Hari was very close to Shatian Singh (later Major and PVC) as not only were they classmates at school, but cadets together and both in Durga Horse, prior to the integration of the states. Hari was awarded AVSM, although he deserved a MVC, but such is the state of our bureaucracy. Apart from taking part in Sino-India war, he was active in anti-insurgency operations in the North East and was Army Instructor at the DSSC, Wellington, Nilgiris. Hari retired as Brigadier and Commander of the Meerut Sub Area.

Hari married Bindu Kanwar, granddaughter of the Rana of Amarkot (now in Pakistan). They have two sons, Kishan and Mahavir. Kishan joined Hari's regiment in the 2/9 GR. He served in the North East, Srinagar Valley, and deployed in what are flash points of Kargil, Leh and Siachin. In fact he served over twenty years in Kashmir at various appointments.

He married Sandhya Singh from Neri near Sitapur in UP and have a son and daughter. Hanut, their son, married Sneha Kumari Shekhawat and they have a son, Dhruv. Their daughter, Sunaina Kumari now works freelance for various prominent travel publications as well as a script writer in Mumbai.

Kishan was OIC PPO Pokhra, Nepal before returning

to command his battalion. He served as Instructor at the DSSC, Brigade Commander in Udaipur, BGS to the Corps Commander, Jodhpur, Deputy Military Secretary, New Delhi before and as GOC in Pune, from where he took premature retirement at the rank of Major General.

Kishan was awarded the AVSM and VSM, though he was recommended for a 'Chakra' but again the bureaucracy played up.

Mahavir joined the Taj Hotels after graduation from Rajasthan University where he excelled in cricket and if it hadn't been for an appendix operation a day before the selections, he would have been in the Indian cricket team. Apart from being a fine all rounder, he was proficient in tennis, squash, hockey, football and horse riding.

Staying loyal to the Taj Hotel group, he rose from Security Officer to Director Corporate Security and was in charge of security of every Taj hotel in the world. His response and actions during the terrorist attack in Mumbai earned him laurels from the government and industry.

Chandan's youngest brother, Mohan was like Hari, a student of Chopasni School and a good sportsman. Though his elder brothers were keen that he should join the Indian Navy, Mohan joined the Rajasthan police after graduation. He was awarded the President of India's Medal for Gallantry and Indian Police Medal for outstanding service.

Mohan was more of a spiritualist and kept away from the evils of what ails the police these days. He was married to Krishna Kumari Shekhawat from Jaipur and though he served in various capacities in Jaipur, Hanumangarh, Bikaner, Jodhpur and Jaisalmer, it was Jaipur where he was most comfortable. He, not conforming to the 'buttering' and flattering of senior officers remained at the rank of Superintendent of Police (SP) in the CID.

Mohan and his wife joined the sect known as 'Dadu panthi' and devoted their lives to the service of this sect. Not blessed with children, they lived in Vaishali Nagar, Jaipur after retirement. Sadly neither are alive today.

Regarding Chandan's own family, he married Junu Kumari, daughter and youngest child of Raja Bhom Singh of Umaidnagar, in 1963 in Jodhpur. They had two children, Sajjan and daughter Namrata.

Namrata completed her schooling from St. Patrick in Jodhpur after having studied at various schools where ever Chandan was posted. An undergraduate at the time of marriage, she did her graduation after marriage with a degree in Sociology. She is married to the current Rawat of Deogarh, Veerbhadra Singh.

They have a son, Mayurdhwaj and daughter Pavitra. The family runs an 80-room heritage hotel, a converted fort, in their village of Deogarh near Udaipur. Mayurdhwaj runs a quartz grinding factory, a petrol pump, looks after his farms and is married to Kritika Kumari from Vijaynagar, Gujarat. Pavitra has her own high-end fashion label venture.

Sajjan completed his schooling from KV AF, Jodhpur after having studied at various schools in Assam, Delhi, London and Allahabad (now Prayagraj). A graduate of English Literature from Jodhpur University (now unfortunately called Jai Narayan Vyas Vishwavidyalaya), Sajjan joined his father in the limestone and lime business, which they ran for over 32 years before the failing health of parents and worldwide slow down resulted in their selling the business.

Sajjan was a keen sportsman, who played squash at the national university level, followed tennis, horse riding, hockey and football. He was appointed as Squash Secretary, Additional Honorary Secretary, Honorary Club Secretary and finally Honorary Secretary of the Sardar Club Trust.

Sajjan married Mumal Kanwar, daughter of Thakur Ranvijay Singh, from Sohangarh Punjab, in 1988 and they have two sons. Harshveer, the elder son joined the Indian Army and at present is a Captain in the Infantry, whereas the younger son, Divyveer joined the Taj Hotels in Mumbai and is currently posted in Udaipur as Duty Manager. Both sons are alumni of Mayo College Ajmer.

9
Liberation of Bangladesh

"The moment the creative warmth of Pakistan cools down contradictions will emerge and acquire assertive overtones. These will be fuelled by clash of interests....and consequently both wings will separate within twenty-five years...and West Pakistan will become a battleground of International Powers."
— Maulana Abul Kalam Azad

"Of the events of the war, I have not ventured to speak from any chance information, nor according to any notion of my own. I have described nothing but what I saw myself, or learned from others of whom I made the most careful and particular inquiry."
—Thucydides, *History of the Peloponnesian War,* 413 BC

Background to the War

Prophetic words indeed by Maulana Azad, one of India's greatest men, his prophecy came true almost to the day, exactly as he foretold. The genesis of the breakup of Pakistan lay in the very principles of its creation. When after the Second World War Britain realised that it could no longer hold on to India and an independent India blessed with a large area, rich in agricultural and mineral resources and a population, next in numbers only to that of China, and this population having a great sense of civilisational identity, an educated elite and an entrepreneurial class equal to any in the world, would within a decade or two emerge as a super power equal to and a rival of the other great powers.

Japan under the Great Emperor Meiji had already proved how a country with medieval institutions and stage of development could transform itself into a rich and powerful nation in only two decades and with China likely to follow suit, European hegemony would be challenged.

From the port of Gwadar, India would control access to the Persian Gulf and the Humroz Straits through which most of the trade in petroleum products passed. Britain which like other Western European nations was entirely dependent on petroleum products from the Middle East, did not want India to control their lifeline. Sir Olaf Caroe, the former Governor of the North West Frontier Province, wrote to the British Government that the solution to the problem of safeguarding British interests lay in splitting India into two countries divided by religion. A weak Pakistan would emerge and it would always be dependent on the Western Powers for its survival and Indian frontiers would be shifted almost a thousand kilometres away from the choke point of Humroz.

Maharajah Narendra Singh of Sarila, a kinsman of mine and India's former ambassador to France, after researching from the recently declassified secret cabinet papers at Whitehall has discussed this in his book *Partition of India*. Besides having accessed the secret British Cabinet papers, Sarila was also in the know of behind-the-scenes manoeuvring going on in the higher echelons of the British government because during Mountbatten's tenure as Viceroy and later as Governor General of India, Sarila was his ADC.

Pakistan, a state divided in two by several thousand kilometres of Indian territory with the people in the eastern wing having nothing in common with the western part was a doomed state from the day of its inception.

Having been created with weak foundational principles the ruling military, political and civilian elites of Pakistan who were all almost entirely from the western wing treated the east as a colony to be exploited, its resources extracted for the benefit of the west and to make matters worse, the people from the eastern wing who were highly civilised and cultured were despised as a lazy dark-skinned race possessing no martial traits and who could always be depended upon to serve their masters in the west.

How wrong they were. In less than two weeks more than a hundred thousand strong Pakistani Army supported by even a larger number of para-military troops and with all the American political and war materiel support surrendered abjectly to the non-martial freedom fighters of Bangladesh and the equally non-martial Army of Hindu India.

When the final break up occurred instead of serious introspection the Pakistanis put the blame on India and till today create a psychosis of hatred for India among their populace from which come most of the Jihadis of the world. This sense of grievance and lamentation is a trait shared by Pakistanis with people subscribing to cultures and religions that have emerged from the harsh climatic and geographic landscape of the Arabian desert and who live in the lands extending from Pakistan right up to the eastern coast of the Mediterranean and extending even further to include Northern Africa.

Perhaps it has something to do with the very nature of a belief in a monotheistic God who excludes all else, this exclusiveness leads to hatred of the other. This is a self-destructive emotional condition bordering on the psychotic for the other can even mean others in your own family, village, tribe, town, social and religious groups and to other nations leaving no one out but one's own self.

The Shia-Sunni divide and the Roman Catholic-Protestant wars are examples. This state of heart and mind puts themselves and their countries into perpetual turmoil and mutual bloodletting. The world would not be concerned about it but for the fact but they have exported their irrational behaviour to other countries making Jihad into a global phenomenon.

The sad fact is that even today when East Pakistan is history and a prosperous and progressive Bangladesh has emerged in its place the Pakistani establishment continues to be in an extractive mindset and selfish elites led by the military extract the cream from the resources of their own nation and people for their own selfish purposes leaving the average citizen disillusioned and poverty-stricken, a fertile breeding ground for Jihadi terror groups and suicide bombers who as youth have been brainwashed in madrasas financed by equally selfish but wealthy Saudi princes. Some other Arab groups who thanks to the boom in oil prices have overnight become rich within one generation, a typical rags-to-riches story.

Their Porsches and Patek Phillipe watches are an attempt to put a veneer of sophistication over their barbaric inner selves. To those of you who may think that my language is intemperate and unduly harsh all that I ask is please look at the photographs of the atrocities inflicted on the Bengalis by the Pakistan army. I, like many of my colleagues, were witnesses to it. We will neither forget nor forgive.

In order to justify their own failures the Pakistani establishment led by the military would have their people believe that we were responsible for their troubles in East Pakistan. Nothing could be further from the truth and I should know for I was posted for two years prior to 1971 close to the border of East Pakistan and when the trouble started in March 1971, we were caught completely unawares. Even our intelligence agencies knew nothing and when we asked them for information, we found that they were as, if not more ignorant than us.

If we had a hand in fermenting trouble in East Pakistan, surely we and our intelligence agencies would have known, this lack of intelligence would plague us even later when the refugees first started pouring in and we had neither plans nor means to handle them and had to build and improvise from scratch. It is only later when the huge influx of refugees became an unbearable burden and confirmed evidence of genocide and atrocities started pouring in that we started providing covert help to the freedom fighters.

But lest the Pakistanis start using what I have written here as proof that it was India that began the war we did not actively intervene till they began to shell Agartala in November. Agartala is no ordinary border town, it the capital of the Indian State of Tripura. Nor should Pakistan ever forget the overt and covert role they played in starting and sustaining the rebellion in Nagaland and Mizo Hills. I had myself taken part in operations in which we recovered irrefutable proof of their role and General Sagat Singh's account of this crossing and subsequent events also mentions and confirms this.

In writing this chapter which covers the Bangladesh Liberation War 1971, I have been fortunate to have in my possession the audio tape recording of 1974 vintage of the Air Marshal's own account of the events. So for the greater part, I am writing this chapter in the first person as recounted by the Air Marshal himself. His account is corroborated by similar accounts by Gen Himmeth Singh and Gen Sagat Singh and interviews and of Group Captain Sandhu and Air Commodores Singla and Shridharan.

Then Squadron Leader C.S. Sandhu was the Squadron Commander of 110 Helicopter Squadron which along with a detachment from 105 HU gave Gen Sagat Singh the tools to overcome all riverine obstacles and capture Dacca, a task that was neither visualised nor planned for by Army Headquarters. I too was a part of the heliborne operation on December 9, 1971 that got us across the Meghna River. My Commanding Officer, Colonel Himmeth Singh and I were in the leading helicopter that was piloted by Sandhu. Sitting on the floor of the hold like the rest of us but at the far end towards the cockpit was the then Group Captain Chandan Singh.

In between were crammed about fifteen of my men. Colonel Himmeth Singh and I sat on the open side of the hold as the doors had been removed to facilitate quick boarding and exit. One had to hold on for dear life to whatever one could for there was nothing between us and the ground below, the vibration and the blast of wind from the rotors making the whole thing more dramatic. But the view was grand and the sight of the mighty Meghna River below us was awesome.

Soon we were joined by two Gnat fighters flying protective cover. The scene resembled a Hollywood war movie. The only thing different was that this was the real stuff and instead of John Wayne accompanied by a saucy news reporter in hot pants it was just us, dirty, scruffy and very un-hero like.

A broad stretch of the river almost sixteen kilometres wide was selected for the crossing for this was precisely the place where the Pakistanis would least imagine or expect us to cross. Logically it was an impossible task for a conventional commander to even contemplate but Sagat Singh and Chandan Singh were neither conventional nor ordinary commanders.

The only exchange that I had with the Air Marshal during this bone rattling ride was a salute and a 'good afternoon Sir', the normal service greeting. At that time I did not even know his name nor who he was except that he was a senior Air Force officer which fact was obvious from the broad band of stripes on his shoulders.

It is this operation visualised by Gen Sagat Singh and executed by Chandan Singh's and Sandhu's pilots and my Unit 4 Guards which got us across the sixteen kilometres wide Meghna River, a task that was considered impossible by both the Pakistan army and Indian Army Headquarters. The helicopters placed us deep in enemy territory and behind his fortified positions cutting them off from Dacca and making a mockery of his tactics of defence based on the fortresses concept.

We now had a clear run to Dacca with virtually no opposition and this created such a panic in the Pakistani Headquarters that barely twelve hours later on 10th December after the culmination of our operation which had started at 4 pm on 9th December they approached the United Nations representative in Dacca and sued for a ceasefire. Sagat had skilfully ensured that the enemy, particularly their senior commanders with their HQ and major part of their forces were bottled up in three or four towns out of touch with each other and Dacca, with no hopes of relief or reinforcement.

The rest of the country was ours and we had a free run. As a participant in this operation and other operations in the theatre, I not only have firsthand knowledge of the events but also know all the principal players at a personal level and have video/audio recorded their accounts. But in order not to interrupt the Air Marshal's personal narrative, I have included some of these accounts which I feel are relevant to his story as separate accounts. These accounts not only corroborate the Air Marshal's account but also bring in different and fresh perspectives. These accounts are also of importance for future historians and scholars. Each of these accounts though related to all the others stand on their own and complete stories.

Air Vice Marshal Chandan Singh's Account

"In 1969 I was posted as Commander of the IAF Station Jorhat which was a relative backwater for the IAF where all the glamour and pride of place was given to the fighter and bomber bases. But nonetheless, Jorhat was one of the most important logistics bases as far the Indian Army was concerned. Jorhat had two transport squadrons of the Second World War vintage Dakotas, a flight of MI-4 helicopters and a detachment of Hunters and Gnats.

The transport squadrons provided logistics support to the far flung Army posts in the North East States along the China and Burma Borders and also to the formations deployed in counterinsurgency role in Nagaland, Manipur and Mizo Hills, the helicopters provided communication support and casualty evacuation facility to the isolated Army Posts which in many cases were several days march on foot from the nearest road head and the only way of maintenance was by para dropping of supplies including rations."

"As there was neither electricity nor refrigeration facilities at these remote posts it was a common sight to see a dozen or so sheep and goats (in service terminology MOH which was the official army term for meat on hoof, i.e. live sheep or goats) crammed tightly into a wooden crate and fastened to a parachute and loaded into the Dakotas for dropping over the posts. Many of the animals would be injured and nearly all that were dropped in high altitude areas would become blind, for some reason probably low atmospheric air pressure.

Before the animal rights activists led by Maneka Gandhi start howling in protest it must be remembered that our men at these posts had no availability of fresh vegetables nor dairy products for months on end and had to subsist on wheat flour, rice, dal, potatoes and onions and so MOH and rum were not luxuries but essential survival rations. The jawans at these posts had a wonderful racket going. They would declare some drops of rum, sugar and MOH as lost, damaged or un-retrievable and so claim replacement drops. Small mercies, for all the senior commanders knew what was going on but chose to ignore the situation for they too had done the same when they were young post commanders."

"Jorhat is located on the southern bank of the Brahmaputra in north east Assam. It is in the middle of the tea country where the finest teas are grown. The true connoisseurs prefer Assam Tea to that from Darjeeling for its full body and rich taste. The tea planters' clubs where we were all honorary members provided a welcome social diversion.

The airfield was one of the several dozen built by the British and Americans during the Second World War to support their operations against the Japanese in Burma and also as bases for transport aircraft which flew over the Hump carrying supplies for the Chinese for their war effort against the same enemy. It is from these bases that the Chindits and Merrils Mauraders which operated behind enemy lines were supported. The people of the plains are mainly Assamese, an Indo-Mongol race. But the remote valleys and hills are peopled by diverse tribal people of different racial and linguistic groups. Some of these tribes in the remote areas still live in Stone Age conditions.

Having several helicopters under my command, I visited their settlements as often as I could because for one it was a way of showing the Indian flag plus their lives and customs fascinated me. No other part of the world has such an anthropological, floral and faunal diversity crammed inside a relatively small geographical area."

"My immediate problem was of another kind. Assam is a

high rainfall area and tall grass and scrub would grow faster than our limited funds allowed for its manual cutting. This was extremely hazardous to aircraft operations because it attracted many birds and bird hits had become a menace and posed great danger to the jet engine Hunters and Gnats. The low lying areas were filled with water and a breeding ground for mosquitoes which affected the health of the airmen and their families. So looking for a solution, I converted the low ground areas into fish ponds and stocked them with carp and a species of fish which fed on mosquito larvae would bring this menace to an end. For reducing the menace of bird hits and fire hazards, I found out that if we replaced the existing grasses with Citronella grass which the birds avoided, we could solve both problems and also earn some money for welfare measures for the station.

We managed to procure some seeds and planted them adjacent to the runway and then went around the tea gardens looking for a disused boiler and other equipment. This too we found and had our workshop repair and install it in a disused shed.

We were soon making money by selling citronella oil, our first batch got us Rs. 52,000 for the station. Encouraged by this, we started a dairy, a piggery, and a fish tank. I was fortunate to have with me Fl Lt Jai Singh from Kota whose father Gopal Singh was a farmer and well known horticulturist. So I made him the first officer in charge.

Jai Singh was also a graduate from an agriculture college and this helped in getting the project off the ground. Jai Singh's successor was another famous and maverick pilot Flt Lt Unni Kartha who acquired the nickname chief pigman after a P.G. Wodehouse character in his Blandings Castle novels. Unni like all Wodehouse characters has the ability to keep his audience in splits of laughter. This name followed Unni even later in his career. When I relinquished command at Jorhat, the station had a welfare fund amounting to Rs. 1 lakh. A huge sum in those days which we used to make the living conditions of the airmen somewhat better."

"When the trouble in East Pakistan started, I had no role, firstly because Jorhat is some distance away from Bangladesh and secondly no task had been given to the IAF as yet. Events had moved so fast from 25th March onwards the day on which Sheikh Mujibur Rehman was arrested and Major Zia ur Rehman announced the declaration of independence on Radio Chittagong that the Government of India and the Service Headquarters were taken completely by surprise and were slow to react."

"No contingency plans had been made to cater to face such a situation, a problem that persists with our establishment even today. We are always reactive rather than proactive and hence lose the opportunity to exercise our options at the correct time. Sometime in July 1971 I was detailed by Air Officer Commanding in Chief Eastern Air Command Air Marshal Devan HQ at Shillong to take charge of the training of about a dozen Bengali pilots and a hundred airmen who had defected from the Pakistani Air Force and come over to our side, and create a nucleus for the future Bangladesh Air Force.

The aim was to build up to at least a squadron strength but sufficient pilots and aircraft were not available. I was given two Otter passenger aircraft and one Alouette helicopter for training and to make them operational eventually on Hunters. But this was a long-term task and at that time we found the pilots and the airmen under qualified. I started with training the pilots on Otters in night time ultra low level flying. I had a satellite field at Dimapur where I moved the Bengali pilots and airmen for here I could train them without interruption of our regular operations at Jorhat."

"Anticipating that with the aircraft provided we could only operate at night against the enemy, I started them on low level night time flying training. This type of flying is called horizon flying and is both difficult and hazardous. I had trained on this type of flying with the CIA in 1963 and was the only such qualified pilot in the IAF. This training paid great dividends when the war broke out in December. The

Bengali pilots performed magnificently.

The aircrafts were modified and fitted with two chutes to drop 25 pound bombs and two rocket pods each carrying 14 rockets, in addition a light machine gun was mounted in the cockpit behind the pilot. The training was done at my satellite airfield at Dimapur. Within one month we trained five pilots to fly solo in all roles of bombing and rocketing at night. The enthusiasm of the pilots and ground crew was remarkable and they learnt quickly."

"This was fortunate for at the end of November the AOC in C asked me to move with my small Bangladesh Air Force to Kumbhigram and launch operations against Pakistani troops even before the war started. Kumbhigram is in the Cachar District in South Assam bordering Bangladesh."

"We arrived at Kubhigram on the morning of 2nd December and there learnt that IV Corps in retaliation of shelling of Agartala, the capital of Tripura by the Pakistani army had launched offensive operations in East Pakistan and heavy fighting was going on over the entire Corps frontage of more than five hundred kilometres all along the borders of Meghalaya, Cachars, Tripura, Mizo Hills and some parts of Burma.

The same day I was ordered to launch bombing raids on the fuel storage tanks at Chittagong and Narayanganj. We were prepared to go but at the last moment our operation was postponed by twenty-four hours." (This postponement of some operations by the army and air force is interesting, did we have information that Pakistan would be launching its pre-emptive strikes at night on 3-4 December, so by delaying our own main offensive, Pakistan would be held responsible for starting the war.)

"On 3rd Decemeber night under a brilliant moon the first sorties took off, the Alueotte piloted by Flying Officer Alam to Narayanganj and one Otter piloted by Sqn Ldr Sultan to Chittagong. An hour and a half later, I took off in the other Otter and flew towards Chittagong where I saw a bright glow on the horizon towards the harbour which indicated that Sultan had been successful in his mission. I then turned northwest towards Dacca and saw another glow coming from the vicinity of Narayanganj, confirming that Alam in his little Alueotte too had accomplished his mission."

"In the overall plan our contribution may have been small but it did a whale of good to the morale of the Bengalis and had a very negative effect on the Pakistanis for it brought the war deep into East Pakistan and conveyed to the Pakistanis that the gloves were off and there was to be no turning back.

Later in the morning, I was told that the Pakistan Air Force had launched pre-emptive strikes on some of our airfields on the Western Front. These however did little or no damage as we had dispersed our aircraft in bomb proof bays, having learnt our lessons from the dramatic Israeli air attack on Egypt in 1966 when they destroyed the entire Egyptian Air Force on the ground in one morning. The Egyptian Air Force aircraft were lined up on the airfields as if on an inspection parade.

Before proceeding further, I would like to mention the gallantry and enthusiasm of the Bangladeshi pilots Sultan, Alam and Ali. They continued with their bombing and strafing runs throughout the war in support of IV Corps actions with whose actions I now got involved."

Operations with Gen Sagat Singh's IV Corps

On the 3rd morning I was to go to Tiliamura, the HQ of IV Corps and meet Gen Sagat Singh. I arrived there that afternoon but couldn't meet him as he was out visiting troops as nearly all the formations in his command had gone on the offensive on the entire five hundred kilometre frontage. I met him later that evening when he arrived and stayed the night; it was quite an experience. He was full of energy, dynamism and go; over several large whiskies he talked about his Corps current operations and future plans.

He then asked me as to what our little Bangladesh Air Force could do. As a starter he said we must leave Kumbhigram and move closer to any one of the border airstrips available— Kailashaher, Kamalpur or Khowai. I selected Kailashehar as that was where the action was. He asked me about target transport movement, lines of communication and troop concentrations and if possible destroy a bridge or two. He didn't have much time so I couldn't discuss details with him and in any case I didn't have much of an air force to be of much use to him.

I arrived at Kelashahar with my little Bangladesh Air Force on the morning of 4th December and mounted a total of thirty-six sorties on 4, 5 and 6 December, mostly disrupting the lines of communications between Munshibazaar—Fenchigunj and Brahamanbaria. I am not sure of the success we had with these three aircraft, but on the sorties I was on we did attack road transport and convoys.

On my sorties with Flt Lt Singhla and Flt Lt Sultan BAF we managed to hit three troop transports. My log confirms two transports totally destroyed, in the other missions it states targets hit but results not known. I am sure the sorties would have had similar results.

On the 5th evening I was told over the radio telephone by Gen Sagat Singh that I was to call on Gen Krishnarao, General Officer Commanding 8 Div and inquire if I could be of help in his operations. I called on him on the 6th morning. That particular day a battle had been raging at Alinagar tea estate near Shamshernagar airfield in East Pakistan.

I had been observing the progress of the battle from Kelashahar and when the guns fell silent I got airborne and landed at Shamshernagar. I had thought of using the Shamshernagar airfield to move further forward, but found that the airstrip had been so badly cratered by our shelling that it was unsuitable even for helicopters. There were craters even in the parking area.

Nevertheless we landed there and commandeering an Army jeep I asked the driver to take me to the Division Headquarter. I noticed several bunkers and trenches damaged by our fire.

The HQ was in the centre of the tea estate and in a clearing was parked the Division Commander's caravan in which he stayed and also had his office and next to it was an open ground where a helicopter could land. I called on the Div Comdr and before we could start a conversation, we heard a helicopter landing and saw Gen Sagat Singh emerge. He had a half hour discussion with the Div Comdr and then I was called in and told to act as the eyes and ears of the Division Commander. I was also told that some more MI-4 helicopters were arriving and I was to take charge of them.

Somewhat later the same morning, he called me again and said that he had received information that the enemy at Sylhit was wanting to surrender and since our ground forces were not close enough, I was to fly to Sylhit and accept the surrender and bring him the Instrument of Surrender. It was a great moment and an honour and I was thrilled that he had chosen me for this task.

On the 7th morning I got airborne and went towards Sylhit where I saw a dead town with not a soul stirring in the open. I did two orbits around the town and then flew to Sylhit airport expecting the Pakistanis to be lined up awaiting to surrender, but saw no one. I had half a mind to return but then against my instincts and better judgement decided to land thinking that the enemy troops were hiding under cover and would emerge once they saw the helicopter land.

I was just about to touch down when I heard the rattle of machine guns from all directions and bullets striking the fuselage of the helicopter. This time I followed my instinct. I came up on the collective, opened throttle and got away flying low level between the trees and out of range of enemy fire.

I did not know the extent of damage but managed to climb up to 4,000 ft to see what was happening. Once again there was no movement and I had half a mind to try and land again but better sense prevailed and I returned to Shamshernagar and drove straight to Div HQ and sure enough Gen Sagat Singh was there and so I told him—'Sir I have gone to Sylhit but there was no reception party waiting to surrender and instead my helicopter is perforated with bullet holes.'

Gen Sagat Singh did not bat an eyelid, it made no difference to him to him whether I was hit or not. He said 'in that case we should launch a heliborne operation against Sylhit.' He didn't express any sympathy or even apologise that the information about the garrison wanting to surrender was incorrect. Such was the man, he had only the mission in mind regardless of all else.

He told me, 'now that you are with us, you stay with us', and also informed me that at this very moment 110 Helicopter Squadron under Sqn Ldr Sandhu was landing at Kelashahar and I was to take charge of them. He said that by 1200 hours this very day, i.e. 7th December I was to go to Kalora and pick up Brig Quinn (Bunty) Commander of the Brigade and go to Sylhit and select a landing place for the helicopters, then use the newly arrived helicopters to launch the operation.

Sylhit Operation

As ordered, I went over to Brig Quinn, whose troops had just come out of the Battle of Ghazipur, a few kilometres from Kalora. Kalora is a small railway station with a couple of sheds, a school building and some barrack like structures. One of Bunty Quinn's battalions 4/5 Gurkha Rifles was resting in the buildings after having suffered heavy casualties at the battle of Ghazipur.

When I went to meet the Commanding Officer of the Battalion he said that all his officers were casualties and there was only himself and one other officer who were fit to carry on with the operation. I understood that what he was wanting to convey was that his unit could not undertake this operation immediately. I told the Brigade commander that I didn't know whether he had received these orders as yet but my orders from the Corps Commander and the Division Commander were explicit.

These were that I must start mounting the heliborne operation with our troops on board at 1200 hours and that the operation must be completed by sunset. So time was of the essence, and whatever troops they had were to be reorganised quickly as this was a new operation which had to be completed before sunset. Bunty Quinn also stated that it would be very difficult for these troops to undertake an operation of this type immediately, so I had to tell him that if this was the case he should contact his Division and Corps Commanders and inform them accordingly and I would stand down the helicopter pilots. Bunty then decided that 4/5 GR were to go in irrespective of the state they were in. Sagat had a formidable reputation of being a go-getter in peace and war and his junior formation commanders some of whom were unsure of their own competence in war were hesitant to approach him and put their views across.

The Gurkhas had never ever been inside a helicopter, most had not even seen one at close quarters. So their apprehension was quite understandable and then there was the fact that they had been badly mauled in the preceding battle and pulled back just this morning. I too after my experience at Sylhit in the morning wasn't expecting things to be easy. On the recce, Bunty and I had selected a position for our landing ground between the River Surma and Sylhit town close to the rail and road bridge over the Surma River. The capture of the bridge intact would facilitate the advance overland of our forces to Sylhit.

I came back to Kelashahar Airfield to get acquainted with the newly arrived helicopter crews. I had no idea who they were or which unit they belonged to. So I called them together for a chitchat, certain names stand out in my memory. One was Sqn Ldr Sandhu, a very courageous young man and his two very bright and enthusiastic flight commanders, Flt Lt Vaid and Flt Lt Jayraman.

All three of them were fully operational pilots with lots of flying experience and were raring to go. The helicopters too were in a very good state and they were hoping to start operations as soon as possible. I told them that I had good news for them, they had to be ready to undertake an operation immediately. They were to lift a battalion and put it behind enemy lines near Sylhit and that they should brief their pilots and get them ready. Pre-flight briefings, aircraft inspection, operational checks, etc. were all carried out.

By 11.30 hours I had 5 MI-4 helicopters with me all capable of carrying twenty fully armed troops and we landed in the paddy fields in Kalora near the 4/5 GR location to commence the operation.

I must digress and inform you of certain limitations that helicopters suffer from. During peacetime the helicopters must be launched from well prepared helipads and must land on similar ground. The reasons are not that they require a pucca hardened tarmac or concrete runway but the dust that the downward thrust of rotors kicks up is a great flying hazard at the time of landing. It may well lead to the helicopter crashing while it lands as the pilot is blinded by the dust.

This worried me a great deal as the ground at this time in most parts of East Pakistan had gone dry and dusty. The day time was all right but what of flying at night, this was uppermost in my mind. In war there is no time to prepare a helipad so I decided to take the risk and land in the paddy fields. Fortunately the paddy had been harvested only a few days earlier so the ground was still slightly moist but not boggy and the dust was manageable. It was hard enough for several sorties to land without roughing and gorging the surface too much.

On landing we went to see the Commanding Officer of 4/5 GR. He was having a hard time organising his troops who were now without most of their officers as they had become casualties in the last few days. Instilling enthusiasm for a new operation was an almost impossible task. Brig Bunty Quinn, the CO and I discussed the time frame of the operation and we decided that the takeoff time for the first sortie would be 1500 hours.

Before that we rehearsed the troops in getting in and out of the helicopters with the main and tail rotors running. The troops had to be warned to avoid running into the spinning tail rotors. The rear hold doors of the choppers had been removed to facilitate quick entry and exit and also to reduce weight. But as the take off time approached there was no sign of the troops. I again went over to the barracks where the troops were housed and contacted the authorities. The men were getting ready but without officer supervision this was not an easy task and not going as per plan. I mentioned this to Bunty who then took charge of the battalion and gave them a pep talk, telling them that there was no cause for worry and that he himself would be participating in the operation and was keeping a battalion in reserve ready to help them out if needed.

I had worked out the time frame for the operation, the time it would take from Kalora to Sylhit, turn round at Sylhit, Sylhit to Kalora and turn round at Kalora. It would not be possible to launch more than two waves before sunset. This caused me great concern. I did not want to participate in an operation where only a part of the battalion could be lifted. I was also not sure of the night operational capability of the new pilots.

But I had no choice and besides my fears about the pilots, night flying ability was partly misplaced as at this stage. I was not aware that Sandhu had been preparing his flight commanders and some of his boys for such an operation right from the moment he and his squadron had arrived in the Corps Theatre in September and Gen Sagat Singh had warned him to be ready for such an eventuality. (Note Sandhu's account to the author of meeting with Sagat on 19th September and requirement to keep this info to himself).

The first wave was launched at 1400 hours. All five MI-4 helicopters, I was in one of them, landing without any opposition at our predetermined landing ground. We came back and picked up the second lot of troops and went back and landed them. As we were airborne after this second wave, I heard the rattle of machine guns. I saw the helicopter to the left of me getting grounded and unable to lift off. I didn't know the reason why, so I enquired on the radio and was told by the pilot that his helicopter had been hit.

I instructed the remaining helicopters to fly back to Kalora, and on landing there found that three other helicopters had bullet holes but these did not affect their serviceability. However it was getting dark and I decided to take just one more wave. I also decided to take two armed helicopters to provide suppressing fire if needed. When the second wave landed not a shot was fired. I visualised that the Gurkhas had fanned out and cleared the enemy from the area.

The armed helicopters had gone in a few minutes before us and were hovering overhead ready to launch their weapons should the enemy rear his head again. But the enemy did not oblige and the third wave had no problems at all during ingress or exit from the landing ground. When we landed back at Kalora it was pitch dark and I decided to halt further operations and do some stocktaking.

All the helicopters had landed an hour after dark and I along with Sandhu, Jayraman and Vaid had a good look at the helicopters. Though most of them had been hit they were in good flying condition. We asked the engineers to go through pre-flight and post flight inspections. In the meantime the fifth helicopter that we had left behind after the second wave rejoined us after some on site field repairs to the rotor and fuel tank.

I asked the Tech Officer to inspect this helicopter in the greatest possible details and make it serviceable for night operations. At 2000 hours we collected all the pilots of the MI-4 Sqn and the Bangladeshi pilots and discussed what we should do for the rest of the night.

I found that some of the pilots were not night qualified so Sandhu and I decided to train these pilots immediately on the spot. We practised these pilots on night take off, landing and flying till we were confident of their ability to do so. By 2200 hours we had seven pilots on the MI-4 and three on Alueottes ready for night operations.

This being accomplished, I had a moment of respite and time to contemplate our present and future actions, and it suddenly struck me that all that we had done and planned to do had no formal clearance from the Air Force authorities. Moreover I had no business lording over the operation, Sqn

Ldr Sandhu as the Squadron Commander was the rightful person to carry out the operation. So I decided to check back with HQ Eastern Air Command as soon as possible. The second factor was that there were no proper night landing and takeoff facilities at Sylhit and Kalora and even at Kelashahar where we were now.

There had to be minimum aids for making the landings safe. On the other hand, if I was to use these aids it would be a clear target for the enemy in the vicinity. We discussed these issues and I decided that we would light up at the paddy fields at Kalora and have unidirectional GLIM lamps at Sylhit. I detailed Sqn Ldr Chowdhry of the Dakota Group at Kelashahar to be responsible for the ground facilities at Sylhit.

The plan was for the Bangladesh pilots to provide a protective umbrella with the armed Otters, a difficult task but still good deterrence. The plan was carried out this time with six MI-4 helicopters as another one had joined us from Mizo Hills. I was in one of the Alueottes with Singhla flying protective air cover. We had a grand time firing rockets and machine guns at Pakistani machine gun positions which were revealed by the trajectory of the tracer rounds fired by their machine guns.

I do not know how much damage we did but as the night progressed the firing became less intensive. Singhla and the Bangladesh pilots flew all night returning only to refuel and rearm.

Initially I had flown protective air cover but later did two sorties on the MI-4s. All was going well and I was keeping abreast of the happenings on the radio, but at 0300 hours one of the MI-4s was badly hit and grounded at Sylhit. I told the pilot not to attempt to recoup the helicopter, but to stay with the ground troops and we would evacuate him in the morning. One more aircraft force landed en route, possibly due to bad servicing or sheer engine fatigue or enemy action. So now out of six MI-4 we had only four left."

"It was only in the morning that I could have a look at our machines which we collected at Kelashahar for servicing and regrouping. I then took an armed Alueotte to look at the two grounded helicopters. The one that landed en route had engine trouble but could be repaired in situ and noted the spare parts required and told the crew to stay on. The other helicopter was badly damaged and it was not possible to repair it immediately as the Gurkhas were still engaged with the enemy less than half a kilometre away. So we had to abandon it for the time being. The other one we had repaired and retrieved in a few hours followed soon afterwards by the one at Sylhit."

"The Heliborne operation carried on during the day and we were now flying in the reinforcement battalion. In the meantime, I received a note from Gen Sagat Singh congratulating us on the success of the operation and urging us to continue. The man once having got the enemy by the throat was not going to let him go. By now though exhausted, we had a sense of satisfaction at a mission well done.

Our air effort Sylhit around was now augmented with MIG-21s from Tezpur, while the rest of the IAF having achieved complete mastery of the skies over East Pakistan the MIGs, Hunters, Canberras and Gnats were hammering away at the enemy's positions and lines of communication, and I with my Bangladesh Air Force was having a field day bombing and strafing enemy convoys moving from Maulvi Bazaar and other places to reinforce Sylhit. They had to abandon their vehicles and start moving in total disarray on foot becoming easy picking for the now emboldened Mukti Bahini boys and our own advancing troops".

"So fast was the advance of our ground troops that information on their advance and locations could not reach the Joint Operations Rooms in time and our planes working by predetermined bomb lines sometimes strafed our own forces. On 12th December the leading battalion 4 Guards was strafed and in spite of Flying Officer D.S. Shaheed who was the Forward Air Controller with the battalion contacting the pilot on the radio and informing him of the mistake, the pilot could not believe that we were so far forward and that it was the Pakistanis who had broken into our radio frequency and speaking to him.

Fortunately Shaheed was able to convince the pilot soon and further strikes were called off. This lack of coordination between the higher commands of the three services was to have tragic consequences when some civilian boats commandeered by our forces and manned by the Mukti Bahini for operations against the Pakistanis were strafed by Sea Hawks flying from INS Vikrant and planes of the IAF.

Several lives were lost because HQ Eastern Command did not or could not coordinate the operations with the other services. The excuse that operational situation was fluid and fast changing is not acceptable. Senior Commanders of all the three services and their staff should always be located in one place and be in constant touch with each other 24X7".

"By the end of the day, i.e. 8th December when this mission had been completed our small band of six MI-4s, two Otters and one Alueotte had carried out twenty-two sorties on 7th December, thirty-four sorties on night 7/8 December and ten sorties on day 8th December. Considering the fact that two or three aircraft were always out of commission at any one time it meant that each aircraft had carried out twelve sorties on an average, a tremendous achievement. We carried twelve hundred troops and ten tons of stores and equipment in about twenty-four hours of non- stop flying enabling the army to achieve its objectives".

"The helicopters encountered heavy small arms fire during the operations and all helicopters had the fuselages punctured like garden watering cans. But no pilots Indian or Bangladeshi gave any thought to the danger and carried on with their mission, something that makes me proud to this day.

General Sagat Singh handsomely acknowledged the dedication and gallantry of all the pilots. Very early on the 8th morning at about 3 am I decided that I must get official sanction for the operations from AOC in C Eastern Air Command so decided to fly to Shillong stopping at Jorhat to get a few hours of rest and change of uniform for my meeting.

At about 5 am I lay down to get some rest but at 5.30 was woken up by a call from the Senior Air Staff Officer congratulating me for the success of the operation and asking me to get back to Kelashahar. I took this as an approval of our operations and so the anxiety of being hauled over the coals for undertaking a mission which had no sanction from higher authorities was removed from my mind and I returned to the war zone ready to undertake anything which Gen Sagat Singh might conjure up.

He was a magician and conjuror who could juggle half a dozen balls at the same time, for balls read battles. He not only had the enemy guessing about his moves and plans but even we could never guess what and where his next move would be".

"Summing up the operation at Sylhit, I would like to say a few words. Firstly, this was a unique type of operation for it was the first time in the history of India that such a kind and magnitude of an operation had been undertaken. It was also unique because it was not pre-planned. The Corps commander saw an opportunity, seized it and launched the operation knowing full well that the air resources were inadequate but we would deliver.

At the commencement of the operation neither Bunty Quinn nor I had a clue about enemy disposition and strength. But even the enemy could not quantify us and take counter measures for we had achieved total surprise and speed which is the essence of heliborne operations".

"The impact of the operation was that it opened the eyes of the Higher Army and Air Force Commanders to the fact that here was the answer to the problems posed by the terrain in Bangladesh which was made more intractable by the destruction of nearly all bridges by the Pakistanis and in some cases by the Freedom Fighters. Of course the commanders had planned to use the MI-4s in an operational role but only in a very limited way and sanction was given for only a company sized operation.

At no stage was an operation of this magnitude visualised

and as to what was to follow now that is the crossing of the Meghna it was unthinkable except by Gen Sagat. The Sylhit operation helped us to iron out operational procedures, lighting of landing and takeoff pads, other was that understanding and cooperation between the Army and Air Force must be total not only at the level of headquarters but also between the aircrew, chiefly pilots and the assault troops. This was so at Sylhit.

There was one incident in which I was involved that was unpleasant and avoidable but about which I do not wish to go into details. It involved a young army officer and I attribute it to battle fatigue. His unit had just come out of a difficult operation in which they had suffered very heavy casualties and were now involved in a joint operation. But being unfamiliar with air operations attempted to intervene in the conduct of what was a purely air force function. Fortunately I was able to defuse the situation before it got ugly."

Crossing of the Meghna-9th December

"If any one single operation were to be cited as the turning point of the war, without doubt it was the heliborne crossing of the Meghna river by 4 Guards which was lifted across the Meghna by 110 and 105 Helicopter Squadrons on 9th December. This was Gen Sagat's masterstroke and it broke the back of the Pakistani army. The operation was conducted with such precision and efficiency that there was not a single hitch and we suffered no casualties but for the Pakistanis the war was over.

The operation started at 4 pm on 9th December and concluded at 3 am on 10th December and by midday on 10th December Gen Niazi, the Pakistani Army Commander approached the United Nations Representatives in Dacca and GHQ Rawalpindi to sue for a ceasefire for all his plans had come unstuck. His fighting formations had been bypassed and contained, Dacca cut off and rendered defenceless.

IV Corps was now bearing down on Dacca with all the resources at its command. In fact the Mukti Bahini and some of our Artillery OPs had infiltrated inside Dacca to prepare for the final assault while the IAF kept up constant day and night attacks on targets inside Dacca making sleep impossible for the Pakistani defenders and their commanders."

"On completion of the Sylhit operation on instruction of the Corps commander, I moved my entire air assets to Agartala by late evening on 8th December where I had orders waiting for me to go to Brahmanbaria and meet Maj Gen Ben Gonsalves GOC 57 Div. I met him at 11 pm and discussed operations in his area.

His division had advanced on a broad front and his lead battalion 4 Guards had reached the Meghna river at Ashuganj by last light on 8th December and the rest of 311 Brigade and 73 Brigade had been asked to build up on the bridgehead. He said that though the bridge was intact crossing the river by the bridge was not possible with the resources and time available for on the further bank at Bhairab Bazaar was Pak 14 Div. with two brigades."

"The GOC Gen Gonzalves asked me if it was possible to launch a river crossing operation with a battalion group, to be undertaken immediately. I went back and discussed this with my boys. By now some more helicopters had joined us but their pilots were not qualified for night operations. So I decided against undertaking the operation in haste and instead asked Sandhu and Vaid to put the newly arrived through some night flying training and also decided to carry out an armed recce of our probable landing area early in the morning."

"At first light on 9th December, I told Gen Gonsalves that we were ready but would first undertake an armed recce of the area and select the landing area. In the meantime, Gen Sagat had also arrived and decided to come along on the armed recce to Raipura. We did a few orbits of Raipura and they decided on a landing area for the operation some distance away from Pakistani positions at Bhairab Bazaar and Methikhanda. I suggested that we start the operation late in the evening and continue through the night to minimise the chances of interference by the Pakistanis.

216 Cavalier in the Sky

This was a agreed to by both the GOCs and by now we had eleven MI-4s available for the operation. They also decided that the operation would be undertaken by 4 Guards. This was odd because at this time 4 Guards was at Ashuganj. Hence the furthest away from Brahmanbaria and in contact with the enemy and two other battalions of 311 brigade and the entire 73 Brigade were close to Brahmanbaria and not engaged with the enemy. Therefore any battalion from this group should have been the natural choice.

But both the GOCs and Commander 311 Brigade, Brig Mishra felt that 4 Guards under their Commanding Officer, Col Himmeth Singh was the battalion most suitable to undertake this special operation."

"The choice of 4 Guards and their Commanding Officer Col Himmeth Singh for this operation reflected the complete confidence of the senior commanders in the ability of Himmeth Singh and his boys to deliver. In fact when this operation was being discussed in the presence of some battalion commanders, Sagat noticed a marked lack of enthusiasm in them and it was then that he asked Gen Gonsalves to withdraw 4 Guards from Ashuganj even though at that very moment they were involved in a battle with the enemy and have them assemble at Brahmanbaria. He also asked for Col Himmeth Singh to be sent for and taken on another armed air recce of Raipura."

"This decision by the GOCs of switching battalions was to have some unforeseen and unfortunate results for some units that replaced 4 Guards at Ashuganj and it has been a source of many recriminations by some individuals. Withdrawal while in contact with the enemy is one of the most difficult operations. But 4 Guards managed to pull it off without a hitch even though at the moment Himmeth was not present with the battalion as he was on ariel recce of Raipura and Major Chandra Kant was standing in for him.

The time between 4 Guards breaking contact and 18 Rajput and 10 Bihar taking their place gave the enemy time to recover and launch a counter attack which resulted in heavy casualties to the two Bns and the Indep Armoured Squadron."

"All the helicopters had assembled at Brahmanbaria stadium ready for the lift off by 1500 hours and 4 Guards had arrived about a few hours earlier and the troops were all seated in groups of helicopter loads and at 1550 they started mounting the helicopters and everything was well organised and proceeded according to script, were it not for the fact that at about this time some casualties incurred by 18 Rajput and 10 Bihar the battalions that had replaced 4 Guards at Ashuganj started arriving at the helipad awaiting evacuation to Agartala.

This was a great distraction and not good for the morale of the troops and pilots. Our priority at the moment was the river crossing operation and so casualty evacuation would have to wait. Commanders in war have to constantly make tough choices. It is not easy and I was already in a disturbed state of mind for Sandhu, the Squadron Commander had pointed out to me the bodies of forty-four Mukti Bahini boys which lay in a ditch next to the stadium. Their hands were tied behind their backs and they had been executed by retreating Pakistani troops."

"At precisely 1600 hours the first sortie of four helicopters carrying about sixty troops and twenty local porters took off, I was in the lead helicopter which was piloted by Sandhu and sitting in the hold with me was the CO of 4 Guards, Col Himmeth Singh and the lead company commander, Maj Chandra Kant. Flying protective air cover were two Gnat fighters ready to take on any opposition in the air or from the ground.

We did twenty-seven sorties during the day and another thirty at night. This time everything proceeded very smoothly. The pilots and the ground crew performed magnificently and 4 Guards gave the impression that this sort of thing was a daily routine for them notwithstanding the fact that they had been involved in a serious fire fight with the enemy till about two hours ago and had suffered several casualties including a company commander, Major Kharbanda during the last twenty-four hours.

The turn around time was considerably speeded up and

for us it was merely flying in and flying out as no enemy opposition was encountered. 4 Guards encountered opposition much later and not at Raipura."

"As the landing was not too far from the enemy Div HQ at Bhairab Bazaar, we could not use lighting aids to mark the landing zone but instead used dough made from atta(wheat flour) to mark the field. Later we shifted the LZ to a fresh location some distance away as the old LZ had become unusable owing to constant landings and take offs. We also started using torches and GLIM lamps to guide the helicopters as no enemy interference was encountered.

So smoothly had the whole operation gone off that at that time we hardly felt that we had undertaken the most audacious and momentous operation of the entire campaign in East Pakistan, it was army and air force cooperation at its best. For me it was a source of immense satisfaction and great pleasure to see, how well led and motivated troops and pilots accomplished as possible a task which many thought was impossible."

"By the morning of 10th December, 4 Guards had not only secured the bridge head but had also expanded it to facilitate further crossings by air and ferry. On successful completion of the operation all the higher commanders were very happy and we were congratulated by everyone.

But Sagat would not rest on his laurels and wanted me to lift two more battalions immediately. When I appeared hesitant he even tried invoking our Rajput sense of gallantry, duty and mutual loyalty. But this time I had to firmly tell him that though the pilots were willing the machines which had been flying non-stop for four days needed servicing and maintenance and would be ready only on 11th December for further operations. Gen Sagat understood our problem and agreed to postpone the helilift of the rest of the brigade and Arty guns."

"The ground crew at Agartala worked round the clock for the next twenty-fours to get the machines ready for another round of operations. The crossing of the Meghna river on 9th

December was a textbook operation that went like clockwork even though the battalion involving 4 Guards had come out of an operation that very morning and had to march back fifteen miles to reach the launch pad at Brahmanbaria. However in the shortest possible time they managed to organise themselves and were prepared for the airlift and crossed the Meghna. A few hours after the crossing their patrols had established contact with Pakistani positions at Bhairab Bazaar in the North and Narsingdi towards the south east."

Narsingdi—11th December

"By the 10th morning, 4 Guards having secured a bridgehead close to Bhairab Bazaar, 19 Punjab was able to cross the Meghna river by ferry and were deployed to contain HQ 14 Pakistani Div with two brigades. This one single BN performed this task with great elan forcing the Pakistanis to think that they had more than a brigade opposing them. It came as a great shock and sense of disbelief to Gen Abdul Majid GOC 14 DIV when he surrendered with six thousand troops on 17th December to learn that all we had against him was an infantry battalion 19 Punjab and a battalion of the Mukti Bahini.

In bottling up Pak 14 Div at Bhairab Bazaar the air force also played a role. All sorties which could not find suitable targets were diverted to Bharab Bazaar and at night the modified Caribous of the IAF and the Otters of the Bangladesh Air Force kept up a constant bombardment with 500 lbs bombs shaking their morale and giving them sleepless nights.

At no time could they figure out the strength of the forces that we were lifting across the Meghna, the constant and unbroken chain of helicopters flying night and day over several days made them highly exaggerate our force levels and instilled a sense of great fear among them.

"But for me and helicopter crew including the maintenance team there was to be no respite. Early on the 11th morning, Gen Sagat Singh and GOC 57 Div contacted me, both were very happy with the success of 4 Guards operation at Raipura. 4 Guards now advanced towards Narsingdi along the railway line and were likely to secure the town which was lightly held before the last light. Both Sagat and Gonzalves saw this success of 4 Guards as an opportunity to be seized and exploited now by crossing the Meghna in a big way and get as close to Dacca as we could. When I requested for some time to service the aircraft, Gen Sagat said that it was no time to rest and we had to finish the task we had undertaken."

"This time his plan was to lift an entire brigade and an artillery regiment entailing 150 sorties. Each helicopter had to do at least 14 to 15 sorties, the human may undertake the mission but the machine might fail. I did not mention this to him, as time was of great essence and these considerations were for subordinate commanders like me to bother about. If the machines had to be used they had to be brought to Agartala and put under scheduled maintenance, which was done.

In the meantime, the pilots and the crew along with their army colleagues were brought to Brahamanbaria for a thorough briefing. This time the loads were going to be different with the guns and their ammunition being lifted. The centre of gravity of the loads had to be factored in and this was going to be a tricky operation. Having had the experience of lifting tanks to Ladakh in 1962 I knew how tricky the task was where standard operating procedures were not going to be adhered to, but then this was war and risks had to be taken."

"By the afternoon on the 11th the helicopters had been assembled at Brahamanbaria. At the same time, we received word that 4 Guards had occupied Narsingdi and were mopping up the remnants of the Pakistani troops in the town. Earlier we had undertaken an armed recces and Gen Sagat as was his wout had come along and selected the landing area.

Then I took along the GOC Gen Gonzalves, Brigade Commander Brig Mishra and the Arty Brigade Comdr, Jungi Bawa for a survey of our landing zone which was about three miles south east of Narsingdi close to the Bhairab Bazaar-Narsingdi-Dacca road. We could take this risk as 4 Guards had already occupied Narsingdi and there was no chance of any interference from the enemy. Soon after midday the sorties started and continued uninterrupted till the morning of the 12th.

By now we had got used to such operations except for the transport of artillery guns where the centre of gravity was unknown and the pilots had to continuously correct the aircraft using the collective and throttle. This was taken in their stride and the operation was completed without any mishap. At the end of this massive helilift operation, a total of 1628 troops, plus several hundred Mukti Bahinis, artillery guns and several tons of ammunition and other stores had been lifted."

"By the morning though the pilots were willing to go on in spite of having been in the cockpit for over twenty-four hours the machines showed signs of fatigue and three helicopters had engine failure and had to force land en route. They were repaired on the spot and recovered within six hours of having force landed. It was a grand experience and accomplishment and we were all justifiably happy and proud. These machines had put the army across six wide river obstacles which they would have had to cross if they had moved overland. In less than twenty-four hours we had carried out 135 sorties."

Narayanganj

"By the use of helicopters most of 57 Div had been positioned just short of Dacca in the central sector. The rest of this division had crossed over in captured river craft that the Army engineers had requisitioned. The army had some problem in finding the crew to man these boats and ferries. But in the end with the help of the Mukti Bahani some of the crew were located and persuaded to take our troops and stores across. Taking the heavy 5.5 inch arty guns was also a problem but somehow it was managed.

The positioning of our arty guns within firing range of Dacca was not only a tactical necessity but firing into Dacca coupled with bombing by the IAF gave the Pakistanis sleepless nights and lowered their morale, whereas on the local population it had the opposite effect for they now knew that their hour of deliverance from Pakistani tyranny was close."

"On our side a sense of great urgency prevailed to get the job done and finished. The United Nations was proving difficult and the US 7th fleet with its flagship the nuclear propelled and armed USS Enterprise had entered the Indian Ocean through the Straits of Malacca and was making threatening moves. So Gen Sagat decided that he would move a brigade from 23 Div which was on his left flank towards Dacca and so asked me to move a brigade from Daudkhandi across the Meghna to Narayanganj which is just south east of Dacca.

I had to tell the General that the helicopters were at the end of their tether but he said, "Chandan the war is on and let us get on with the job" and issued orders to the effect. This order came as a surprise to 23 Div and some of the units under its command which had seen some very intense fighting in the preceding days. There appeared to be some hesitancy but Sagat was not one to brook this and there was no one who could openly stand up to him. So in the early hours of the 14th we started our fourth heliborne operation and carried out 80 sorties by day and about 40 by night.

Once again the enemy was taken by complete surprise and we encountered no opposition but two more helicopters literally dropped out of the sky. They were of course recovered on the 15th morning."

"At the same time, wireless intercepts and intelligence sources indicated that the Pakistanis were seeking a ceasefire which was agreed to by us effective from the same evening onwards. So the war barring the celebrations was over and a sense of jubilation and satisfaction prevailed among the ranks of our Armed Forces.

The pilots could now have their well earned rest and sleep but the maintenance crew had to again work overtime to service all the helicopters for there was no saying when they would be needed again. With Sagat you could not take anything for granted knowing that Chittagong and Cox Bazaar several hundred kilometres to the south could be probable beach heads for the US 7th fleet to land troops and Sagat might want to pre-empt that from happening by occupying them first.

He had already tasked a Brigade, some Mukti Bahini units and Establishment 22 under Maj Gen Obhan to capture Chittagong but in case of any delay he could ask us to reinforce them with additional troops. Gen Obhan and Est 22 which consisted of mainly Tibetan troops were well known to me from my Charbatia days, when I had the responsibility for the air part of the operations and General Obhan the land warfare part. We both operated under the Cabinet Secretariat."

"The night of 15/16 December was a night of celebrations for the pilots and I dare say that many of them made much of it with too many whiskies. But for the army it was a time to position their troops and logistics for the final assault on Dacca should the ceasefire not hold. It was also a time of stocktaking for unlike the helicopter pilots the infantry had suffered heavy casualties particularly amongst the officers.

In one Brigade that is 311 Brigade of 57 Div it was as high as more than 75 per cent among officers of the rank of major and 50 per cent among captains and lieutenants. This indicates the intensity of the fighting and the leadership of the combat level officers."

16th December, the Surrender

Once the negotiations for the surrender of Pakistani Forces was agreed to by Gen Niazi, Gen Aurora the GOC in C Eastern Command, Air Marshal Dewan and Vice Admiral Krishnan assembled at Agartala. They were accompanied by Gen Sagat and GOC 57 Div Gen Gonzalves who were flown in by the MI-4 and Alouette helicopters. Here I ensured that all the pilots got to see the signing of the surrender document by Gen Niazi.

We were also joined by the helicopter unit from Hashimara commanded by Nanda Cariappa, son of Field Marshal Cariappa who had served with 4 Guards earlier when it was designated as 1 Rajput.

For Nanda it must have been a proud moment to be with his father's battalion at the moment of their triumph. It was also a moment of personal satisfaction to Nanda for five years earlier in 1965 the Hunter he was flying had been shot down over Pakistan and taken prisoner. FM Ayub Khan who had served under Gen Cariappa learnt of Nanda's capture and offered to repatriate him immediately. But Gen Cariappa refused to accept the favour and said that every Indian soldier was his son and Nanda could wait to return till all the others were released.

The jubilation and the release of emotions among the Bangladeshis was something that anyone who was a witness can never forget. The troops of 4 Guards whom we had lifted on 9th December and were in the suburbs of Dacca from last light 12th December onwards and 2 Para who had been airdropped at Tangail on 11th December had arrived in Dacca on 16th December after the announcement of the surrender, had a hard time keeping the crowds away from the airfield and the venue of the signing of the document of surrender.

The Guards had entered Dacca from the south and the Paras from the north and I am glad and proud that the Air Force had it made it possible for both these two battalions to enter Dacca first. In cordoning off the airfield and surrender venue they were assisted by the soldiers of the Pakistan army who were allowed to keep their personal weapons for self-protection. Otherwise they would have been lynched by the Bengalis.

It is a rare moment in history that a new nation which has never existed before in history is born and at the same time millions of people are released from a tyranny more inhuman than that imposed by the Nazis on captured countries and on the Jews. That night I came to know and feel what the term sleep of the blessed means".

For his courage, leadership and planning during the liberation war Gp Capt Chandan Singh received the Mahavir Chakra.

"Looking back at the momentous events and what the

small band of helicopters and their pilots achieved, I cannot but marvel but also feel that like Sagat all commanders both from the army and the air force have to factor the full potential of helicopters in their operation plans and helicopters have to be integrated in the army formations. It does not matter whether the pilots wear the air force blue, the army olive green or navy whites but command, control and training have to be integrated."

Kilo Flight and the Birth of the Bangladesh Air Force

I am singularly fortunate to have obtained an account on the raising of the Bangladesh Air Force and operations undertaken by it during the war written by Air Commodore C.M. Singla is reproduced below with his permission. This event is not only important but is also not well known and I have therefore included the full account of Air Commodore Singla even though parts of it have been covered in the Air Marshal's own account.

The BAF was formed at Dimapur, Nagaland on September 28, 1971 under the command of Air Cmde A.K. Khondakar (later Air Vice Marshal and Chief of Air Staff of the Bangladesh Air Force.) On the Indian side the overall responsibility of raising, equipping and training was of Group Capt Chandan Singh and in this he was assisted by a team of officers, foremost among them was Flt Lt Singla whose account I have reproduced verbatim.

This account is not only a continuum of the preceding paragraphs but also corroborates it and lends it an authenticity and excitement which only firsthand accounts can do. I am grateful to Air Cmde Singla who was my senior by a year at the NDA for permission to reproduce his account.

At that time, the nucleus of the BAF was formed as Kilo Flight to assist the Mukti Bahini. Initially Kilo Flight consisted of three aircraft (one helicopter and two Otters) provided by the IAF, 9 officers and 47 airmen all of whom had deserted from the Pakistan Air Force and crossed over to India earlier in the year. Sqn Ldr Sultan Mahmud who later went on to become an AVM and CAS Bangladesh Air Force was appointed Flt Commander of Kilo Flight.

According to Air Commodore Singla, "It all started on September 26, 1971. War appeared imminent and our 112 Helicopter Unit was on daily dawn to dusk standby. As a Flt Lt, I was one of the four flying instructors in the unit. I was summoned by the CO Sqn Ldr Naresh Kumar, " You are to move tomorrow morning to Tezpur". Apprehending a desk job during the war my "but-Sirs" were not entertained and I got back crestfallen to a cup of milky, sugary tea in the crew room. I thought of several reasons why I must continue to fly with my unit.

Firstly I was fresh out of instructional tenure, I had little experience on [Alouette] Chetak helicopters. Soon after getting my head in, the CO sent me to AEB in AF Station Hindon for getting categorised and rated on type to start flying training, I was given D/White rec B/Green for want of flying hours on the Chetak. If I stayed with my unit, I would soon acquire day and night hours on Chetak and get upgraded. Secondly I was assigned to fly some missions in Bhutan which would earn me the Videsh Seva Medal. Thirdly why me?"

"Taking courage, I walked into the CO's office again. Gave him my reasons and requested that I be permitted to continue with the Unit and that someone else be deputed. He heard me and said, an aircraft would pick me up at 0800 hours tomorrow".

Resigned to my fate, I asked " Sir, what is my assignment and for how many days must I pack?" The reply, "Pack for 4-5 weeks, carry your bedding and you will be given your task in Tezpur." 4-5 weeks meant that I was to be equipped with baggage to stay forever! Ours was a training unit as also responsible for helicopter support to West Bengal, Sikkim and Bhutan sectors. In addition to normal aircrew complement, we four instructors, Air Force and Army pilots came to us from Helicopter Training School for type and operational training before moving on to other Chetak Units."

"With morale in my boots, I conceived a war in which my

role would be pushing files in some office while other pilots saw action. Where had I gone wrong to deserve this? To me it appeared that I was more being sinned against than sinning."

"Promptly next morning at 8 am a Dakota stopped on Bagdogra tarmac. With engines running, I was waved to step on board. OC 115 Helicopter Unit Sqn Ldr Mehtani was waiting at Tezpur to receive me. For a Flt Lt like me it was a VIP reception indeed. "Let's go and meet the AOC", he said. I was expected. Without 'preliminaries', the AOC AF Station Tezpur asked me if I could fly the Chetak alone. He went on to say that 'Mama' has a helicopter ready for you. Take it to Dimapur. You will be further briefed there. You will get complete maintenance support for the Chetak on immediate priority. Any questions? Carry on."

"In the Helicopter Unit I obtained a map, VHF and NDB frequencies, signed up for the machine and for the first time flew it alone to Dimapur. On switching off at Dimapur, a rickety jeep rolled up and when I was seated it refused to start and so had to get off and help push start it.

Dimapur was commanded by a Flt Lt who had a staff of about 15 men. Their role was to provide support to Dakotas of AF Stn Jorhat which were involved in carrying out air maintenance of troops in forward locations in Nagaland and Manipur. I was given a cot in the ramshackle ATC building. The food was spicy and oily from the Airmen's Mess. The rest of the creature comforts matched the kot and the food. I was told that Stn Commander Jorhat would brief me further."

"On 28th September, Stn Commander Jorhat Gp Capt Chandan Singh landed in a Dakota. He was accompanied by Sqn Ldr C.M. Choudhary, a Bengali-speaking Dakota QFI. Gp Capt Chandan Singh quietly climbed up to the Flying Control and lay down on a bench. In hushed tones I was informed that it was his day of total fast.

A short while later, I was tasked by him to train on the Chetak. Three former Pakistani Air Force pilots had defected and come over to our side. They had escaped persecution and along with the Airmen were assembled at Dimapur. He introduced me to them. They were Badrul Alam, Shahabuddin Ahmed. The third Sqn Ldr Sultan joined me a few days later. By then a maintenance team led by Flt Lt Ramakrishna had been assembled. They were handpicked and gave us excellent support throughout."

"I was asked to commence immediately and make them operational within a week. I informed Gp Capt Chandan Singh that if the IAF syllabus for day and night conversion was to be followed then seven days did not have adequate hours. He clearly instructed that I was to ignore all rules of the IAF hereafter and complete the task as directed. Without any delay I took my pupils in hand, got hold of writing material and started preliminary ground training in right earnest. The Bangladesh Air Force considers this date, i.e. September 28, 1971 as its birth date. It is a great feeling to have been a midwife to the birth of a new country's air force."

"I flew morning, noon and night with them, their age, mature fixed wing habits, distressed state of mind and barely acceptable living conditions made teaching and training a challenging and formidable task. Their attempts at hovering resulted in moving all over and frequently blocking the only runway. It was difficult to make them reduce speed on finals, yet bordering on exhaustion I was able to report to Gp Capt Chandan Singh on schedule that each pupil was now comfortable flying by day and night".

"For your navigational phase I want to see you over Jorhat ATC at midnight tonight." I took off with a pupil on a pitch dark night with 8/8 low cloud ceiling. About halfway to Jorhat it started pouring. The Chetak has only instrumentation with air driven gyros. Flying blind without a visual horizon was bad enough, but entering clouds even in plains with zero instrumentation has resulted in disasters. I kept reducing altitude and speed, maintaining heading. Obviously instead of the pupil I had controls till suddenly I saw tree branches rushing past the helicopter. I had descended below the canopy of trees. That was enough, I did a gentle 180 degree turn and returned safely to Dimapur in pouring rain. However I was questioned for not being seen or heard over AF Stn Jorhat at midnight."

"We barely got a day off to rest. On October 8, 1971, I was summoned to Jorhat. One Chetak had been brought in by transport aircraft. Its serial number is recorded as 364 in my log book."

"This Chetak had two Mystere rocket pods mounted on either side. They carried 7 rockets each, capable of being fired in pairs or salvo. The selection switch for pair/salvo firing was mounted on the Captain's control column. A twin barrel machine gun that was side firing was mounted on the floor. The sliding door on the left had been removed. Gp Capt Chandan Singh flew with me on its copilot's seat to Dimapur.

Armourer Fitters were flown in and so were loads of rockets. Without preliminaries I was told to get my pupils ready to fire rockets accurately. I took the Gp Capt aside and told him that it had never been done in the Air Force before and that I had no clue about how to go about doing it. Harmonisation of the pods, gun sights, ground attack, tactics practice and targets were unprecedented, original and revolutionary. "Who will guide me Sir?" I asked. He smiled and said, "You will learn. I am confident." This was to be the first of the several pioneering flying tasks that were entrusted to me in my career."

"We now had two Chetaks—one armed and the other a passenger version. As part of preparation for the war, for self-protection we were each issued a machine carbine with two loaded magazines and we had to practise firing it. The rocket pods were synchronised, ring and head gun sight installed. On test flight I noticed that the helicopter handled sluggishly—what with the extra load and aerodynamics burden. At night, I reported that the gun sight was mounted very low and it was so bright that I could not see a target through it. Resources not being a constraint they were rectified and a rheostat on the stick gave the realigned gun sight operational viability".

"Gp Capt Chandan Singh discussed the need of a target to enable us to practise firing the RPs. He came up with the idea of parachutes. He said that next morning I was to fly over the nearby dense jungle and a Dakota would come and drop three parachutes with bundles of hay slung underneath. The jungle canopy being dense the parachutes would cover the trees. I could fire at them and they would be replenished when required.

The Dakotas dropped the parachutes on schedule. From my helicopter I observed that all of them went through the canopy of trees and could not be seen from the air. Gp Capt Chandan Singh arrived a little later and asked me for suggestions. I proposed that as some of the neighbouring hill slopes were covered with grass, I could hover low over the slope since the high gradient would not permit a landing. From the hover three airmen could jump out with a parachute and fix the parachute on the hill with hammer and nails.

I would fly overhead and pick them up once the parachute had been spread and nailed down. Returning to Dimapur a short while later, I reported that we had a clear and safe target for day and night firing. I got a prompt go ahead. I now really enjoyed the freedom from rules, regulations and red-tape."

"I evolved the aiming procedure, elevation of commencement of dive and the approximate height above ground for release of rockets and procedure for pulling away. We soon burnt and re-laid several parachutes and I reported that all three of my pupils could now fire RPs with reasonable accuracy by day".

"Gp Capt Chandan Singh now asked Sqn Ldr Sultan to design an emblem to be painted on the armed helicopter. He also asked them to give it a name and number. This created great excitement and animated discussion among them. Finally they decided that the helicopter's vertical stabiliser was to be painted with a red roundel having a map of East Pakistan superimposed on it in green. Also the call sign would be EBR for East Bengal Rifles.

Gp Capt Chandan Singh approved and the armed Chetak donned Bangladeshi colours. I believe it was the first for Bangladesh Air Force. In all my subsequent log book entries

IAF serial no. 364 stands changed for EBR."

"I used to fly to IAF Tezpur for my helicopter maintenance. Word of my activity reached no. 28 Sqn located there. My one time squash partner Flt Lt Manbir Singh called me over and said that Dacca was their target and whether I could get first hand and accurate intelligence. In answer to his series of questions, I asked him to pause and jotted them down. My pupils willingly gave details of anti-aircraft gun locations, fuel dumps, etc. Manbir said that the details obtained were somewhat different from those provided by Air HQ."

"Another incident is worth mentioning. Flt Lt Ghoshal brought in an Otter Aircraft with rocket pods mounted under each wing. One of his pupils was Flt Lt Shamshul Alam. On being sent solo one morning Shamshul failed to return beyond his fuel endurance time. The entire camp anxiously waited for his news. He returned somewhat later after sunset safely. I was told that he flew right over East Pakistan to Calcutta, was given fuel and returned.

After dinner the next night Sqn Ldr Sultan loaded his revolver and called Shamshul and they walked off to a dark part of the runway. We feared the worst. In the ensuing hush the noise made by the insects sounded deafening. A while later Sultan returned with a chastened looking Shamshul following behind much to our collective relief."

"On 15th October I was told that I had successfully completed my assignment and that I was to return to my unit in Bagdogra. I was also made aware that I was instrumental in creating a deadly air element of Bengali Freedom Fighters. My log book now records to what now appeared to be very boring circuits and landings and having to ask permission from ATC to take off and land every time. On 19th October my army pupils were Capt K. Singh and Capt Dullat. On 27th October I was flying VIPs around Barrackpore and Dum Dum airport in Calcutta when my CO asked me to take an Indian Airlines flight to Bagdogra. He told me that I was needed at Dimapur even though by now several pilots had volunteered I was asked for by name."

"On 1ˢᵗ November I was back in Dimapur. At Dimapur I was told that Gp Capt Chandan Singh had given instructions that he was planning some night operations and I was to learn and then train the Bengladeshi pilots on night firing. Night firing was not to be guided by the phase of the moon. Ability to fly and fire in the dark was a requirement. The only operational limitation would be visual sighting of the target on a dark night. By the end of November we were operational by day and night."

"On 1ˢᵗ December, I was asked to fly to Jorhat by myself to meet Gp Capt Chandan Singh. He told me that he was planning to launch night strikes within a few days from an abandoned airfield at Kailshahar near Agartala in Tripura. Could my pupils navigate, strike accurately and return? I said yes to all except that returning to an unilluminated airfield on a dark night without having any homing device could be disastrous. I also suggested that even if I had a hand held RT set we would not be able to lead them in should their course steering go wrong in the likely prevailing strong winds.

He responded by saying what if we were to light up the runway with petromax lamps covered with perforated empty kerosene tins, would it suffice, more so if we covered and uncovered the lamps periodically. This I felt would certainly work and I said so. On 2ⁿᵈ December I flew to Kailashahar but the strike was to be launched from Teliamura which was closer to the East Pakistan border. Here too was located the HQ of IV Corps commanded by Lt Gen Sagat Singh whose reputation as a can do leader was widespread. We all believed that if anybody could deliver East Pakistan it would surely be him.

Gp Capt Chandan Singh also arrived during the day with complete ground support staff. On the night of 3ʳᵈ December, Sqn Ldr Sultan along with Flt Lt Alam got airborne with a full load of fuel and rockets. Their checks and procedures were well imbibed which got them to keep their navigation lights on. They were so visible. I got on to the hand held radio set and told them to switch off the lights which they did and immediately became invisible but remaining audible. Their target was Narayanganj fuel depot.

They were not expected and therefore received no opposition. The mission was accomplished and the fuel storage tanks along with the fuel was destroyed. The glow from the burning fuel could be seen from the Indian border fifty kilometres away. On return locating and landing went without a hitch. Early next morning I retrieved the element back to Dimapur."

"The war with Pakistan started on 4th December when they attacked our airfields in the Western Sector so now that the gloves were off we had a free run to do as we pleased. By then our Kilo Flight was well equipped and organised with adequate manpower, spares and loads of ammunition. Now that war had been declared, Gp Capt Chandan Singh directed that I was to fly all combat missions as pilot in command. We were given Pakistani currency and personal weapons. I moved both our helicopters to Kailashahar and thereafter lived in tents and managed our food from the nearest army units."

"Ground attack and close support missions started in right earnest. Gp Capt Chandan Singh directed my flights and flew with me as passenger from time to time, to gauge the enemy status and our efficacy."

"I flew three missions on the night of 6th December. On the first night of my attack, I recalled that the only way I could become aware of coming under fire from the enemy rifles and machine guns was when I looked directly into the flashes from their muzzles. Also the muted thuds that I heard were direct hits on my Chetak and not because of collusion with bats. Flying from Kailashahar I engaged targets at Kalaura, Maulvi Bazaar, and Shamshernagar".

"Next morning, i.e., 7th December I looked at the bullet holes. The bullet had gone through the fragile cowling. There was no armour plating of any kind for the vital engine parts or the pilots and the gunner."

"I told the technicians to number the bullet holes and

also paint the name of the place over which we had been hit. This was done, but later when the helicopters started taking frequent and several hits the exercise was abandoned. The first few sorties I remember handing over my wallet and watch to our engineer Flt Lt Ramakrishna, just in case. Later when the frequency of the flight increased, I discontinued the practice. As for the Sten gun it being cumbersome to carry on the body, we strapped it to our seats."

"Also we established helicopter airworthiness norms early after the bullet holes in the fuselage and the resultant vibration Ramakrishna and his team would do some patchwork then he would ask me "Will you fly the machine?" "Yes", I would say "Then she is serviceable." Despite several bullet holes in the cowling, main and tail rotors we never grounded the helicopters. So much so that army jawans used to come to our camp to look at the flying sieve."

"I flew eleven missions on 7th December. For the first day flight I was given fighter cover. Soon after getting airborne, we established RT contact. But after a few minutes the fighter escort lost visual contact with me, which could not be re-established despite our mutual effort. Perhaps it happened because he was high and fast and I low and slow in camouflage colours which merged with the green landscape. This effort was given up hereafter. But a few days later I was assured and highly relieved to learn that our Air Force had established complete air superiority. Their runways had been rendered unserviceable

Operating out of Kailashahar, I attacked enemy positions in Darbat, Brahmanbaria, Daudkhandi, Narsingdi Road, etc. By the 7th night there were signs of the Pakistani army retreating from Kalaura. I was given a location by the army on a river bank where en masse crossing was taking place by the retreating enemy troops. Sure enough the river was clogged with boats of different sizes and I hit the biggest boat with a pair of rockets, only to realise that the enemy transport and troops were nowhere near and the crowd on board appeared to be civilians. When my co-pilot confirmed this I called off the attack and reported it. To this day I regret harming civilians that night,

Dates and matching them with salient and memorable features have got mixed up over the years. IV Corps of our army pushed forward in all sectors giving the enemy no respite. 8 Div was moving towards Shamshernagar on the Maulvi Bazaar axis and also on the Kalaura-Sylhit axis. I had already supported their advance.

Airborne one night, I was surprised to hear on the RT "Singla Sir, how do you read me?" "Loud and clear", I responded "Station Calling?" "This is Fg Offr Saikia, your pupil from Bidar". I remembered him from my instructional days on HT2. He directed me to Bn Hq in Sylhit. Gp Capt Chandan Singh was on board as observer. Saikia who was the Forward Air Controller with the infantry battalion confirmed my direct hits on target. Intensive action followed. My helicopter EBR took several hits.

Early next morning our engineering officer Flt Lt Ramakrishna said the damage to the machine was beyond permissible limits. But if I should fly her she is serviceable. Rockets were loaded and I took off. Shamshernagar airfield in East Pakistan was now with our Army.

On the 7th afternoon special heliborne operations were launched. The battalion of Gurkhas was flown deep into enemy territory and landed close to Sylhit. On landing the helicopters and troops came under heavy fire. I expended all my ammunition and came to base to reload and then returned to engage the target. I did this several times. But the light was fading and only part of the battalion had been landed and the troops on the ground were in an intense firefight with the enemy. In the dark I was afraid of hitting our own troops. Further sorties were put on hold owing to darkness. It was then that Group Captain Chandan Singh was threatened."

"A Gurkha Officer approached him and asked why further troop induction was stopped. Gp Capt Chandan Singh explained that night landing was not possible' The officer lost his cool and yelled, "My boys are dying. They need reinforcement. Commence flying now", etc. etc. Group Capt Chandan Singh explained that night operations would result in more casualties to both his troops and the helicopters." But he would not be pacified. Group Captain Chandan Singh told him, "There will be no more sorties tonight. You can pull out your pistol and shoot me." With that the officer turned away and we could breathe easily."

"It turned into the second week of December and now IV Corps was rushing forward to all its objectives. One morning at about 0600 hours Ramakrishna came into my tent saying that Gp Capt Chandan Singh was sitting in a helicopter and wanting an immediate take off. I said I did not know that and would he please load the helicopter with fuel and ammunition and inform the Group Captain that I would join him in a few minutes. As I approached he said we needed to go to Sylhet Airfield. Taking a few minutes to flight plan we took off. He said we were required to ascertain if the Sylhet airfield had been vacated by the enemy and also see if as reported by our intelligence sources they were preparing to surrender."

"If the intelligence was correct then we were required to accept their surrender. This was heady stuff. Orbiting over the airfield it appeared to be deserted. After looking for a while he asked me to land on the dumbbell of the runway. I was approaching to establish hover and was perhaps about 10 feet above ground and at 10 knots forward speed when a machine gun opened up at us from a bunker close by whose roof was about two feet above the ground.

Obviously we got away even faster than we approached and lived to tell the tale. The fool could have taken us prisoner if he had held his fire till we landed. Having gained height and distance, I suggested we take out the bunker with a salvo of 14 rockets but was asked to hurry back and report the correct situation and prevent a disaster."

"Returning to base one evening, my co-pilot, I think it was Akram, said that we should buy fish for dinner. We could do that because the Pak army had vacated the sector and we had Pak currency. I readily agreed. He asked me to land in a field next to a river. He stepped out with his carbine held in readiness in his hand and I kept the rotors running. People started running away, but were summoned in Bengali. I observed that the fishermen kept their catch alive in a small fenced portion of the river. Some were pulled out and paid for. All of us had a pleasant addition to our menu for dinner after days of potatoes and more potatoes and even more potatoes."

"On December 16, 1971, the day of the surrender, I flew into Dacca with S/C Choudhury. The airfield was a desolate patch of potholed ground. Things were strewn all over. There was no owner, no security. People loitered around all over and the Pakistan Army and Air Force which had lorded over the place only a few hours earlier were nowhere to be seen. People were picking up whatever they could as mementoes.

What did I take? I picked up a belt of F86 sabre jet cannon shells! At Dimapur it was broken into smaller lengths and shared. We flew back to Agartala at night and chatted till late with a sense of great relief and elation at what we and our comrades in arms in olive greens had achieved. We had removed a major threat to our country by breaking it into half and created a new nation which had never ever existed in the past. We wondered how the political leadership would handle this hereafter. About the direction the new nation would take and its relationship with India."

"On 18th December I was instructed to return my students to Dacca as also to hand over the bullet-ridden armed Chetak to them and fly back in the other Chetak. We shook hands with Sultan, Badrul Alam and Shahabudin Ahmed who were now the founding fathers of the Air Force of an independent Bangladesh and the bullet-ridden battle Chetak their first aircraft.

Shahabudin wrote his Dacca address on a Pakistani currency note and invited me to his home. I still have that note. Sultan, on behalf of the others, refused to hand over their carbines. We spent the night in what was till a few days ago the PAF Officers' Mess but now the BAF Officers' Mess in Dacca."

"Next morning Sultan saw me off with thanks and a case of Scotch! My report about the retention of the carbines was absorbed silently by Gp Capt Chandan Singh. On 21st December I wound up our Dimapur detachment and returned to Jorhat and on 24th December after handing over the Chetak to its rightful owners 116-HU at Tezpur I reported for duty to my parent station Bagdogra and peace time rule bound functioning as an instructor of my new pupils, Karandikar and Shakleton."

"For our role in the war I was awarded a Vir Chakra and Sultan a Bir Uttam by the Government of Bangladesh. The first and only time that a crew of one aircraft has been awarded by two nations."

10

United Kingdom

After the Bangladesh Liberation War, Chandan Singh was a marked man for promotion and future assignments. His gallantry and exceptional service in the 1962 and 1971 wars, and pioneering of Standard Operating Procedures for Air Logistics Support in remote Himalayan Valleys had already been recognised but there was a lot more he had done in Tibet after 1962 and over Pakistan during the 1965 war that has gone unrecognised and unrewarded because the missions he undertook are still classified.

If it were not so he would have been awarded gallantry awards for both these operations. Similarly for setting up the Aviation Research Centre Base at Charbatia and for his own actions and for training of pilots to operate in and over Tibet he would have become eligible for at least another bar to his AVSM if not PVSM.

Because of the declassification of the CIA papers, we have some information about his operations with ARC and I have included them in an earlier chapter. But of his operational missions over Pakistan in 1965 little is known because they are still classified as 'Top Secret' and he himself reveals nothing. But from the little that I know from other sources the missions he undertook were extremely dangerous as they involved flying at treetop level at night across enemy territory and on accomplishment of the mission returning home. The return journey was even more dangerous because by then the Pakistan Air Force would have become aware of his presence over Pakistan.

Within the Air Force itself his achievements were

acknowledged by all and he had become a legend. He was now selected by Air Chief Marshal Lall, a legend himself for a course at the Imperial Defence College London. For this course only officers of the rank of Air Commodores and equivalents in the Army and Navy are selected and that too from among the officers who have the potential to attain the very topmost ranks. But Chandan Singh as a group Captain was still one rank below, so his selection for the course not only came as a surprise to him but to the others too.

It was a signal that the Air Chief considered him as an exceptional officer who needed to be prepared to assume greater responsibility in future. The first person to inform him that he had been selected for the course at the IDC was his old friend from their CIA ARC days, Lulu Grewal who later rose to the rank of Air Marshal.

The tenure at the Imperial Defence College was interesting and fun, firstly because Mrs Chandan Singh could join him with the children and secondly though Britain was no longer a great power but the Directing Staff seemed not to be aware of their changed circumstances and went about as if the Empire still existed. This Chandan found most amusing.

In fact one of the speakers was openly racist but apart from him, the faculty and guest speakers were to rate.

He was very popular at the College both among the faculty and students not only because of his affable personality but also because among the students he was the only one who had combat experience both in the Army and Air Force from the Second World War onwards.

He could bring to the discussion table his vast and unmatched first hand knowledge of combat and logistics planning in overt and covert operations against both a communist country China and an ally of NATO, Pakistan. Add to this his stint with the CIA at Fort Peary and Langley and balance it with his six months with their arch rivals the Russians in 1959. It was a heady cocktail of knowledge and experience that he brought to the discussions among the students.

The students at the IDC were from all over the world, NATO partners, Commonwealth countries, Middle Eastern nations and even Japan and South America. Interacting with them was an experience in itself. However when it came to professional matters compared to him even the senior Directing Staff were greenhorns. US military doctrine with its overwhelming reliance on hardware and fire power at the expense of quality of manpower dominated the discussions. One would have thought that their own experience in Vietnam where a poor and ill equipped army had defeated them would have taught them some lessons.

The real take away from his time at the IDC and interaction with his fellow students was that whatever the Western or other governments may want us to believe that their foreign policy was determined by ideological, moral, democratic and human rights issues in practice it was real politic and security of their economic particularly their oil supplies that dictated their foreign policy in which morality and ideology had no role.

During his tenure at the IDC the name of the institute was changed to the Royal College of Defence Studies keeping the changed circumstances into account. The students were taken on three conducted study tours.

The first one was to the Midlands and Yorkshire where during a visit to the great Cathedral at York he was pleasantly surprised to see Col Loring who was a deacon at the Minister. At the Royal Hospital at Chelsea Barraooks he met Brig Duncan former Commander Jodhpur State Force who was in not very happy circumstances. To top it all his daughter who should have been looking after him was instead stealing from him. Chandan left behind whatever money he had with him, hiding it under his mattress. During the other tours they went around Europe, the Middle East and North Africa.

One of the papers Chandan was asked to write was on China. At the presentation both the students and faculty were presented and the paper was widely appreciated. It was decided to publish it in the RCDS Journal. However permission to publish it was denied by the Government of India on the ground that it contained sensitive information.

Tenure as Air Attaché in the Indian High Commission in UK

On completion of the course at the RCDS he was promoted to Air Commodore and posted at the Indian High Commission as the Air Attaché. Besides UK he was also accredited as the Defence Attaché to Sweden. The 1970s was the time when the Indian Armed Forces were going in for major acquisitions and upgradation of equipment particularly aircraft, missiles and electronic hardware and both the UK and Sweden were major producers of original equipment.

His work required him to travel to Sweden and other Nordic countries frequently because the Indian defence forces were examining the possibility of inducting the SAAB fighters, tanks, Carl Gustav anti-tank rocket launchers and 155 mm Bofors heavy guns. He had to see the performance of these weapons systems and determine the ability of the Swedish arms industry to fulfil India's requirements.

From the UK India was negotiating for the purchase of Jaguar Fighter Bombers, spares for the aging fleet of Canberras, Hunters, Gnats, Sea Hawks, VTOL Hawker Harriers (for the Indian Navy), Super Constellations, Hawker Sidley 748 transport aircraft and Sea Cat and Tiger Cat anti-aircraft missiles. As the assembly lines producing the older aircraft had closed down years ago sourcing spares for these aircraft was a time-consuming and difficult task.

At times the only source of spare parts was from countries that had earlier imported these aircraft from the UK and had now decommissioned them. In some cases the spares were obtained by cannibalising them from junked aircraft. These parts had first to be located then negotiated for and after removal from the old airframe inspected and certified for use. This was a time-consuming task but he managed to keep the IAF fleet of British origin aircraft flying.

His work also required him to attend social functions and other events associated with duties and lives of diplomats in both the countries that he was accredited to. This kept him fully occupied but thanks to the five-day working week with an extra day's leave he was able to take his wife and children around the United Kingdom and Europe on motoring holidays. Having owned MG sports coupe in his younger days motoring is something that he has always enjoyed and the tenure in Europe with its good motorways and regulated traffic gave him an opportunity to share and enjoy his travels with the family.

He had been working for two years at the High Commission when they were visited by a senior IAF Officer who told the High Commissioner B.K. Nehru that the Air Force wished to post Chandan back to India and promote another officer already working in the High Commission to take Chandan's place. B.K. Nehru who had been impressed with Chandan Singh's work replied, 'over my dead body', so Chandan continued at his post for three full years plus.

The three and a half years tenure in the UK was the happiest period of his life. As an Air Attaché he had a large and comfortable flat and adequate allowances to live comfortably. Having married late his children were little more than babies and he still cherishes the time he was able to spend with them.

11

The Final Years with the IAF

On returning to India he was posted to Air Headquarters Delhi and spent a year in the new post which was not too demanding but a worthwhile experience for it enabled him to see the functioning of both Air HQ and the Ministry of Defence closely. He was then promoted to the rank of Air Vice Marshal and posted as Director of the Aviation Research Centre (ARC). What he saw both at Air HQ and ARC was something that he was unhappy with. There was a disconnect between the two and the easy going "chalta hai" attitude of the babus was not something that he could tolerate.

After only a year in the new post at ARC the Air Force wanted him back but the ARC which functions under the Prime Minister's Office was reluctant to let him go. The Air Chief had to personally intervene and obtain Chandan's release on the grounds that his turn for promotion to Air Marshal had come. He required at least one report from the IAF before he could be considered for promotion to Air Marshal.

On his release from ARC he was posted as Senior Air Staff Officer at Headquarters Central Air Command Allahabad. As SASO the work load was heavy. He was responsible for not only the operational but also the maintenance, training, logistics and personnel of all IAF assets in the Command's Area of responsibility which covered almost half the country. He was perpetually on the move on inspections and inquiries. He relished his job for after many years at a desk job in UK he could indulge in his passion for flying at will.

When everything was going his way and his future in the Air Force and further promotions were assured his personal life and career suffered a setback. His wife fell seriously ill and in spite of the best possible treatment her condition did not improve. With two young children to look after this was a huge distraction from his work which had always been his topmost priority.

Feeling that he would not be able to do justice to his job he put in his papers for early retirement from the Air Force. The Chief and all his friends tried to dissuade him but he was insistent on leaving, to be able to devote all his time to the treatment of his wife and looking after the children.

12

Retirement

He chose to make his home at Jodhpur and devote all his time to the care of Mrs Chandan Singh. Modern medicine proved to be of no help and it was in this desperate situation that he was advised by a friend to look for a cure elsewhere. He was referred to a lady who was revered as a living Sati Mata. Even though not a believer in the occult he was now desperate enough to try anything.

What modern medicine could not do the blessings of Sati Mata and a Bhopa (wandering holy man) did.

He was told that he had been neglecting the worship of their Kul Devi (family deity) and that things would only improve if he asked the Kul Devi for forgiveness and then performed the required rituals.

Chandan Singh, not a great believer in rituals and the occult, was now so desperate that he was prepared to even give this a shot. As soon as he completed the performance of the required rituals, Mrs Chandan Singh miraculously recovered fully and has been well ever since.

In Rajasthan there are many such stories and they concern not only uneducated villagers but also well educated and sophisticated men and women of the world. Many people, particularly the urban elites, scoff at these miracles. To them my advice is go out of your comfortable drawing rooms and see the real world and you will find that the truly enlightened souls know that science and spirituality are not in conflict but in harmony with each other. When Robert Oppenheimer, a man of science and a genius, quoted the Bhagavad Gita on seeing the first atom bomb explode he knew what he was doing.

In due course Chandan's two children, Sajjan and Namrata, completed their education and are happily married with children of their own. Sajjan and his wife Moomal continue to stay with his parents and look after them. Sajjan is happy running a small guest house and pursuing his academic interests. His elder son Capt Harshveer Singh is in the Army and the younger Divyavir is with the Taj Hotels.

Namrata is married to Rawat Veerbhadra Singh of Deogarh, a noble family of Mewar and has two children, a boy Mayurdhwaj and a girl, Pavitra. They are owners of most impressive fort/palace which they have converted into a heritage hotel. Their forefathers were great patrons of the arts and their collection of paintings from their own atelier is one of the best in India.

The Air Marshal's younger brother, Brig Hari Singh AVSM has two sons, the elder Maj Gen Kishan Singh AVSM VSM and Mahavir Singh. His youngest brother Mohan Singh was with the police and received the President's Medal for gallantry and the Police Medal for exceptional service. He had no children.

After his retirement the Air Marshal tried his hand at business which met with both great success and failure. He found himself in some difficulty till Jaswant Singh who had become a senior politician came to his assistance which helped him to stabilise his financial position.

The family stays in their house in central Jodhpur which Chandan had built just before retirement. Part of the house has been converted into a guest house for foreign tourists, which Sajjan looks after. The Air Marshal has been gifted with exceptionally good mental and physical health, a gift from God for years of devoted and exceptional service to the country. May we continue to enjoy the blessing of his company for many more years to come.

On 29 March 2020 at the age of 95 Air Vice Chandan Singh passed away peacefully at his home in Jodhpur.

Appendix I

A Helicopter Pilot's Account of the Meghna Crossing

Air Commodore Shridharan's Account: Baptism by Fire

Helicopter Operations: The Bangladesh War

Doc Shridharan was a newly commissioned helicopter pilot who had just completed his operational training at the commencement of the war and his account gives the perspective from an air force pilot's point of view of the events during the war. His account both complements and corroborates the accounts of Air Vice Marshal Chandan Singh as also the accounts of the Army officers who took part in the heliborne operations in 1971. It is interesting to read as to how intensive and continuous the training of pilots in IAF was, As a junior Chandan Singh would have gone through the same process. This professionalism of the pilots was perhaps the key factor in the success of the heliborne operations carried out by the Army and Air Force during the 71 war.

1. On completion of our air force training in the 102 Pilot's course on June 21, 1969, two of us Anil Kumar Oberoi fondly known as Obe and I from a batch of 15 helicopter pilots were posted to one of the remotest placed helicopter units 110-HU of the IAF at a place called Kumbigram in South Assam. Obe and I travelled together by train from Bangalore to Silchar, the nearest railway station to Kumbhigram stuck for a few days. At Silchar we were stuck for a few days on account of floods as it was in the midst of the monsoon season. Consequently we arrived at Kumbhigram a few days late. On 2ⁿᵈ July

we reported in pouring rain at the Officers Mess where we were greeted by total darkness and received by Fg Offr Charles DeSouza, popularly known as Chippy who told us that on the way to Kumbigram from Silchar we crossed a place called Dwarbund, then halfway another town called Udharbund, and finally the Air Force Station known as Batti Bund. The air force station had electricity by its own generator from 1800 hours to 2200 hours at night and from 0500 hours to 0700 hours in the morning. On entering the mess, we found that all the other pilots had gathered to greet us and we were ushered into 110-HU with a night of partying at the end of which Obe and I were dead drunk.

2. On 3ʳᵈ July with a groggy head we both reported for work on another dull miserable day. The monsoon was in full fury and Kumbhigram as with the rest of Assam has to bear with creepy crawly creatures of all shapes, sizes and colours who escaping the flood waters vie for living space on higher ground where our work and living accommodation was. They were all over on the floor, walls, ceiling and even on us in spite of liberal doses of insect repellent rubbed on to our skins and clothes. There was no escaping them. The mosquitoes harassed us at night and the leeches came in all sizes and after having gorged on our blood the larger species known as elephant leeches would become the size and shape of medium sized sausages which incidentally were a great food and protein supplement relished by some tribal groups. The unit crew room was a large tent. The only building was the CO's office along with that of the Adjutant. The technical DSS (daily servicing section) was also housed in another tent. The unit helicopters, the magnificent MI-4, were parked in blast pens dispersed around the base along taxi ways on the southern side of the only runway 06/24. The runway itself was on elevated ground as the surrounding areas were flood prone.

3. We were quickly interviewed by the Flt Cdr then Flt Lt

A. Mehtani, who later left on promotion to take over 115-HU at Tezpur. Later the CO Sqn Ldr S.S. Anjla interviewed briefed us on various aspects of our future training and conduct, etc. He had to leave shortly afterwards as he met with an accident at one of the helipads in Mizoram and badly damaged his tail rotor. He had gone there for a tryst with an old lady friend. I attended his Court Martial as an officer under instruction. It was quite an experience watching your CO being grilled.

4. On 17ᵗʰ July after a strict general test on the MI-4 and other allied aviation subjects conducted by then Flt Lt T. Jayaraman we both had our first sortie on the MI-4. It was a great helicopter to fly but initially the flying was difficult because after our training on the Bell 47-G3 this helicopter was huge and the pilot's cabin itself was a problem climbing into. But I was quickly launched into action and shortly on 28ᵗʰ July, barely three weeks after reporting to Kumbhigram, was sent with Fg Offr Solomon better known as Solly to a detachment at Aizwal, then a district headquarters now the capital of Mizoram. Here we were tasked to operate with 61 Mtn Brigade which was involved in counterinsurgency operations against Mizo hostiles who were motivated, trained, financed and based across the border in East Pakistan. Here we did several sorties to transport troops to remote areas which were otherwise several days march away on foot. But the poor troops though transported by us into action had to march back to base on foot after the action. (I along with some of my men suffered this fate several times. I suppose when I willingly choose to join the PBI—poor bloody infantry—at the Academy I cannot blame anyone else but myself) On return from a very interesting and intriguing tenure in Aizwal, Obe and I were off to civilisation at Chandigarh for the ground training technical course known as MCF. It was a good and interesting course and we also had a great time during the weeks that we were there, coming up for a

solo check when the conversion was curtailed as there was no QFI to send us solo on the type. By that time the CO had been court martialled and the Flt Cdr posted out and they were the only Qualified Flying Instructors. However Eastern Air Command came to our rescue and gave permission for us to be given a solo check and sent solo by another class of instructor known as Right Hand Instructional Pilot and Right Hand Check Pilot (RHIP and RHCP). Many years later, I became one of this kind on the MI-8 and MI-17 as I never had a godfather to make it to FIS and QFIS course at Tambaram.

5. On February 22, 1970, I was declared U/T Ops day on MI-4. After flying my quota of copilot flying and area familiarisation in the area of operation of the unit from Meghalaya, Mizoram, Tripura, Manipur and some parts of Nagaland my operational conversion started in November 1970. Finally in May 1971, I was declared fully operational Day on type.

6. In September 1971, I appeared for my first categorisation test with the Command Examiner on type Sqn Ldr DC Kaushik and was declared D White Day only as I was only Day Ops then. I continued.............

7. Subsequent to that I did a few long ferries of MI-4s from 3 Base Repair Workshop with our flight Commander Flt Lt Pushpendra Vaid known as Palokha and the other with Flg Offr S.S. Hundal fondly known as Sukhi from 109 Helicopter Unit at Jammu. These were great experiences for me as trainee captain at first and full-fledged captain later from Jammu all the way via Chandigarh, Delhi, Lucknow, Allahabad, Patna, Hashimara, Gauhati to Kumbhigram. These were done between August and October and I really built my hours as captain on type, by this time though we were not directly involved, we knew that the Army was already engaged with the enemy. There were daily reports of skirmishes and some casualties on our side who had to be evacuated by us.

8. Then finally just prior to the commencement of the war,

we were sent by an Otter aircraft of 59 Sqn Chabua to their base to appear to appear with Air Force examiner Wing Commander C. Rama Rao who was also the Station Commander Chabua at the time. We arrived at night and soon we had a briefing by the Examiner and our night flying test was carried out. At night we all had to undergo a oral viva test and a short written test at the officers' mess by the examiner. After a brief rest at night, early next morning our day test was carried out by Wing Commander Rama Rao.

OP Cactus Lily

The lights went off as usual in the Officers' Mess at 2200 hours on the night of 3rd December but early the next morning we were abruptly woken up with a general recall to all our respective units as war had been declared by Pakistan on the Western Front by attacking our airfields. The balloon had gone up and we were plunged into a full scale war on a clear and wonderful morning of 4th December.

We regrouped at the unit and I who had been briefed by the Station Commander Gp Capt J.P. Latta came to the unit and briefed the unit. The Station Commander had mentioned the Pakistani attack and also told us that our attack aircraft had struck back and the PAF in the Eastern Sector had been almost neutralised. But we had yet to disperse all our helicopters to various locations with a set of ground crew to service the helicopters.

The main body of the unit along with the CO and Flt Commanders would move to Teliamura in Tripura and report to HQ 4 Corps to support the army in communication, casualty evacuation and special helicopter borne operations. Me and Fg Offr S.S. Krishnamurthy (Kruts) were detailed to proceed to Dharmanagar also in North Tripura.

We were back at base for the night. Next day the helicopter was dispersed to Imphal in Manipur but once again in the evening we were back to our base. On the 5th morning we were told to ferry the helicopter to Aizwal. We spent the night at 1

Assam Rifles Officers' Mess and spent the day listening to the radio reports of the progress of the war. Late on the afternoon of 7th December we received orders from the Army to report to Kailashahar in North Tripura where a major operation was in progress. At dusk we set course with the ground crew for the Advance Landing Ground at Kailashahar which was an old airfield used by Dakotas of both the IAF and Indian airlines for short hopping flights. It had an old disused Air Traffic Control building and we stayed in the buildings next to it. The unit had started the helilift of the 4/5 Gurkha battalion to the south of a railway station in Sylhit. The CO Sqn Ldr C.S. Sandhu and Vaid had already done two sorties along with a few other pilots.

Kruts and I were inducted into battle soon after midnight when it was still dark as the moon had still not risen and it was total darkness when we did our first sortie. We flew VIC formation of three aircraft and proceeded from Kailashahar with a load of 8 to 10 troops or a gun and six troops to Sylhit. The landing ground was marked by Goose neck lamps by party led Fg Offr S.C. Sharma who was a course mate of mine and had come over from his parent unit 49 Sqn at. He had been brought over by Gp Capt Chandan Singh who was the Station Commander at Jorhat but was now operating with 4 Corps. He also commanded the Bangladesh Air Force who provided cover for this operation with their armed Otters and helicopters.

The helicopters would land in a VIC formation in front of their respective goose neck lamps and after disembarking the troops give the readiness call to the leader on R/T. Then the leader would take off to the left avoiding a building in the front from where the Pakistanis were firing at the landing ground.

My first sortie or baptism by fire was very interesting. I was number three in the formation and hence the last to land. It was a bright moonlit night and the landing area was visible almost as in the day. We landed and disembarked the troops and guns as planned. I did another sortie immediately after that and on return carried out an external examination of the aircraft and found bullet holes on the fuselage but no other damage. I carried out seven sorties by night and day during this operation always flying in the difficult No. 3 position.

15. During one of the missions, Flt Lt P.N. Rao whose air craft was under fire while on the ground at landing area took off to the forbidden left and the helicopter was hit from below and one of the Gurkhas was killed and another seriously wounded. He had to return with these two casualties and landed back safely at Kailashahar. Fortunately the aircraft was not seriously damaged and had only a few bullet holes on the floor of the passenger cabin. He was awarded a mention in dispatches for this after the war.

16. In another incident, Flg Offr Chatwal's helicopter came under fire and a bullet came in from the left and landed between Chatwal and his co-pilot Jagdeep Singh popularly known as Martian. The bullet had grazed Chatwal's leg. The troops jumped out and Chatwal returned to base and did several more sorties as there was no structural damage to his helicopter. Chatwal was also mentioned in dispatches. By the 8th evening the entire 4/5 Gurkhas had been heli-lifted to Sylhit. On conclusion of the operation the Squadron moved to Agartala and the unit pilots and other officers were put in the old Air Traffic Control building while the ground crew were in tents close by.

At Agartala we were under the overall command of Gp Capt Chandan Singh and were given a briefing about our future operations which were likely to be at Brahmanbaria, Raipura, Narsinghdi, Baidya Bazaar, Dwarkandi and Daudkandi. Like the Sylhit operation these operations entailed carrying units and formations of IV Corps across various rivers, the largest of which was the Meghna. The operations would culminate in the final assault and capture of Dacca. Here Chandan Singh who was a veteran of the Second World War and as an army officer warned us that the assault on Dacca would involve street fighting by our infantry and we should be prepared for many casualties among our troops.

In order to carry the maximum numbers of troops and their weapons and other supplies we would be exceeding the permissible weight limits. However with a slightly longer than normal take off run it was possible to do so. At this time we did not realise how much more we would actually carry once these operations started. Sometimes we ferried more than double the permissible weight limits and even today some people doubt that we did actually carry so many troops and their arms and equipment across the rivers with only about 8-12 helicopters available at any one time.

Our first helilift was on the afternoon of 9th December when we lifted 4 Guards from Brahmanbaria to Raipura and then on 11th December the rest of the 311 Brigade and supporting artillery to Narsingdi which had been secured by 4 Guards a battalion I knew well from my days in Mizo Hills where we had jointly carried out some counterinsurgency operations. When working with 4 Guards, everything functioned like a well-oiled machine that is not to say that the other units were not good but 4 Guards under Col Himmeth Singh was exceptional and an example to the rest of the Army.

The conduct of the officers and men whether in war, counter-insurgency operations and even in peace time when I enjoyed the hospitality of their officers' mess was a delight to behold. Perhaps I am biased because the battalion had some friends of mine from our days at the National Defence Academy but that was the general view of this unit by all IAF and even Army officers who came into contact with them. Later after the war I came to know from the Pakistani prisoners of war that even they held the same views about 4 Guards who had chased them without respite from the beginning of the war on 1st December from Akhaura to their final surrender at the Dacca Race Course on 16th December.

At Agartala our helicopters were augmented by aircraft from 105-HU bringing the total helicopter fleet up to fifteen. After 4 Guards had secured the Western bank of the Meghna, we had no interference from the ground by the enemy but the danger of fire from boats on the rivers was always present and also although the IAF had achieved total air superiority a lone wolf attack by a PAF F 86 Sabre could not be ruled out. Another problem we faced was from the dust and paddy straw lying on our landing zones. The straw and dust would be churned up by our rotors sometimes making the final landing almost blind. However, we did not allow it to affect our operations and luckily there were no mishaps either.

At Agartala 110-HU was augmented by some helicopters from 105-HU at Chaubatia and some from 111-HU at Hashimara under the command of Nanda Cariappa bringing the total fleet strength to fifteen helicopters. These operstions were done from the 10th to 15th December. During this time the weather gods were very kind to us. We had clear days and moonlit nights. Every day we had a mass briefing conducted under the supervision of the task force Commander Gp Capt Chandan Singh and a debrief when all aircraft were back. The operations were very smooth and good coordination with the Army was ensured for which due credit must be given to the personal equation that existed between Gp Capt Chandan Singh and Lt Gen Sagat Singh. A lot of credit must also be shared by the pilots and junior Army officers who developed and nurtured deep bonds of friendship from their days together at NDA. We knew and understood each other and were not going to let anything interfere in achieving our common aims. One day when Col Osmani, the overall Commander of the Mukti Bahini, was flying in one of the helicopters of 105-HU from Chabua piloted by Flt Lt R.V. Singh the aircraft was fired upon from the ground and on landing some bullet holes in the fuselage and minor damage to the rotors was detected.

I carried out 38 sorties from Agartala with different co-pilots and it was an enthralling experience operating so closely with 57 Mountain Division and all its battalions and not one helicopter was damaged during our operations with 57 Div unlike at Sylhit with Mtn Div under command of Maj Gen (later General) Krishna Rao.

On the 15th December evening, we came to know that the Pakistanis had sued for a ceasefire and that we had accepted it. So all offensive operations were halted. But not knowing all the details and terms of the ceasefire and whether it would lead to their surrender there was tension and anxiety mixed with hope and exultation. Finally on the 16th morning, we came to know that Maj Gen Jacob Chief of Staff Eastern Command had gone to Dacca by Helicopter to negotiate the terms of surrender.

In the afternoon 5 MI-4-3 Chetaks were prepard at Dacca to fly to Dacca carrying the Indian brasshats and some press people to take the surrender of the Pakistani Forces. I was flying as a co-pilot with Sqn Ldr Nanda Carriappa CO of 111-HU. Obe and I had been rewarded to fly in as co-pilots as we were the junior most pilots in the Sqn and we had also done the maximum number of sorties. It was a clear and lovely day and as we approached Dacca, Nanda Carriappa started looking for the golf course. I learnt later that he and Col Himmeth Singh CO 4 Guards, Brig Mishra Comdr 311 Bde and Maj Shamsher Metha OC 5 Indep Armd Sqn had made a wager to play at Dacca. They made a four ball even before the ink on the surrender document had dried, I however was least interested in golf. After we landed, we were taken by 4 Guards who had entered the city earlier and secured the airfield to the maidan to witness the surrender.

What a sight the maidan was. It appeared as if the entire two million people of Dacca had congregated there. Even today I wonder as to how the guardsmen were able to control the crowd and prevent the Pakistani Generals from being lynched by the crowd. This was a moment rarely if ever experienced by any one in their lifetime and I felt privileged to have been part of the team that made it happen. In a lighter vein, I must mention that the famous photograph of the surrender document being signed and Aurora and Niazi sitting at the table and being overlooked by the rest of the Indian Brass hats all very serious and solemn as befitting the occasion. But in the corner you can see me carried away by the moment elbowing aside Jacob to have a look at the surrender document. I suppose that being a good South Indian Brahmin, supposedly with a very high intellect, I wanted to see for myself that the terms of the surrender were correct.

Appendix II

Meghna Crossing, December 9, 1971

Account of Maj Chandrakant Singh
Vrc OC A Coy 4 Guards

If any one single operation were to be cited as the turning point of the Bangladesh Liberation war, undoubtedly it was the heliborne crossing of the Meghna river by 4 Guards which was helilifted across the Meghna river by 110 and 105 Helicopter units of the IAF on December 9, 1971. This is an army man's firsthand account of his unit's role in this operation. As such it may appear that I have not given adequate credit to the brave pilots of the two Helicopter Units who flew us across, but that is not my intention. These magnificent men and their flying machines performed wonders far in excess of what could be legitimately expected of them. Throughout this and other operations they displayed the highest levels of professionalism, airmanship and gallantry. My salaams to them and their crews for without them we could not have achieved what we did and Dacca would have remained a distant dream.

8ᵗʰ December

We had harboured for the night at a village called Arhand on the Comilla-Brahmanbaria Highway effectively cutting off Pak 14 Div at Brahmanbaria from their other Division at Comilla. In the last seven days of almost continuous battle we had punched a wide hole in the outer crust of defences along the border, captured Akhaura and penetrated about forty kilometres deep and cleared an area forty kilometres wide, creating a suitable launching pad for further operations.

Early in the morning we were joined by our Brigade

Commander, Brig R.N. Mishra who asked my Commanding Officer Lt Col Himmeth Singh to accompany him to recce a possible crossing place on the Meghna. Major Tuffy Marwah with Charlie Company had been sent on a search and destroy mission a day earlier and reported back on the radio that the area was clear of enemy troops and he had encountered only light resistance. So the Brigade Commander with our CO accompanied by a small protection party took off for the recce and I was left in charge of the battalion.

With us was Major Shamsher Metha and his 5 Indep Armoured Squadron. At about 0700 hours I got a call on the radio that GOC 57 Mtn Div Maj Gen Ben Gonzalves wanted to speak to me. This was odd for rarely in battle do Divisional Commanders talk to lowly Company Commanders. But before the war we had worked out a system of coded call signs where by using nick/first names commanders at all levels could talk to each other.

So it was Ben for Paunchy. He said he was unable to contact either Brig Mishra or Lt Col Himmeth Singh and he wanted the battalion to reach Brahmanbaria as soon as possible. I told him that both the Brigade Commander and my CO had gone on a recce and were out of range of our radio set. So as soon as I established contact with them and got their orders, I would move the Bn. Now the army has a well established chain of command which must be always adhered to, especially in war. I hated to think of what my Commanding Officer's reaction would be when on his return from the recce he found his battalion missing.

Sensing my hesitancy in implementing his order he said "Paunchy this is Ben, get your Bn to Brahmanbaria immediately and I will meet you on the Bridge on the Pagla river, and I will ask the GSO1 (the chief operations officer at the Div HQ) who has a more powerful radio set to inform Himmeth." Senior Commanders are not expected to break the chain of command and issue orders three levels down just as junior commanders are expected to first approach their immediate senior and not go over his head and approach directly commanders higher than him.

As expected, Himmeth on return to Arhand, was not too pleased to find his Bn missing and even though when explained the circumstances was still slightly cross. But the GOC left me with no choice. I assembled the Bn and leaving a small party behind to receive my CO and Brigade Commander on their return and inform them of the GOC's orders, we took off for Brahmanbaria mounted on Shamsher's tanks and some captured vehicles. Shamsher now had 17 tanks, three more than his authorised holding. We had captured these three Pak PT-76 tanks at Akhaura. Shamsher's men after repairing them got them on the road and they were now a part of his Squadron. These same tanks had played hell into my Company a few days earlier. Supported by two companies of infantry they had overrun one of my platoons and captured seven of my men. But now they were a welcome addition to our force.

Brahmanbaria was about 15 kms from Arhand but the PT-76 is a fast moving tank and we got to Brahmanbaria in less than an hour and met Gen Gonzalves at the Bridge on the River Pagla. Two spans of the bridge had been blown up by the retreating Pakistanis. With the General was his ADC, Helicopter pilot, Maj Goraya BM of the Arty brigade and some other officers and men. It says something about the quality of our commanders that the first man in Brahmanbaria was the GOC himself, having been brought up on the stories of Rommel and Patton. Now seeing the same qualities being displayed by our own commanders it was very inspiring. The General was fuming and fretting with Brig M.L. Tuli Commander of 73 Brigade and from what we could make out he was expressing his severe displeasure at Brig Tuli for not having closed in with the Pakistanis during the last twenty-four hours. Not having sent out patrols, Brig Tuli was not aware that Brahmanbaria had been evacuated twenty-four hours earlier. Had he been more energetic, we had a fair chance of capturing all elements of PAK 14 Div at Brahmanbaria. It was only when the GOC flew over the town in his helicopter that he realised that the town had been abandoned by the Pakistanis. Brahmanbaria was an important objective considering the fact that here was located the headquarters of both PAK 14 Div and 27 Bde. The GOC ordered me to take the Bn into Brahmanbaria and clear the town, but it was easier said than done. The bridge was down, the river was not fordable and the tanks though amphibious could not carry the extra load of infantry while swimming across. We had therefore to scrounge for some country boats which we found but with no oars. So some of my men had to swim across and by joining some bed lining ropes which are standard equipment of our jawans, we managed to organise a ferry service, pulling the boats to and fro across the river.

In about an hour we had managed to get the battalion across. Shamsher had some problem getting the captured Pakistani tanks across as these tanks leaked because of faulty watertight seals. How he got them across, I do not know for by then I had taken off with my men. In the meantime, Brig Mishra and my CO Col Himmeth Singh joined us and so had Tuffy Marwah and his company. They had crossed the river a few kilometres downstream and also fought a few actions on the way to our rendezvous that very morning.

By improving and lots of good luck, we managed to cross the river. If the enemy had left behind even a small party to contest our crossing they could have delayed us by at least a day. But it appears that the stuffing had been knocked out of them at Akhaura and they wanted to find safety behind the Meghna.

We now fanned out and commenced securing Brahmanbaria, during our search of their Division Headquarter and in one of the HQ bunkers which according to Gen Sagat Singh were built as if to withstand a nuclear strike and a siege of several months we found the bodies of six jawans of 10 Bihar. They had their hands tied behind their backs and had been shot in the back of their heads. I pointed this out to our GOC. He was furious and declared that should we capture Maj Gen Abdul Majid GOC Pak 14 Div, he would have him tried by a court martial and sentenced to death for war crimes and violation of the Geneva Convention on treatment of prisoners. Alas this was not to be because our political masters decided otherwise.

We also saw the bodies of forty-four local Bengalis, probably Mukti Bahini lying in a ditch near the stadium. They had their hands tied and had been shot in the head. Today's generation brought up on 24X7 television and seeing the work of the ISIS in Iraq and Syria may be able to understand the affect it had on us. We not only could not give them a decent burial or even cover their faces but the smell of rotting bodies bloated to unrecognisable shapes and the sight of bottle green flies buzzing over their faces and maggots crawling over and eating into their flesh is something one wants to forget but can never do.

The butchered Mukti Bahini's bodies lay in the open and dogs and vultures had got to them. However having a job to do, we had to move on leaving the bodies behind but taking the memories with us. Over the years, I have heard many people calling us war veterans as aggressive right wing war mongers whenever we espouse strong action against lawless anti national forces. My answer to them is that we who have seen the ugly side of war are the most pacifist of people for we don't want to go through it again. But if surgery is required to excise a sore to save the rest of the body it must take place and in time so that not only is the body cured but a message is sent out that we are prepared to take timely and drastic action.

During the securing of Pak 14 Div Headquarters, we recovered several top secret documents which indicated the haste in which the Pakistani HQ staff had abandoned their positions. These documents were handed over to the ADC to Gen Gonzalves. We now expected 73 Brigade to take over the advance from us as after the first day of the war when they had been involved in a supporting role they had seen no action, whereas our brigade that is 311 Bde had been involved in continuous fighting and needed time to rest and replenish our ammunition and food supplies, but it was not to be.

Gen Gonzalves was still fuming at the Commander 73 Bde and so ordered us to resume the advance to Ashuganj about

20 kms away. Ashuganj is a large town on the east bank of the Meghna which is a twin to a still larger town Bhairab Bazaar on the West bank. Linking the two is more than a kilometre long Coronation bridge, the only bridge on the Meghna. At about midday we resumed our advance once more mounted on tanks, D company under Maj Kharbanda along the road and A Company which was my Company on the right flank. A and D company were mounted on Shamsher's tanks but the rest of the battalion was in some civilian transport and captured Pakistan Army vehicles.

Our most prized and visible possession was a red fire engine from the Brahmanbaria fire station, this was requisitioned by Tuffy Marwah OCC Company who donning a fireman's shiny helmet and vigorously ringing the bell and sounding the hooter followed close behind, hoping to scare the Pakistanis or may be just for fun.

At first we met with slight resistance which we brushed aside but the constant shelling and exploding air burst shells was a constant danger. Just short of village Talashahar, we hit the enemy's screen position, Shamsher's tank on which some my men and I were riding was fired upon by an anti-tank gun. Fortunately the shell exploded a few feet away. We jumped off and Shamsher with another three tanks charged the enemy position capturing it and scattering the enemy troops. But Kharbanda OC B Coy was not so lucky. In an attempt to clear an enemy position he charged their machine gun post and received a burst in the upper leg. He also lost a few men who were killed and wounded.

It was here that 2 Lt Rajendra Mohan and his troop of tanks came to his rescue. They charged the enemy position and cleared it. Otherwise Kharbanda and some of his men would have either been taken prisoner or killed. We advanced another kilometre or so and as the light was fading took up defensive positions for the night. There was no way that we could have got into a street and house-to-house fighting that night inside Ashuganj, because firstly we were just not prepared for it. We were tired, had carried out no reconnaissance. Our Artillery had not fetched up because the Engineers had not yet bridged the Pagla River at Brahmanbaria. But most importantly, we had received no orders to do it.

On the other hand, the enemy was at Ashuganj in full force. Their Pak 27 Brigade with HQ Pak 14 Div totalling about 6,000 troops were against us. To make matters more difficult, they had an Arty OP sited on top of a 300-ft grain storage Silo on the river bank inside Ashuganj. From his position he could observe and bring down effective fire for miles around as either 18 Rajput and 10 Bihar from our Brigade or 73 Brigade who had done no serious fighting till date had been earmarked for this task. Once my men had taken their positions and dug down, we could dig our fox holes in fifteen minutes flat in the soft and moist soil of Bangladesh. I went to the Bn HQ which was located in a Masjid in the hope that it would be marked as such on their maps and so the Pakistanis would not shell it. Our guess was right for though all our other positions were shelled that night the Masjid was spared.

At the Bn HQ over whisky which was miraculously produced by the CO's batman Guardsman Hari Singh, Col Himmeth Singh told me that he had received orders to meet the Brigade Commander at Brahmanbaria at 0600 hours and I was to take charge of the Bn in his absence. After a hot dinner much appreciated by everyone for we had subsisted on cold and wet shakarparas for over a week. Even they had been finished some days ago and I returned to my company.

Here I was met by my Senior JCO Sub Makhan Lal. He was a veteran of the Second World War and the Kashmir war. No one could have asked for a better senior JCO. He was cool, calm and a steadying influence on all including me. But now he was very agitated, on inquiring why? He let me know that the reason for his anger was that the four jawans from the Engineer Regiment who were attached to my Company had gone missing. He had asked them to dig their fox holes some distance from where my batman was digging a fox hole for me. But thinking that the safest place would be next to the company commander they had dug their fox hole close to mine. So he had given them a piece of his mind and asked them to move some distance away and dig fresh fox holes for themselves. They were not too pleased to have to dig once again and just then the company position was shelled. After the shelling ceased, Sub Makhan Lal had gone around the Company position to check if all was well with the men. He found the engineer boys missing and in spite of his best efforts, he could not trace them and presumed they had run away and deserted. There was nothing that we could do at this time. So I said we would resume the search in the morning, till then we could get some rest.

Early in the morning, I took off to the Bn HQ where the Adjutant Capt Vijay Dewan, popularly known as Glucose, met me and informed me that the CO had left a few minutes earlier in a jeep which the engineers had managed to get across the Meghna on an improvised raft. As soon as there was sufficient light, I took a round of the battalion's position. The forward companies were occasionally still being fired upon by the enemy with small arms. But as it was doing no damage, we held our own fire, not wanting to expend our own ammunition as replenishment was not easy.

We had been operating behind enemy lines for about nine days and therefore were particular about conserving ammunition which we knew was difficult to replenish. It was when I was seeing my own company that Sub Makhan Lal informed me that he had found the engineer boys and that they were all dead. When the shelling had started a shell had fallen into their trench and they had all been blasted to smithereens. Pieces of their bodies were strung up on the branches of trees above and around the trench.

At about 0900 hours I received a radio message from the CO to bring the Bn back post haste to Brahmanbaria and he would give further orders there. I asked him as to whom I was to hand over our positions for we were in contact with the enemy and exchanging sporadic small arms fire. He told me not to worry about that as 18 Rajput and 10 Bihar from our Brigade and 73 Brigade were in the vicinity and they would be moving in from the north and the south. Having collected the Bn, we started marching back after having to shed Shamsher's tanks who joined 18 Rajput.

This constant marching to and fro much like the famous ditty about the Duke of York marching his men up the hill and then down again was getting to be irritating. However as every infantryman knows that this has always been the fate of the Poor Bloody Infantry. By about 1300 hours, we had reached Brahmanbaria stadium which was our designated RV. Here the CO met us and told us that we had been tasked to cross the Meghna and helicopters would be landing soon to take us across.

My reaction to this is best summed up in Col Himmeth Singh's own words in an article he wrote "Paunchy who has a wonderful sense of humour when told about the heliborne operation made this absolutely unbeatable remark. He said that Sagat always felt that the battalion could do anything. Thank God that this time he had chosen to give us helicopters and hadn't decided that the battalion should swim across the Meghna." For whatever faith Sagat had in the capabilities of the battalion the miles wide Meghna was outside our swimming capability.

We were given new maps which covered the area from Brahmanbaria to Dacca and also included our next objective across the Meghna, the Landing Zone at Raipura. We immediately started preparing our men for the task. The first thing to do was work out the load tables. We could load about fifteen troops and three or four Bengali porters who carried our extra ammunition in each helicopter. We had also to warn the men about being hit by the tail rotors of the helicopters which could be fatal.

Fortunately for us nearly all our officers, JCOs, NCOs and senior guardsmen had some experience of the MI-4 Helicopters first in 1964 at Hashimara on the borders with Bhutan and then in 1970 in Mizo Hills. This stood us in good stead. While we tied up loose ends the helicopters started landing and at the same time an unending stream of bodies and wounded jawans of 18 Rajput started arriving at the stadium. 18 Rajputs had met with a setback at Ashuganj after we had withdrawn. Not a very auspicious way to begin a new operation, particularly when undertaking something which the Indian Army had never done before.

In the next few minutes, fourteen MI-4 helicopters were lined up in the stadium. All were without the rear boom doors of the holds to facilitate easy boarding and disembarking. Precisely at 1600 hours four helicopters carrying a platoon plus forming a sortie took off simultaneously after taxing a short distance as the helicopters were overloaded.

My CO Col Himmeth Singh and I were in the first helicopter of the first sortie. The pilot was the Squadron Commander of 110-HU Sqn Ldr C.S. Sandhu and sitting at the far corner of the hold was Group Captain Chandan Singh, the senior Air Force Officer in the IV Corps theatre.

Col Himmeth Singh and Gp Capt Chandan Singh had already carried out a recce of our landing zone earlier in the morning along with Gen Sagat Singh and Brig Mishra. Their helicopters had been shot at on the way home and Gen Sagat Singh received a bullet which passed through his beret grazing his forehead. A lesser man than him would have been perturbed but Sagat being Sagat it made no difference to him. As soon as we were airborne, two Gnat fighters flying CAP (combat air patrol) joined us. With the miles wide Meghna below us and noise of the rotors the scene was straight out of a Hollywood movie but we did not have even a box camera to record the event.

In about fifteen minutes we were over Raipura and landed on our designated LZ each helicopter only a few metres from the other. Such was the skill of the pilots that even at night with no or very primitive landing aids not one mishap occurred. As soon as we landed the platoon took up positions to secure the LZ and Flying Officer D.S. Shaheed began to mark the LZ with wet wheat flour dough. Before the second sortie landed, I was asked by my CO to take a recce patrol to Methikhanda Railway Station which was reported to be defended by a platoon of para military. Like any recce patrol, I had only a small party consisting of my radio operator Ved Prakash and two men as protection. I was to approach the Railway Station stealthily and report back what I observed. I had gone only about a kilometre when from out of nowhere thousands of Bengali natives emerged, all of them were shouting 'Joy Bangla-Joy Indira'. The crowd soon swelled to several thousand and my men and I were lifted on to their shoulders and carried forward. My men and I had never experienced anything like this before.

In our earlier actions the villagers would simply disappear. However now sensing that the tide was firmly in our favour and the Pakistanis were on the run the locals had taken heart and were emboldened to come out openly in our support. The Bengalis are normally a noisy people but when excited a Bengali crowd can perhaps be even heard several miles away. All pretence at stealth was given up and my men and I were carried by the crowd right upto Methikanda Railway Station.

When we got to the station, we found that the Pakistanis hearing our helicopters and then the crowd had panicked, they hastily loaded their belongings into a goods wagon and collecting some locals at gun point to push the wagon they took off towards Narsingdi, a large town about thirty kilometres away. So that is how we secured our objective without firing a shot and reported thus to my CO on the radio. He said that he would soon be sending the rest of my Company to link up with me. They would be coming with D Company which was commanded by young Surinder Singh because Uppal, the regular Coy Commander had been wounded some days ago.

There is a saying in the army that nothing is more dangerous than a subaltern with a map and compass. Sure enough, Surinder got lost with my company and his own company. It should have taken him at most about forty-five minutes to reach me. But even after five hours there was no sign of him. This caused me considerable anxiety because in the meantime, we had got into a faceoff with some local Mukti Bahini boys who were Urdu-speaking as they were deserters from the Pak army.

The situation could have got out of hand and it took quite an effort to establish our identity. When Surinder turned up in the morning he naturally got a mouth full from me and Col Himmeth. It transpired that instead of depending on his compass and map he had relied on a local guide who instead of taking him to Methikhnda took them towards Bhairab Bazaar where Pak 14 Div had withdrawn after blowing up the bridge on the Meghna. Surinder had hit their main defences and the Pakistanis reacted violently with heavy shelling. Six of my men were wounded and D Coy too suffered some casualties. But there was a positive outcome to this too.

Maj Gen Abdul Majid the GOC of Pak14 Div thinking that we had put a large force across the Meghna and were attacking them went into a shell from which his Div emerged only on 17th December to surrender to Gen Gonzalves. In the meantime, C Company under Tuffy Marwah secured the west bank of the Meghna to provide cover for 19 Punjab to cross over by ferry and it is they along with a battalion of the Mukti Bahini who contained a superior force of 6000 enemy troops of 14 Pak Inf Division at Bhaiarab Bazaar 6000 till their surrender.

With Pak 14 Div holed up at Bhairab Bazaar and showing no attempts to breakout, the way to Dacca was clear. The enemy had no troops to stop us and it was only a question of building up our strength which was done on 11th December when 18 Rajput and 10 Bihar were helilifted to Narsingdi which we had cleared earlier in the day. This was a remarkable feat of putting across the river one full brigade with its supporting artillery consisting of over three thousand men.

Before the war when Gen Sagat Singh had asked for permission to use helicopters for river crossing operations, both Army and Air HQ had thought that with the number of helicopters available it was only possible to lift an infantry company of about 150 men. In the next two days these helicopters ferried another six thousand troops across the Meghna at Daudkhandi. I had no further role to play in the war as in the process of clearing the town of Narsingdi, I picked up a bullet in the leg, but the show, bar the shouting, was over.

In another four days of little or no fighting the Pakistanis surrendered, and though I would have liked to have witnessed the surrender it is not something that I regret. Having captured dozens of buses, trucks, cycles and auto rickshaws and one fire engine the perennial favourite mode of transport of OCC Coy Maj Marwah's favourite, he had used another one to take him to Ashuganj from Brahmanbaria on 8th December. We were now well on our way to Dacca but this time on wheels and thank heaven not on our sore feet. On the 12th evening, we were in Demra three miles from Dacca and occupied the Adamjee Jute Mill.

Our patrols accompanied by artillery OP officers had crossed the River Satya Lakha and on the 13th we had started shelling Dacca Cantonment. Niazi and the civilian Governor of East Pakistan, Dr. Mullik approached their government in Islamabad and the United Nations asking for an immediate ceasefire.

This was without doubt Sagat's show and his finest hour, we were the tools that he used. Gp Capt Chandan Singh and the helicopter pilots deserve all the credit for making the impossible possible. Without them my battalion and other units of the army who followed could not have done it. I end with Dandin's words in the *Daskumar Charitra*–

> *A doer of things made possible*
> *He is counted amongst the immortals.*

Air Vice Marshal Chandan Singh
(Rtd) AVSM, Vrc, MVC

Service No. 3460
Branch in IAF : GD (P) later F(P)
Date of Birth : July 08, 1924
Date of Commission : July 27, 1946
Dte of Retirement : April 30, 1980

Honours and Awards

Ati Vishist Seva Medal (AVSM)

Award Date January 26, 1962
Announced January 26, 1961
Unit: No. 43 Squadron IAF (Jorhat)
Reference: Notification No. 15-Pres/62 dated January 26, 1962 published in Part 1, Section 1, Gazette of India dated February 3, 1962.

Citation

Sqn Ldr Chandan Singh was seconded from the Rajasthan State Forces to the Indian Air Force in the General Duties Branch with the rank of Flying Officer in 1946. He qualified as a service pilot in 1949. He was promoted Squadron Leader in 1957. He devised new techniques for training young pilots in high altitude flying, and was responsible for the selection of routes which have added to the safety of flights over the hazardous mountains of Ladakh. He is one of our outstanding transport pilots.

Note

43 Squadron, then operating from Jammu & Srinagar air fields, under Wg Cdr J.F. Lazarao (later AVM) were the pioneers who started supply dropping operations to support J&K Militia, after the PLA attack on Kongka La in October 1959. 43 was the only fixed wing squadron operating to Ladakh. The road through Zoji La was closed in winter. And there was no road between Leh and Thoise. So, for the Army personnel in these two sectors, 43 was truly their "Nabhsa Jeevan Dhara" [Lifeline Through the Sky].

Around 1960, Sqn Ldr Chandan Singh was a flight commander in 43 Sqn. It was his excellent professionalism which helped discover safe valley routes, and air dropping techniques, for operation to Kargil, Leh, Thoise, Fukche and Chushul airstrips and to many DZs like Galwan in Ladakh. Soon after, the C-119-G Packets operated in strength and the AN-12s entered the scene, using the same routes and techniques of Chandan Singh. Fukche and Chushul were handed over to the Packets while Leh, Thoise and DBO became the mainstay of the AN-12s. In 1962, No. 43 squadron operated to Kargil, Leh and Thoise airstrips and to Sultan Chushku DZ. Except for Leh, Daks were the only fixed wing aircraft operating to these places. In winter, Zoji La was snowed under and the whole of Ladakh was purely air maintained. Thoise and Sultan Chushku were air maintained even in summer.

When AN-12 aircraft entered IAF service in early 1961, based at Chandigarh, Chandan Singh was once again a pioneer to shift the air maintenance logistic base further forward to Leh, in support of operations in Ladakh. He is the one who conceived and led a formation of four AN-12 aircrafts, which airlifted AMX tanks from Chandigarh to Chushul, in the nick of time, when PLA was poised to overrun Chushul. This was an incredible feat of valour in the 1962 war, surprising everyone including PLA as well as Soviet designers. Because neither was the AN-12 designed for this task nor was Chushul fit for operations of such a large aircraft.

Vir Chakra (VrC)

Award Date October 20, 1962
Announced January 26, 1963
Unit: 44 Squadron IAF (Chandigarh)
Reference: Gazette of India, February 16, 1963 - No. 18-Pres/63, dated January 26, 1963

Citation

On October 20, 1962, Squadron Leader Chandan Singh was detailed to carry out supply dropping in the Chip Chap area in Ladakh, in an AN-12. On reaching the dropping zone, he noticed that the outposts were under heavy fire from the Chinese forces. He successfully dropped vital supplies to our garrison although his aircraft was hit 19 times by enemy ground fire, Squadron Leader Chandan Singh displayed courage and devotion to duty in carrying out the task in complete disregard of his personal safety and returned safely.

MAHA VIR CHAKRA (MVC)

Award Date December 7, 1971
Announced January 26, 1972
Unit: 10 Wing (Jorhat)
Reference: Gazette of India, February 12, 1972 - No. 20 - Pres/72 dated January 20, 1972

Citation

Group Captain Chandan Singh, AVSM. VRC is the officer commanding of an Air Force Station in the East [Air Force Station, Jorhat]. During the war with Pakistan, he was in the forefront of the air operations conducted for the liberation of Bangladesh. Group Captain Chandan Singh was also responsible for the planning and execution of the special helicopter operations to airlift two companies of troops of the Sylhet area. When it became necessary to overcome the obstacles in the advance of the army towards Dacca, he planned and executed the move of nearly 3,000 troops and 40 tons of equipment and heavy guns with the extremely limited helicopter force at his disposal. This operation entailed landing the troops and equipment near heavily defended areas by night. Prior to each mission he personally carried out reconnaissance in the face of heavy enemy fire. On the night of December 7/8, he flew eight missions, deep into enemy territory to supervise the progress of the helicopter airlift and to guide and inspire his pilots who were facing heavy opposition from ground tire. Later he undertook a further 18 missions in the same operation, always leading the landings at new places. On many occasions his helicopter was hit by ground fire, but this did not deter him from further missions. The success of this major airborne operation contributed significantly to the fall of Dacca and the capitulation of the Pakistan armed forces, in Bangladesh. The leadership, drive and determination coupled with the bravery shown by Group Captain Chandan Singh over an extended period of time, are in the highest traditions of the Air Force.

Appendix III

Princess Pema Tseuden (Coocoola) of Sikkim who was a source of intelligence of Chinese activities in Tibet

Chandan Singh as Captain in Jodhpur Lancers

Chandan Singh (No. 8) at the Air Force Selection Board Cairo, Egypt 1946

Twin Engine VSTOL Helios used by Chandan Singh to
fly from Charbatia into Tibet

Helios being unloaded at Charbatia from a CIA DC 46

Lt Col Revat Singh and his men of the Dogra Regt recovering the bodies of
Major Shaitan Singh PVC and others killed at Rezangla

A Mi4 Helicopter in Ladakh

An Alouette helicopter of Kilo Flight mounted with
rocket pods and machine guns

Chandan Singh briefing pilots of Kilo Flight

AN 12 over Ladakh

Maj Shaitan Singh PVC

Maharajah Sir Pratap Singh with Marshal Joffre
and Gen Haig in France 1916

A camel ambulance Haifa 1918

Jodhpur Lancer, Painting
by Capt Lovett 1910

Sir Pratap on the cover of Hisory book of First World War

AVM Chandan Singh with the author

Jodhpur-Meherangarh Fort and Jaswant Thara in the foreground

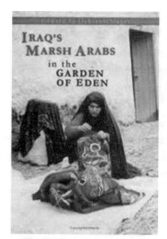

Marsh Gypsy in Iraq 1942

Kamal Attaturk

Umed Bhawan Palace, Jodhpur

Officers and JCOs Jodhpur Lancers

Abdul Baha and Sir Pratap

Maharajah Umed Singh of Jodhpur

Chandan Singh's children—Sajjan and Namrata Chandigarh 1966

Chandan Singh with Defence Minister Jagjivan Ram

Brig Hari Singh receiving the Ati Vishist Seva Medal from the President

Chandan Singh with Maj Gen
Ben Gonzalves GOC 57 Div

First shelling of Dhaka

Chandan Singh with his Russian instructor
during training on AN 12 in Russia 1961

Chandan Singh with cadets of 20 Course Kilo Sqn NDA

An Otter light aircraft of Kilo Flight used to bomb enemy positions

Chandan Singh with ACM Arjan Singh

Chandan Singh with his brothers

Chandan in Russia

Chandan Singh on holiday in Simla 1948

Mrs Chandan Singh

Mi4 Helicopters being unloaded after the Meghna crossing

Spitfire fighter of the IAF 1949

Daimler Armoured cars used in Persia 1941

Nehru and Indira Gandhi with the Chogyal of Sikkim and his sisters

Author with Prof Stanley Wolpert

Chandan Singh (sitting first left) with fellow cadets at OTS Bangalore 1941

AMX 13 Tanks
deployed for action
Chushul 1942

Chandan Singh's
brothers and
parents
(from left, Mohan
Singh IPS, mother
Roop Kanwar, young
Mahaveer son of
Brig Hari Singh,
father Col Bahadur
Singh, Kishan later
Maj Gen,
Sayar Kanwar eldest
sister, Hari Singh
later Brig)

Chandan Singh at the wheel of his MG with AD Datt (sitting) later AVM 1957

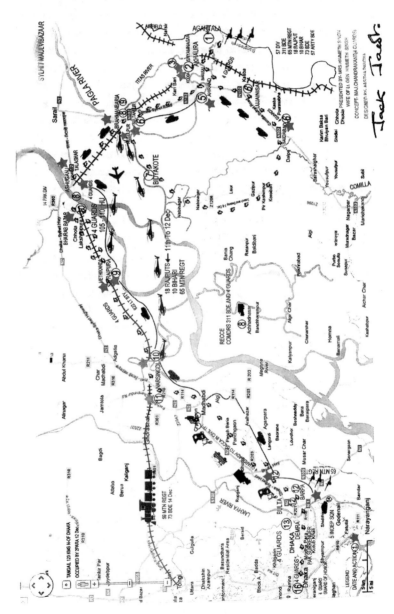

Map of Meghna Crossing